THINKING THROUGH KIERKEGAARD

PETER J. MEHL

Thinking through Kierkegaard

EXISTENTIAL IDENTITY IN A PLURALISTIC WORLD

UNIVERSITY OF ILLINOIS PRESS
URBANA AND CHICAGO

Manufactured in the United States of America
This book is printed on acid-free paper.
c 5 4 3 2 1

Library of Congress Cataloging-in-Publication Data
Mehl, Peter J. (Peter John), 1956–
Thinking through Kierkegaard : existential identity in a pluralistic world/ Peter J. Mehl.
p. cm.
Includes bibliographical references and index.
ISBN 0-252-02987-9 (alk. paper)
1. Kierkegaard, Søren, 1813–1855. I. Title.
B4377.M44 2005
198′.9—dc22 2004021718

To Shelley, Rachel, and Maggie,

my girls

The struggle itself toward the heights
is enough to fill a man's heart.
One must imagine Sisyphus happy.

—Camus, *The Myth of Sisyphus*

Contents

Preface

My relationship with Kierkegaard is like my relationship with my wife. I fell in love with her as an undergraduate. Over time our differences began to surface but we had developed a bond of mutuality and affection and had influenced each other in ways that now constitute each of us. Even further down the road we have had deeper ups and downs, sometimes more engaged with one another, sometimes less. But we have not divorced and I do not think that we could. Our relationship remains central to each of us. Our relationship has spawned other events: children, social projects, career shifts and advances, new adventures. She is part of who I am; this book is dedicated to her and to our daughters. So too has my relationship with Kierkegaard gone: until it is now a mutually critical partnership. We will never divorce and I do not think we could. He will always be with me, yet he is not as immediately infatuating as he initially was. He now occupies a place in my consciousness that is pervasive but not all consuming.

As my thinking has developed, I have come to see problems and perils in the Kierkegaardian perspective. Many Kierkegaardians, scholars of the master, have developed very lucid and accurate explications of his thought. Yet they do not often consider his thought critically; they do not look comparatively at thought that poses a serious challenge to Kierkegaard's. This book poses some serious questions for some Kierkegaardians. Kierkegaardians who struggle with and follow the contemporary discussions about moral and religious identity, about existential and spiritual issues in a pluralistic world, and who see Kierkegaard as providing positive resources or even as solving these struggles will be interested. Other

Kierkegaardians, who see themselves firmly with the hermeneutical circle of the orthodox Christian tradition, will have less interest. As well, this project is not a complete analysis of Kierkegaard's works; many important works are not discussed at all. Rather, it is a selective analysis in the interests of thinking about a Kierkegaardian approach to existential identity and how this approach fares in terms of certain strands of contemporary thought, especially more pragmatic and contextualist veins. If the widespread interest in Alasdair MacIntyre's, Richard Rorty's, and Charles Taylor's works, or more popular works such as Robert Bellah et al.'s *Habits of the Heart* or Marcus Borg's *Meeting Jesus Again for the First Time,* is any guide, even those with only marginal interest in Kierkegaard may find my project of interest. And I hope that students new to the writings of Kierkegaard, and thinking about existential issues in their own lives, will find this work engaging. Of course, in many respects I write about struggles and questions I have posed for myself, and I must wrestle existentially with the questions, since I am, after a fashion, a Kierkegaardian too. And is not the existential (and not the scholarly commentary) what Kierkegaard thought life was about anyway? This book is a result of some of my reflections; the existential, however, is for me alone.

This book draws on ideas from several papers published over the last few years. I thank the journal publishers for permission to utilize ideas that first saw public light in their publications:

— "Kierkegaard and the Relativist Challenge to Practical Philosophy," *Journal of Religious Ethics* 14.2 (1986): 247–78; reprinted with a new postscript in *Kierkegaard after MacIntyre,* edited by John J. Davenport and Anthony Rudd (Chicago: Open Court/Carus, 2001), 3–38.

— "In the Twilight of Modernity: MacIntyre and Mitchell on Moral Traditions and Their Assessment," *Journal of Religious Ethics* 19.1 (Spring 1991): 21–54.

— "Despair's Demand: An Appraisal of Kierkegaard's Argument for God," *International Journal of Philosophy of Religion* 32 (1992): 167–82 (reprinted with the kind permission of Kluwer Academic Publishers).

— "Moral Virtue, Mental Health, and Happiness: The Moral Psychology of Kierkegaard's Judge William," in *International Kierkegaard Commentary: Either/Or, vol. 2,* edited by Robert L. Perkins (Macon, Ga.: Mercer University Press, 1995), 155–82.

— "Matters of Meaning: Authenticity, Autonomy, and Authority in Kierkegaard," *Philosophy in the Contemporary World* 4.1–2 (Spring–Summer 1997): 27–32.

— "Edifying Hermeneutics: Kierkegaard's Existential 'Method' and Its Limits," in *Kierkegaard and the Word(s): Essays on Hermeneutics and Communication,* edited by Gordon D. Marino and Poul Houe

(Copenhagen: Reitzel, 2003), 49–59, first presented at the Fourth International Kierkegaard Conference, June 2001, at the Howard V. and Edna H. Hong Kierkegaard Library on the campus of St. Olaf College.

The first chapter sketches my questions and my argument against the background of contemporary historicist and pragmatist thought. Then I look closely at selected writings of three main pseudonyms: Judge William, the pseudonym of the second volume of *Either/Or* (1843) and his letter entitled "The Balance between the Esthetic and the Ethical in the Development of the Personality," Johannes Climacus's dialectics as they are found in the *Concluding Unscientific Postscript* (1846), and the edifying reflections of Anti-Climacus in *The Sickness unto Death* (1849). In chapter 1 I examine Judge William's vision of the normatively human in *Either/Or II,* building the best interpretation of this vision that I can muster. In many respects I think Judge William's letter entitled "The Balance between the Esthetic and the Ethical in the Development of the Personality" captures much of the core of Kierkegaard's vision. While the quest for ethical self-realization is richly illuminating, questions about moral content and evaluative stopping points already arise; we can see how spiritual despair will be the inevitable outcome. In chapter 2 I shift to a more focused examination of Johannes Climacus's reflections in the *Concluding Unscientific Postscript,* especially epistemological issues and the strenuous moral life that propels one to religious faith. I argue that here Kierkegaard yearns for an epistemological foundation and despairs of finding one, but as he develops his vision of the normatively human and his case for religious faith he is best seen as an edifying hermeneutical philosopher using a pragmatic approach. Chapter 3 is an examination of Anti-Climacus's more (dare I say it) systematic analysis of the structures of human selfhood, the condition of spiritual despair, and how one might arrive at the relief offered by Christian existential identity. Here I claim that the final resting place for Kierkegaard, which eradicates spiritual despair, is his own social and cultural context as he uncovers it in an introspective analysis of his own effective history. But this leads to a truth for all of us: self-conscious reengagement with our social and cultural resources provides an avenue for self-expression, moral meaning, and spiritual identity, a recipe for human flourishing. In the final chapter I make a sustained effort to consider my analysis of Kierkegaard in relation to some important contemporary writers with similar aims and interests. Charles Taylor's views in *Sources of the Self* and Alasdair MacIntyre's views in *After Virtue* are similar to Kierkegaard's theistic efforts, while Owen Flanagan's and Jeffrey Stout's reflections provide a more pragmatic and less moralistic vision of our search for moral and spiritual meaning. I try to state concisely the key features of my reconstructed more pragmatic Kierkegaardian vision of human existential identity. I consider how Kierkegaard defends his vision of the normatively human and how we should judge it today. Throughout, I weave in my criticisms and my suggestions for reconstruction.

Someone asked me recently how and when I encountered Kierkegaard. Although I am not sure, my first memory is struggling to understand the turgid opening passages in *The Sickness unto Death* and reading the rich typology of moral postures he unfolds thereafter with a genuine sense of discovery; I was sure I saw people I knew in the conditions he described. This was before I began my formal study of philosophy and religion. I did not take a course on Kierkegaard or on existentialism in college but Kierkegaard's views (as I had come to know them through my reading and other courses) stuck with me until it was time to write a master's thesis, and Kierkegaard was my choice. So one of my first debts of gratitude goes to my M.A. advisor at Ohio University, the now deceased Stanley Grean. George Weckman and David Stewart also provided valuable insight and advising, and Gene Blocker encouraged my interests in existential thought all along. At the University of Chicago, under the influence of Don Browning, my interests moved toward ethics and the psychology of Erik Erikson. Don encouraged me to wed these interests to my interest in Kierkegaard and to a growing interest in William James and American philosophy. In a seminar on rationality and relativism with Robin Lovin, I encountered MacIntyre's *After Virtue* and was deeply struck with MacIntyre's explicit rejection of, yet clear parallels to, Kierkegaard. A paper from that class became my first published article, thanks to Robin's encouragement. The influence of Browning and Lovin is pervasive in my thought. After leaving Chicago, I have been encouraged and challenged by two colleagues at the University of Central Arkansas: Jim Shelton and Charles Harvey. I owe a special debt to Charlie; a Kierkegaardian of sorts himself, he has always read my work and always critically.

Additional thanks must go to the University of Central Arkansas for repeated reassignment, giving me time to reflect on and write about Kierkegaard, and for a sabbatical in 2001 when this book officially began. The Summer Scholars Fellowship program at the Howard V. and Edna H. Hong Kierkegaard Library at St. Olaf College also provided support during the summer of 2001. Finally, I want to thank my editor at the University of Illinois Press, Kerry Callahan, for sticking with the project and shepherding it forward to publication.

Introduction: Kierkegaard's Existential Anthropology and the Search for Self

This book is a critical evaluation of Søren Kierkegaard's vision of the normatively human and the tactics he uses to defend that vision. It is, to use more contemporary language, an examination of his image of human flourishing and the sorts of epistemic strategies he employs to justify it. But it is more than simply an explication of Kierkegaard's thought. I will consider his thought in light of contemporary descriptive and normative accounts of human beings and their moral and religious life. In this light I will argue that Kierkegaard's central claims cannot be maintained or, better, cannot be maintained with the strength that he asserts. Yet much remains engaging in Kierkegaard's thought, especially when it comes to questions of our existential identity. Kierkegaard still has important truths for us today.

So in the first place my argument is about selected aspects of Kierkegaard's thought and recent interpretations of it. My main focus is his more philosophical and especially his more psychological writings or, as they are often called, his pseudonymous authorship. Indeed, I have chosen to structure this work around three main pseudonyms: Judge William, Climacus, and Anti-Climacus. Using these "authors," I make a sustained effort to sympathetically reconstruct certain of Kierkegaard's core claims regarding selfhood and its effort to gain existential orientation; I explicate the most accurate and plausible interpretation that I can. I draw on several recent studies of Kierkegaard's thought, especially those who are clearly defenders of his thought. In particular, I have been influenced by John Elrod's (1975) study of the pseudonymous writings, and more recently, the valuable studies of C. Stephen Evans (1995, 1997, 1998), Edward Mooney (1996), Anthony Rudd (1993), John Davenport (2001), and John Davenport and Anthony Rudd (2001) are implicitly (and sometimes explicitly) present in my reading of Kierkegaard.[1]

In the second place, this book is a constructive argument about problems and prospects for Kierkegaard's existential project in light of certain strands in contemporary, especially pragmatic, thought. It is an effort to think through Kierkegaard today and to consider what existential identity in a pluralistic world might look like. The contemporary thought that I draw on and find most persuasive is unified by an effort to philosophically address the matters that Kierkegaard addressed: issues of selfhood, our identity and well-being, our moral and social life, existential issues, and religious visions and strategies for defending such matters. The writings of Owen Flanagan (1991, 1996), Hilary Putnam (1981, 1987, 1992, 1995), Alasdair MacIntyre (1966, 1984, 1987, 1999), Charles Taylor (1989, 1992, 2002), Jeffrey Stout (1988, 1989), Thomas Nagel (1986), Richard Rorty (1979, 1982), and Basil Mitchell (1980) have influenced my views here and provide much of the background for my critical analysis of Kierkegaard. All these writers address broad normative concerns with philosophical clarity; they address "matters of meaning." All these philosophers, to various degrees, are exploring implications of postmodern philosophical sensibilities for normative thought, especially for a vision of who we are and might aspire to become, for our spiritual or existential identity. Central to their concerns is our "contemporary moral confusion" and ways to address it; they are aware that we have a plurality of normative perspectives and that no perspective stands as the uncontested horizon for our lives. MacIntyre, Mitchell, and Taylor are all arguing (in their unique ways) that if we are to restore intelligibility and rationality to our moral attitudes, we must restore more classical theistic visions of human life. In some ways these efforts parallel Kierkegaard's. On the other hand, Putnam, Rorty, Stout, Nagel, and Flanagan all (again, in unique ways) think that our situation is not so drastic and that instead of wholesale restoration we can practice a selective retrieval,[2] a sort of "moral *bricolage*"—Jeffrey Stout's term (1988, 294)—within and among the various traditions that provide our resources for thinking and acting. They offer more modest alternatives to the argument for restoration; they affirm moral seriousness but within a pluralistic perspective. Reading Kierkegaard through their eyes leads me finally to a modified and more modest

Kierkegaardian vision of existential identity. (An existential identity, as I use the term, is different from a mere psychological identity in that it explicitly addresses moral and religious matters; issues of ethical evaluation and life-purposes are self-consciously affirmed. Perhaps the phrase *spiritual identity* is preferable, as long as the term *spiritual* can carry cognitive freight and is not associated with any particular religious tradition.)

Sketching Kierkegaard's Thought

Recent studies of Kierkegaard's pseudonymous writing have pointed to an overall coherence in Kierkegaard's thought. In my view Kierkegaard's authorship is unified by a concern with the meaning and worth of human existence, with matters perhaps best called religious or spiritual. He is, in Charles Taylor's words, on a quest for "an ultimately believable framework" that provides meaning and purpose to life and through which "we make sense of our lives spiritually" (1989, 17–18). Such a framework will provide us with more than a practical orientation; it will make sense of our various intuitions and interests, in particular our ethical and religious concerns. It will provide us with a moral and spiritual identity, an existential identity. The lack of such a framework for our existential concerns, to continue with Taylor, will constitute a failed quest, and we will "fall into a life which is spiritually senseless" or, to use Kierkegaardian terms, a life of spiritual despair (Taylor 1989, 18).

In his effort to find an answer to such fundamental existential questions, Kierkegaard developed an understanding of the human self. This understanding forms his conceptual framework for locating our spiritual identity; the self is the point of entry for grasping the meaning and worth of our lives. But this understanding is not simply a psychology, an empirical explication of personality. It is more of a moral psychology, where the focus is on how the self is occupied with moral matters or situated in moral and religious space. But even this is not sufficient, for Kierkegaard does more than describe. He has an explicitly normative interest; he is concerned about the proper human life, the ideal form of human life. In the final analysis Kierkegaard's image of the human being weaves together descriptive and normative claims as he strives to bridge the gap between what a human being is and what a human being ought to become. He presents a vision of the normatively human; he provides a spiritual framework for making sense of our lives, a vision for our existential identity. Insofar as he is successful, he answers the challenge of spiritual despair.

The substantive lynchpin of the whole vision is perhaps best referred to as an *ideal of personhood.* (I do not think Kierkegaard can plausibly refer simply to personhood as a description of human nature, for I will argue that his vision is a specifically normative conception of personhood.) Another way of referring to Kierkegaard's ideal is captured with Owen Flanagan's ideal of the strong evaluator: "The strong evaluator is concerned that her desires, commitments, plans and character satisfy high ethical or spiritual standards. What makes her evaluation strong is that she engages in systematic moral inspection" (1996, 205). But with Flanagan I will argue (against Kierkegaard) that "being a strong evaluator, one who has well-developed capacities for specifically ethical evaluation and even, more implausibly, for whom such evaluation is the pivot on which her being turns, the basis on which all other motives are assessed, is neither a standard feature of all persons, nor unambiguous and unproblematic as a moral ideal" (1996, 154). I will argue, finally, that humans do have a natural tendency toward and can find satisfaction in an ideal of personhood, but Kierkegaard construes this interest as so strong and so high that it becomes implausible, and sociopsychological explanations are more in order. However, *if* more modestly stated, such an ideal has much to commend it. I refer to an ideal of the *modest* ethical and spiritual evaluator.

In his early work, *Either/Or II,* Kierkegaard's spokesman for the ethical way of life, Judge William, says that "personality [*personligheden,* perhaps better translated as personhood] is the absolute, it is its own objective [goal], it is the unity of the universal and the particular, . . . it is itself the Archimedean point from which one can lift the whole world" (E/O 265). The ideal of personhood continues through Kierkegaard's whole authorship; it is a central thread that binds the whole together. In his *Concluding Unscientific Postscript,* Kierkegaard has his pseudonym Climacus use the phrase *becoming subjective* but that is precisely to become an integrated and coherent strong evaluator: "An actual human being, composed of the infinite and the finite and infinitely interested in existing, has his actuality precisely in holding these together" (CUP 302). And then slightly further on, "ethics focuses upon the individual, and ethically understood it is every individual's task to become a whole human being" (CUP 346). In *The Sickness unto Death,* one of his last pseudonymous works, Kierkegaard has Anti-Climacus use the term *self* more often than personhood, but the ideal is the same: I have myself as a task of integration, of becoming whole, a synthesis of the finite and the infinite, or of necessity and possibility. As Anti-Climacus says: "Personhood is a synthesis of possibility and necessity" (SUD 50). Even the culmination of the vision in Christianity ties directly into this ideal; in his *Journals* Kierkegaard writes: "Christianity is rooted in the view of existence which says that all salvation is related to becoming personality [personhood]" (SKJP 3.490).

At the core of the ideal is what Kierkegaard refers to as spirit. Spirit is a rich concept in his writings. Briefly, spirit denotes not simply consciousness or even self-consciousness or simply choice or exercising my will. In the first place spirit denotes a capacity for agency that enables one to sustain a self-conscious and responsible relationship to the material content of one's life. In Kierkegaard's view this capacity is also a reality for me, and the critical spiritual move is to sustain a relation to my capacity to sustain a relationship to my life; in this is my hope of integration and wholeness. Put another way, the core of personhood is the personal "I," an abstract subjective center that appears to transcend all self-constituting relations to the world and can "look over my shoulder" to see just how it stands with my life. As spirit I am radically self-transcending. This spirit or "I" is what some philosophers deny exists at all.

The ideal of personhood is the center of a rich and dynamic vision of the human being and our possibilities for existential identity. As Kierkegaard unveils this vision he portrays a progressive hierarchy of existence-spheres or "stages on life's way," moving from what he calls various esthetic postures to the ethical stance and then to religious forms of existence, with Christian existence as the highest. Each stage is more comprehensive than the previous, encompassing it in a higher, more adequate form. It is not too far-fetched to say that Kierkegaard considered many of the forms of life, or cultural traditions, then known.[3] Everything from Epicurean hedonism to the radically disengaged romantic, to the ethical humanist and the Christian monastic mystic, is mentioned to some degree. The vision's historical roots can be traced as far back as the Jewish prophetic tradition and the classical Greek philosophers, forward into the Christian writings of St. Paul and St. Augustine, and is reaffirmed in an even more pronounced manner in the modern thought of Descartes, Kant, and Hegel. But before we consider historical roots or argue for historical explanations, we need to clarify Kierkegaard's vision.

I have one more preliminary point. Kierkegaard sees the human being as strung between two basic poles or two constitutive aspects of humanness. Our basic interest, goal, task, or *telos* is to put these two poles together, to sustain a relationship between these poles. One pole is our particular internal perspective within finite life; the other is our capacity to objectify ourselves and our world and then see them from the "outside." The dynamics of our life are set by these polarities. The trouble is that putting these together is not an easy project; achieving selfhood, or realizing the ideal of personhood, is putting them together, but this is subject to failure for a variety of reasons. It is, in Kierkegaard's hands, an extremely strenuous project. Kierkegaard's term for our inability to realize this polarity, or to sustain the relationship between this polarity, is despair. As Alastair Hannay puts it, "Despair in Kierkegaard's Pseudonyms is unwillingness to live up to an expectation of selfhood" (1998, 338). In Taylor's terms, it means not having found an "ultimately believable framework" for an existential identity and thereby experiencing a spiritually deficient or a meaningless existence. Despair appears in the Judge's letters and continues through to Kierkegaard's next to last pseudonymous work, *The Sickness unto Death,* where despair is central to the whole analysis of human existence. But to start, Kierkegaard's views on despair need to be explicated carefully, for he has in mind, I believe, a specific sort of despair—one that is intimately tied to his specific conception of the human being. As the pseudonym author of *The Sickness unto Death,* Anti-Climacus, says: "Despair is a qualification of the spirit and relates to the eternal in man" (SUD 17). Insomuch as selfhood refers to a high ideal of spiritual integration, so despair refers to the state of the individual who is unable to realize himself as a Kierkegaardian self. Kierkegaardian despair follows only if Kierkegaard has the normatively human right.

Our Contemporary Context

As a reflection on problems and limits in Kierkegaard's vision and its defense, this book is in part a deconstruction of Kierkegaard's thought. But by deconstruction I mean nothing too specific, just an analytic attitude that is culturally, historically, and psychologically sensitive. I do not aspire to a strong relativism, but a modest objectivism that is suspicious of deep skepticism and yet leans fallibilist. My philosophic posture follows William James; it moves in pragmatic and naturalistic directions, but does not lose sight of moral and religious intuitions and attitudes. As a result, in many respects I point out how what Kierkegaard sees as a discovered perspective on humans and their life-situation is also the result of specific social and historical locations, philosophical commitments, and cultural assumptions. Kierkegaard is not simply discovering but also participating in a cultural construction of the human being. As Charles Taylor says, when considering our "modern notion of the self" and our deep sense of inwardness, "it is in large part a feature of our world, the world of modern, Western people. It is a function of an historically limited mode of self-interpretation, one which has become dominant in the modern West" (1989, 111). Kierkegaard left very creative and insightful descriptions of the conditions of human existence, but to a greater extent than he realized these are conditions that reflect the Western Christian social and cultural context in which he was nurtured. They are not the universal conditions of human existence. They represent one powerful and persuasive analysis of humans as they encounter themselves in late-modern Western Christendom.

Put another way, this book is an examination of Kierkegaard's thought in light of, as Owen Flanagan says, "the twin facts of the social construction of persons and the historical construction of society" (1991, 105). Some of what Kierkegaard ascribes to the human self can, I believe, be justified, but other aspects are overstated and derive less from the basic constituents of the human self and more from the stringent Protestant Christian heritage within which he was nurtured. Discerning what can be confidently affirmed of Kierkegaard's vision of the normatively human and what cannot constitutes a central effort of this book. This portion of the book is an extended philosophical argument that examines the implications of a more thoroughly contemporary view (one more attuned to historical and social context but not ignoring natural and rational constraints) for Kierkegaard's project of normative justification. I judge that Kierkegaard's efforts to bridge descriptive analysis and normative proposals for human flourishing in his vision of human existence are strikingly contemporary and offer much for us today. But although on the right track he is still too insufficiently cognizant of the difficulties of the project, especially given how deeply our natures are shaped by our biology on the one hand and our social and cultural context on the other.

All human consciousness is nurtured in a specific cultural tradition and is subject to specific social conditions; our personal identity, our moral psychology, and even our existential identity are embedded in the communities that helped constitute us. As Alasdair MacIntyre argues: "The individual's search for his or her good is generally and characteristically conducted within a context defined by those traditions which the individual's life is a part" (1984, 222). This is not to say that we fall victim to our times. While thinking and acting from within traditions, I do think (as does MacIntyre, in my view) that we can transcend our times in creative and cogent ways. It does mean, however, that (contra Kierkegaard) there is no noncontroversial vision of the human self upon which we can build *the* ideal normative vision of human life. Kierkegaard has one clear and firm confidence: he believes he has grasped the essence of the human condition as one where human beings qua human beings are compelled toward a specific sort of ethical, religious, and finally Christian existence. This Christian existence is the endpoint of a series of "stages" that all humans are driven to begin, and to traverse, on pain of despair. Kierkegaard's whole project is wrapped around this vision of the normatively human, the essentially human. My central thesis is that this vision is overstated; it can be maintained only if more modestly stated. We can build an ideal of human life, and this ideal can be connected in ways to what we know about human beings and what makes life satisfactory. But we must be careful; we must be sensitive to ways that this ideal will be connected to who we are as participants in late-modern Western culture. That this is the case should not rule our thinking out from the start, for everyone thinks and acts from within some tradition-generated resources. Finding ourselves within cultural traditions is the point of departure for critical thought, not its end. This more hermeneutical approach, or, to use Hilary Putnam's phrase, this "pragmatic realism," comes without finality, but with traces of human interpretative and constructive fallibility everywhere (1987, 17).

This critical thesis has important implications for thinking through Kierkegaard today. Because the lynchpin of Kierkegaard's project is this thesis about the normatively human, it is related to his claim that human existence is despair. We are in despair because we cannot realize our *telos*, yet it exerts its claim on us nonetheless. I argue that Kierkegaardian despair is premised on a human desire for firm foundations, for complete coherence and wholeness, for a point of moral and spiritual transcendence, but that his approach to human existence, his "method" for uncovering this dynamic structure of human existence is an incoherent mixture of foundationalist aspirations and pragmatic and empirical strategies—strategies that seem clearly nonfoundationalist. I think that we must favor the more pragmatic and radically empirical side of Kierkegaard. The implication is that humans are not in such dire straits, hence the solution need not be as radical; more circumspect problems suggest more modest solutions. So I suggest that there are questions with Kierkegaard's "self in despair" image; problems, we might say, in his moral psychology. Much of Kierkegaard's reflection on our moral and psychological selves can be affirmed. For example, our self is relationally constituted, for we are shot through and through by our effective history of social relationships. Equally important, our social/empirical relations do not exhaust us, we still are a relation unto ourselves, we relate ourselves to ourselves; rational and responsible agency plays a role. Our active efforts through the feedback of experience to shape ourselves are crucial to our well-being. But in the final analysis the Kierkegaardian either/or is too sharp: either become a Kierkegaardian self or live in despair poses false alternatives. Kierkegaard makes the existential stakes so high and the conditions of self-navigation so difficult that his stance assures that we will end a cul-de-sac of moral and spiritual frustration.

As I noted above, another intriguing question involves Kierkegaard's "method" for framing the vision of the human self and its situation. How does the "physician of the soul" come to an understanding of humans and their *telos?* What gives Kierkegaard the confidence that he has it right? One thing that seems crucial to his case is the lived experience of humans, their hope and despair, their frustration and fulfillment, their joy and sorrow. What Kierkegaard calls the edifying or upbuilding points to a pragmatic element in his reasoning. What we should accept is what makes an existential difference in our lived-experience. This resource for making his case brings up fascinating epistemological issues. William James refers to the "morally helpful" as a consideration when evaluating religious beliefs (1902). Is there a pragmatic dimension to Kierkegaard's effort to defend (albeit indirectly) his vision? I argue that there clearly is such a constraint operating epistemically for Kierkegaard. In this sense, Richard Rorty (1979, 369) is right to refer to Kierkegaard as a "great edifying philosopher."

In addition, Kierkegaard also expresses a deep skepticism about human knowledge that seems related to a very high standard for what counts as knowledge. Does this skepticism mask a foundationalist demand for absolute certainty? Is Kierkegaard really a strong objectivist? Kierkegaard sought a secure point of departure for life; he yearned for an Archimedean point from which he could have secure thought and action, from which he could live. And I think that he thought he had found it in inwardness; our one certainty is what he calls our own "ethical actuality." But he was also approaching a more hermeneutical perspective, an edifying hermeneutics. When Rorty says that "edifying discourse is supposed to be abnormal, to take us out of our old selves by the power of strangeness, to aid us in becoming new beings," it is easy to see Kierkegaard (1979, 360). I will try to shed some light on his epistemological convictions and reconstruct them in light of contemporary thinking.

Finally, this thesis about humans and their existential *telos* also has implications for Kierkegaard's theological claims. Kierkegaard's apologetics for Christianity rests on the analysis of the human being and the experience of despair. But if the basis of his vision of the normatively human is pragmatic and a relatively adequate analysis formed within the social and cultural resources then available, what of his strong religious and Christian conclusions? Is Kierkegaard willing to see his vision of the normatively human, a vision that culminates in Christian existence, as just the best view to date, or just one of many plausible visions and subject to revision further down the road? How should we understand Kierkegaard's religious psychology and the power that constitutes us? Our pluralistic context affects religion as much as ethics and shakes our confidence in his ethical perspective as well as his inner theological journey. I suggest a revision where the self, at the deepest level, is constituted by cultural frames of significance and by active participation in a living tradition or even traditions. An individual who is only partially or sporadically or unselfconsciously culturally connected lacks resources for generating a purposive perspective that transcends the de facto preferences of her immediate context. Such an individual is threatened by spiritual despair, for such a perspective is a humanly necessary ingredient of well-being.

Textual Issues and Authorial Voices

Anyone who has attempted to tackle the writing of Kierkegaard knows that they make up a diverse and complex authorship. The standard fare served up as "Kierkegaard" in philosophy textbooks or in historical surveys is at best one-sided and often deeply distorted.[4] In one sense, Kierkegaard would have liked that; a reader must grapple with his "authorial voices" for himself or herself. Kierkegaard's work does not fit easily into packages appropriate for undergraduate consumption or for selective placement in narratives of Western philosophy. He is not easily snared in our conceptual nets; he eludes quick categorization and this may be part of the reason for his enduring significance. That unique, yet accurate, readings of Kierkegaard's project are still emerging is not surprising. I, of course, want to provide such a reading, and I will provide ample textual evidence for my reading, but I do not think my reading completely escapes my own history.

Any examination of Kierkegaard's project must face the question of the pseudonymous authorship and its relationship to Kierkegaard's own considered opinions on the matters portrayed in the first person of the pseudonyms. Although Kierkegaard formally admits that he is the author of all pseudonymous works up to the *Concluding Unscientific Postscript to the Philosophical Fragments,* he asks that "if it should occur to anyone to want to quote a particular passage from the books, it is my wish, my prayer, that he will do me the kindness of citing the respective pseudonymous author's name, not mine" (CUP 267). Respecting his wish, I intend to structure my critical analysis around three widely read and studied pseudonyms. These "authors" are three main "voices" for Kierkegaard's vision of human existence as it developed in his writing; no one of them captures Kierkegaard's vision completely, but taken together I think that they provide illuminating perspective on his thought. Temporally, they span his maturing authorship. In chapter 1 I examine Judge William, Kierkegaard's ethical spokesperson and the "author" of *Either/Or,* volume 2 (1843). In chapter 2 I "listen" to Johannes Climacus, Kierkegaard's most philosophical voice and "author" of the *Concluding Unscientific Postscript* (1846). Finally, chapter 3 considers Anti-Climacus's reflections, Kierkegaard's religious psychotherapeutic voice and "author" of *The Sickness unto Death* (1849).

Although Kierkegaard had intended to end his pseudonymous authorship with the *Concluding Unscientific Postscript,* he cast another pseudonym in the figure of Anti-Climacus, the author of *The Sickness unto Death.* But, as the Hongs point out, Kierkegaard struggled with whether to use his own name as author or a new pseudonym. He finally decided on a new pseudonym, Anti-Climacus, and in his journals reveals, still with a sense of distancing, his own relationship to Climacus and Anti-Climacus: "Johannes Climacus and Anti-Climacus have several things in common; but the difference is that whereas Johannes Climacus places himself so low that he even says himself that he is not a Christian, one seems to be able to detect in Anti-Climacus that he regards himself to be a Christian on an extraordinarily high level. . . . I would place myself higher than Johannes Climacus and lower than Anti-Climacus" (SUD xxii). Evidently Kierkegaard opted for a pseudonym even at this stage of his authorship because he aspired to an ideal that he had not existentially reached and over which he still had mixed emotions. Perhaps Kierkegaard sensed that his vision of the normatively human was outstripping all our existential capacities and resources.

Still, despite the pseudonyms and multiple voices, I believe that there is a relatively strong coherence in Kierkegaard's whole authorship. I think this can be demonstrated by a more comprehensive examination of all his works, especially his journals and papers, than I will undertake here. But aside from that point, I am sure that some will argue that I have accentuated certain ideas or themes to the exclusion of others equally or more important for Kierkegaard, and so it may well be. Finally, my explication and reconstruction of Kierkegaard is inescapably bound up with my particularity. But I judge my efforts relatively successful in transcending some of that contingency if I have advanced the conversation in the judgment of those who are informed of Kierkegaard's thought and who grasp the conditions that shape thinking in our times. I also judge my efforts successful if I have added some navigational compass to those of us searching for existential rudders on our pluralistic seas. Both remain to be seen.

Notes

1. The recent volume edited by John Davenport and Anthony Rudd, *Kierkegaard after MacIntyre* (2001), is perhaps the best collection to date that demon-

strates how Kierkegaard's thought remains a fertile ground for contemporary philosophical thought. I have profited from nearly all the essays in the volume, and I am indebted to the authors.

2. To be fair, Taylor (1992, 23) refers to his effort as a "work of retrieval."

3. Asian traditions were just coming to light, and Kierkegaard did not have a deep knowledge or attraction to them, as did Schopenhauer. But Kierkegaard considers mysticism many times; I have noted only one mention that suggests Asian traditions in *Either/Or.* Referring to a young man, the Judge says: "He lost himself one-sidedly in a mysticism not so much Christian as Indian. He ended in suicide" (E/O 245).

4. Unfortunately, MacIntyre's portrayal in *After Virtue* of Kierkegaard's position as a last desperate effort to make an irrational leap out of the failed Enlightenment effort to justify morality is one such distortion. I will discuss MacIntyre in my final chapter.

1 *Judge William: Strong Evaluative Identity*

Either/Or was Kierkegaard's first pseudonymous work and the most popular during his lifetime. In volume two of *Either/Or* we find the letters of Judge William, letters to his younger friend known only as A. The Judge's second letter is entitled "The Balance between the Esthetic and the Ethical in the Development of the Personality," and esthetic/ethical is one way to state the basic polarity within which Kierkegaard frames his ideal of selfhood. Throughout his authorship Kierkegaard takes many passes at stating this polarity, which sets the terms for the dynamics of success and failure for humans as they search for existential orientation. As I mentioned in the introduction, this polarity has to do with being a creature that has a definite particularity as an individual and the capacity to transcend these "accidental" features by "objectifying" them in thought and for action. Kierkegaard's main concern in *Either/Or* is to concretely make the case for the superiority of the ethical way of life over the merely esthetic life-stage. I want to dwell on the Judge's letter at some length, for it contains many critical points for Kierkegaard's moral psychology, for his normative vision and my evaluation of it. In it Kierkegaard conveys his most sustained considerations of the crucial transition from the purely esthetic to the ethical existence-sphere. If we have problems here and it is hard for us to follow Kierkegaard into the ethical stage, then it will be equally difficult to follow him to the religious stages where personhood is said to reach fulfillment. I will argue that several critical problems are already evident in this early writing.

Judge William's Moral Psychology

Judge William's long letter to his young friend begins with an emphasis on the importance of choice. Why is choice important? The first main point seems to be that without choice I do not become a person, my personality does not develop, I do not gain a personal identity. As the Judge puts it, choice "is crucial for the content of the personality: through the choice the personality submerges itself in that which is being chosen, and when it does not choose, it withers away in atrophy" (E/O 163). If I do not choose the course and purposes of my life, what happens? As time goes on, others will choose for me (164), and so I will become one among many, or I will become whatever the others are becoming. And in that defrauding I will "lose myself." Or, if I am relatively isolated from others and so do not become one with them, and I do not choose, the Judge says that I will be shaped by "obscure forces" within the personality: "The personality or the obscure forces within it unconsciously chooses" (164).

The Judge seems to be telling us that we will lose ourselves if we do not choose. Does he mean that we will not be able to identify ourselves; that we will not be able to recognize who we are over time? That would be a radical loss of self. That would be a loss of a most basic sense of psychological continuity. He must mean something closer to the loss of our personal identity in the sense of knowing who we are as the central character in the story that is our life, a loss of our identity in the sense of being some definite personality or character through time. But we should note that he does say that I do become someone even if I do not choose; it would still seem that I gain some sort of identity. What is clear, however, is that I do not *achieve* an identity in the sense of self-consciously determining the course of my personality development; I have an identity, but not by my own doing. In his letter the Judge says that it is not that "the person who lives aesthetically does not develop, but he develops with necessity, not in freedom" (E/O 225).

All of us are, of course, developed by necessity in the first place. I am whatever I have been lucky (or unlucky) enough to inherit in the course of my life. I am an empirical reality, a physical and psychological being that is shaped by the world in which I live. I have a particular physiology, with particular strengths and weakness; I have a particular social location, again with a specific givenness not of my doing; I have a personal bent, a particularity of talent maybe. All this is my finite concretion. As the Judge puts it, I am a "specific individual with these capacities, these inclinations, these drives, these passions, influenced by this specific social milieu, as this specific product of a specific environment" (E/O 251).

Kierkegaard calls this a person's "immediacy." Obviously everybody up to a certain age is just whatever they have become. Their life is largely given, and they take it as it comes. The esthetic individual is simply whatever he or she is by virtue of the givenness of his or her conditions. In the Judge's words: "What does it mean to live esthetically? . . . to that I would respond: the esthetic in a person is that by which he spontaneously and immediately is what he is" (178).

It seems clear that the Judge is not saying that we will not become persons, in the sense that our personal identities will not congeal, that we will not become a specific physical-mental-social "me," or that we will necessarily be in a state of identity confusion, if we do not choose as he is asking us to. For we have an "individuality" as result of the specific empirical conditions that have shaped us—indeed, as a result of the choices we made before we self-consciously made choices! If this is the case, what is Judge William's point? It might seem that the Judge is simply telling us to make a firm choice to think for ourselves, a sort of Enlightenment challenge to become more autonomous. But that is not exactly right either; the Judge is asking for more than being a self-conscious decision-maker. This is a first step on the way to becoming a whole human, to realizing personhood, but it is not sufficient. A person living from the esthetic posture makes decisions, and their decisions can be very reflective. In fact the Judge's young friend A, to whom his letters are addressed, is a virtuoso when it comes to deliberation, and of course he makes choices. The esthetic person does not always live immediately from his or her desires as a child does; the esthetic person may well be oriented around an empirical condition such as a talent, but one orders one's practical life to insure that this talent is cultivated and realized as far as possible. As the Judge says, the esthetic person "will perceive that it is impossible for everything to flourish equally. Then he will choose, and that which determines him is a more and less, which is a relative difference" (E/O 225). So what does the esthetic person lack? The Judge, and Kierkegaard with him, has something more specific than mere ego identity in mind when he says we must choose ourselves or we will lose ourselves, more specific than an awareness and concern for my life. The esthetic person has a life and cares about it, indeed most adult persons do.

The first decisive step out of esthetic postures is self-consciousness. The individual who chooses himself or herself "becomes conscious as this specific individual" (E/O 251). More specifically, the self chosen "has a boundless multiplicity within itself inasmuch as it has a history, a history in which he acknowledges identity with himself; he is the person he is only through this history" (216). It is clear that Kierkegaard understands how we are formed by our interaction with the environment, specifically the identifications with significant others and the rules and roles of our society. I think he sees (although I am not sure how thoroughly) that we are formed, and even have been forming ourselves, although not self-consciously, long before self-consciousness becomes a decisive possibility. Here I refer to all the important work done on identity and ego development by Erik Erikson and the ways that the ego synthesizes and resynthesizes its environment throughout childhood. Hence, as Erikson says when speaking of identity issues: "While the end of adolescence is thus the stage of an overt identity crisis, identity formation neither begins nor ends in adolescence: it is a life long development largely unconscious to the individual and his society" (1980, 122). We have been making choices, unself-consciously, for some time when the sense of self-awareness begins to predominate.

More recently Owen Flanagan has drawn several crucial distinctions in thinking about identity. At the most basic level is mere psychic identity, which is simply a "perceived psychological continuity" (1991, 134). This is a continuity that is simply given for humans, unless they are infants or mentally impaired. More important is our "full actual identity" in distinction from mere psychological identity; full actual identity is "constituted by the dynamic integrated system of past and present identifications, desires, commitments, aspirations, beliefs, dispositions, temperament, roles, acts and actional patterns, as well as whatever self understandings (even incorrect ones) each person brings to his or her life" (1991, 135). This is the real objective me, and Flanagan does not mean to say that it is a "well-integrated" system, just a relatively sound one such that one does not operate in a state of identity diffusion or crisis. Most people have just such an actual identity; if they do not it was probably the result of some traumatic external conditions in childhood. But clearly "actual identity" is Kierkegaard's immediate self, or the immediate self with a bit of self-reflection, the self just as it is; the person I am as given in my history.

But at some point "I" join the process of my identity formation; I become the editor of this emergent configuration rather than simply part of the product. Flanagan also draws this distinction, and he refers to "self-represented identity," which he characterizes as "the conscious or semi-conscious picture a person has of who he or she is. The self as represented is the self from the subjective point of view" (1991, 137). The first step in the activity of self-representing is trying to get our heads around the actual me. That is, we try to track full actual identity in our activity of self-representing identity; we hope that the self we represent ourselves to be is the self we in fact are. As the Judge puts it in this metaphorical passage: "Through the individual's intercourse with himself the individual is made pregnant by himself and gives birth to himself. The self the individual knows is simultaneously the actual and the ideal self, which the individual has outside himself as the image in whose likeness he is to form himself, and which he has within himself, since it is himself" (E/O 259). I am seeking to know myself, to penetrate my whole concretion with consciousness, to become self-conscious, to discover who I am. I take it that many young people face the issue of who they are going to become, the issue of self-represented identity; and the first question must be who they have become up to that point.

If we read on in Judge William's letter we might think that the core of the choice of self is to decide to engage life in evaluative terms. As the Judge says: "My Either/Or designates the choice by which one chooses good and evil or rules them out. Here the question is under what qualifications one will view all existence and personally live" (E/O 169). Now to choose one's self in the Judge's terms is to choose one's self as an ethical, an evaluative decision-maker, and not simply to make decisions but to make decisions in self-consciously normative terms. But although this is crucial it is not the core of his ideal, for the Judge soon adds an important qualification: "Every human being . . . has a natural need to formulate a life-view, a conception of the meaning of life and its purpose. *The person who lives aesthetically also does that,* and the popular expression heard in all ages and from various stages is this: One must enjoy life" (179, emphasis added). This qualification changes things, for now the esthetic person is not seen as merely indifferent, bouncing from one thing to another, and not as a minimally autonomous agent, that intends and chooses courses of action, albeit with a particular aspect of himself or herself at the heart of his life. The hedonist makes a major self-conscious evaluative choice; he or she chooses hedonism. The distinction between the ethical and esthetical does not turn simply on the activity or nonactivity of normative choice; it is something even more specific.

The one thing, says Judge William, that distinguishes all forms of estheticism is that the individual *"posits a condition that either lies outside the individual or is within the individual in such a way that it is not there by virtue of the individual himself"* (E/O 180). What does this mean? In Hegelian language, the Judge says that in estheticism "the spirit is not qualified as spirit but is immediately qualified" (180). Maybe we should begin with what it does not mean! It does not mean that the individual is lacking autonomy in the normal adult sense of being a self-conscious deliberator who can act on the basis of his or her evaluative distinctions. For surely many a hedonist is an autonomous agent; he has chosen, possibly in very elaborate ways, to pursue a path that makes for enjoyment; that is the hedonist's life-project, it gives purpose and meaning in life. So the hedonist will not just take things as they come, but will cultivate himself and his world in order to find enjoyment as he conceives it. The hedonist knows his desires, and his overarching desire is to arrange life so that they are best fulfilled. Presumably to live with the spirit as "immediately qualified" is to live with my capacity for autonomy in the service of something other than itself. It is not that I am not conscious of my capacity for rational and responsible decision-making; it is that it is not the center of my existence. It is that I have not defined my self-identity around the activity of ethical evaluation and agency.

Perhaps an example will help to see how Kierkegaard's ideal, even as we see it in the Judge's meditation, is more than simply one where an individual is self-consciously and responsibly charting their life-course and thereby can be said to have a self-identity. It is an ideal that advocates a *complete identification* with our capacity to objectify and evaluate our lives and to constantly live from or within this process: this is the critical step into the Kierkegaardian ideal of personhood. As Ed Mooney puts it, "Finally, the outcome of self-choice for the Judge is the achievement of full and *self-responsible* personhood" (1996, 17). Suppose I am a professional basketball coach. I work to improve the standing of the team under my care and even spend some time to improve the players' personal life; to a degree I sacrifice my well-being for theirs. My life-project is this task of coaching. While not totally consumed with the task, after all I have some distance from it, I am a "coach" and most of the highs and lows of my life revolve around the results of my chosen profession. In the course of this endeavor my character takes shape: I become a person whose life is defined by this local project, by my relationship to all that this activity involves. I am self-conscious of this; I am not one with my project. Rather I am self-consciously engaged in a project that I know constitutes me; it is what I care about; it motivates me.

If someone asks me about my life and who I am, I can tell them about my life and who I am: my life has a relative coherence and integration in terms of my pursuit of the goods of the game, indeed of my participation in the institutionalized practices, the rules and roles, of basketball. It is not the only thing that moves me, but it is fair to say that this is my central project. My life is not without meaning and purpose; my self is not aimless but built around concrete possibilities and talents that I saw (and still see) as live options for my life. I am certainly not merely following the crowd mentality, blindly following others' beliefs and values. But I am also not single-mindedly and consistently pursuing the ethical life, where that means that I am always considering whether my identifications and concerns are acceptable or where that means evaluating the worth of my beliefs and values and readjusting my life. I make considered evaluative choices, but my thinking and acting rarely go beyond my local projects, especially of the welfare of my team and the strategies of the sport I love. I have never thought seriously and consistently about my life and profession in ethical or spiritual terms; I am generally too engaged in living. My thinking simply stops at this point. Why should it go further?

For Judge William, to live one's life with the spirit as the center of one's existence is the critical point, and it is humanly necessary to live in this way. The Judge, presumably, would tell our coach that his life is lacking; he is, whether he is aware of it or not, in despair. But how so? In this fascinating passage the Judge speaks of the birth of spiritual self-consciousness and suggests dire consequences if spirit is "repressed": "There comes a moment in a person's life when immediacy is ripe, so to speak, and when the spirit requires a higher form, when it wants to lay hold of itself as spirit. As immediate spirit, a person is bound up with all the earthly life, and now spirit wants to gather itself together out of this dispersion, and to transfigure itself in itself, the personality wants to become conscious in its eternal validity. If this does not happen, if the movement is halted, if it is repressed, then depression sets in" (E/O 188–89).

I want to note several things here, and I think they are at the core of Kierkegaard's reflections on the normatively human. First, the human self is enmeshed in a process of development; the self is subject to natural conditions that assert themselves, conditions not of its own making. At a certain age (presumably adolescence) a person's immediacy (which is their full facticity, their nature as it is simply given) "ripens," and the "immediate spirit" (consciousness) apprehends itself, grasps itself through itself, consciousness becomes distinctly self-conscious. And these conditions are arranged in lower to higher levels; they are not all equal. I will return to this more natural-law vision of human spiritual development. It is important because it appears that in some sense Kierkegaard sees the spirit as an interest, a desire, in the heart of the human being—this "natural" desire that can be thwarted only at the cost of despair. But more than simply a consciousness of this "higher form of spirit," more than simply self-consciousness, is needed for Kierkegaard's full ideal of personhood.

Second, the mention of "immediate spirit" suggests my power of conscious deliberation and decision-making, but when it is not part of my image of myself, much less at the center of my whole existence. "Mediated spirit," however, would be ripened spirit, spirit that is aware of itself as spirit or, in more common terms, a person who has the developed ability to represent themselves to themselves. But even mediated spirit is not yet Kierkegaard's ideal. Our coach is self-conscious, he is relatively aware of his actual identity, the identifications and commitments that make him who he is. That is, he is aware of himself as a self; he has a life and he cares about it. What he does not do, presumably, and what leaves him in despair according to the Judge (and Kierkegaard) is that he does not define himself as an ethical evaluator; the seat of his existence, the center of the narrative that is his life, his self, is not "spirit" as responsible freedom.

To correctly grasp the Kierkegaardian ideal one must see that there are different types of autonomy, and the one that frames Kierkegaard's ideal of personhood is not always easy to grasp. Here I draw on Bruce Miller's analysis of autonomy, utilizing three of his types of autonomy: free action, effective deliberation, and moral reflection (1987). First there is basic autonomy, or autonomy as free action, the autonomy constitutive of any entity defined as a person, the ability to think and make intentional choices. Children exhibit this sort of autonomy, as does even an "esthetic" individual thoroughly encased in the shell of the finite. Then there is autonomy that engages in, or can engage in, evaluative reflection; this is the autonomy that ripens and awakens with self-consciousness about identity and considers course of action in terms of evaluative distinctions. This might be called normal adult autonomy, or autonomy as effective deliberation. Nonmentally impaired individuals, by the time of late adolescence, are autonomous in this sense. The hedonist mentioned above is autonomous in this sense; our coach is autonomous in this sense. They have a relatively firm sense of who they are; they have a self-identity (although it may be congealing for only the teenager). They can understand the consequences of their decisions; they can be held accountable for the actions that flow from their decisions, as a child cannot.

But then there is autonomy that takes the activity of self-evaluative reflection, reflection on the desirability of one's aims and interests, as part of identity. This is neither basic autonomy as "free action" nor normal adult autonomy as "effective deliberation." This is what Miller refers to as "moral reflection," and in its extreme it becomes the center of one's self, one's ideal self, and that around which life is to be ordered and in which it is to be lived. Here it can, in Miller's words, "require rigorous self-analysis, awareness of alternative sets of values, commitment to a method of assessing them, and an ability to put them in place" (1987, 107). In its most developed form it is an ideal (to emphasize again) that demands a *complete identification* with our capacity to objectify and evaluate our lives and to constantly live within this process. In its Kierkegaardian guise, it means that I am always considering whether my identifications and concerns are acceptable, where that means evaluating the worth of my beliefs and values and readjusting my life. As a sustained existential posture, I follow Flanagan and refer to the "strong evaluator" or "strong evaluative identity" (1996, 142–70). As I mentioned, I think this is another way of putting Kierkegaard's ideal of personhood, and much of my analysis in the following chapters will develop more fully the ideal of the strong evaluator and argue that while the ideal has much to commend it, it finally must be stated in a more modest form than Kierkegaard advocates.

Finally (to return to the above quote), the Judge declares that the spirit "wants to become conscious in its eternal validity." In the Judge's view the spirit, the capacity for rational and responsible decision-making, for freedom in the sense of perceiving, evaluating, and endorsing elements of our given identity, of our life-situation, is that aspect of the human being that is eternal. Spirit is always present for the self, not like an empirical condition—which stands in a contingent (nonnecessary) relationship to the self. Spirit is the absolute, as that which is unqualifiedly ultimate and does not get its status from anything else to which it stands in relation; it is the universal, as in not merely local, but present in all cases: "The personality [*Personligheden,* personhood] appears as the absolute that has its teleology in itself" (E/O 263). In Kierkegaard's final analysis, the apprehension of spirit, of freedom, is our route to God, although the Judge does not really have this clearly in his existential sights.

What the Judge does declare is that spirit is the only thing that can be chosen absolutely; it is our sure point of practical orientation. Although the Judge is no epistemologist, he is clear that the empirical, the merely historical side of myself, will not do as a foundation for life, for one cannot really choose the relative absolutely. But humans can try to choose the relative absolutely; this indeed is the perennial human confusion on Kierkegaard's view, the problem that creates all our spiritual problems, the hedonist's confusion and presumably our coach's problem. If I choose anything but personhood, anything but spiritual freedom, I choose what is merely finite and accidental; spiritual freedom, however, is infinite and essential. To make this volitional blunder in navigating life is to end up in despair, it is necessary for human well-being, for my "soul," to put spirit in the driver's seat and not to allow any other merely finite realities to serve as the constitutive basis of my self-identity. This is the essence of strong evaluative identity. Kierkegaard's claim is that to deny spirit the driver's seat is a recipe for despair; despair is the cost of denying the ideal of personhood.

As early as Judge William's reflections in *Either/Or II,* despair plays a critical role in Kierkegaard's vision of human existence, both psychologically and as an element in his defense of the ideal. Although Kierkegaard's mature statement is *The Sickness unto Death,* Judge William has a good deal to say about despair. He clearly advocates strong evaluative identity over forms of estheticism for psychological reasons related to the consequences to the human being. Strong evaluative identity is that one point of departure that can adequately ground my practice, that can serve as a secure basis, for it is not subject to the shifting sands of the empirical. As we noted above, if the individual denies or otherwise ignores the capacity for self-consciously navigating life, if, as the Judge said, "the movement is halted, if it is repressed, then depression sets in" (E/O 188–89). If a person tries to float through life distancing himself or herself from the conditions of life and not self-consciously committing to various definite projects, a deep dissatisfaction will overtake him or her. If a person lets others decide their life for them, if they try to follow the crowd, again despair sets in. Ignoring the human interest in being able to oversee one's own life, to make self-conscious choices, to (as we say) express yourself through some medium, is a recipe for dissatisfaction. This (it seems) is a truth of psychology. But these are all preliminary sorts of despair, finite despairs, esthetic despairs, to speak with the Judge. In the final analysis, *all* postures that do not take a decisive step into the infinite ethical requirement, any life that does not choose the self in its capacity for self-transcending spiritual freedom, and thoroughly identify with this, ends in despair.[1] This, it seems to me, is not a truth of psychology, but a specific normative ideal.

So the point finally is to choose despair, says the Judge. Not despair in a finite sense, where I acknowledge that I am frustrated by the collapse of a particular finite element in my life that is identity constituting, say, for example, my marriage or vocation. But to "despair completely," to see that life in the finite empirical world is despair and to choose this is to see that any and all possible finite empirical realities can never provide the grounding for myself, the absolute point of departure, the firm foundation for praxis, that I seek. If I am to choose absolutely I cannot choose the relative. What is left for me? Myself as spirit, as self-transcendence. In this passage, a passage that gets us very close to the Judge's religious sensibilities, he makes it clear that he desires a point of departure that is outside the vicissitudes of time and context, that is not merely empirical or finite: "The atheist perceives very well that the way by which the ethical is most easily evaporated is to open the door to the historical infinity. And yet there is something legitimate in his behavior, for if, when all is said and done, the individual is not the absolute, then the empirical is the only road allotted to him, and the end of this road is just like the source of the Niger river—no one knows where it is. If I am assigned to the finite, it is arbitrary to remain standing at any particular point" (E/O 265). When the Judge says "the individual" he means the personal I, the self-transcending agent; this is what he understands as absolute, as eternal. And notice how closely the ethical, which is now the *telos* of spiritual freedom, is tied to religion; the atheist knows how to undermine the ethical.

But then there is one more danger, in the Judge's view at least. There is a danger of an intellectually refined despair, a position that tempts the spiritually well developed. When the individual first apprehends herself as spirit, as harboring the absolute, she is deeply affected, and if this experience is not tempered by a reengagement with temporality, with my finite concretion, it can also lead to defeat and despair! Both denial of spirit and a certain sort of preoccupation with it spell disaster. Judge William again:

> When the individual has grasped himself in his eternal validity, this overwhelms him with all its fullness. Temporality vanishes for him. At the first moment, this fills him with an indescribable bliss and gives him an absolute security. If he now begins to stare at it one-sidedly, the temporal asserts its claims. These are rejected. What temporality can give, the more or less that appears here, is so very insignificant to him compared with what he possess eternally. He sinks into contemplation, stares fixedly at himself, but this staring cannot fill up time. Then it appears to him that time, temporality, is his ruination. (E/O 231)

Again one can see that religious dimensions are intrinsic to the ethical, to the ideal of spiritual freedom, and we will return to these. But what is happening here? Presumably this individual has clearly realized the capacity to distance herself from all possible content, to abstract from every conceivable element of her finite life, to disengage. She has fastened on to her reflective imaginative capacity, her power for objectifying, and notices that it seems unaffected by the particulars of her life. It is, I suppose, a sort of Stoic stance, a willed distancing: I am not this or that, I am simply and essentially my will. Possibly it is an opening into a more Asian religious stance, a path to the higher Self. But what is interesting now is that the Judge says that she has "not chosen in the right way" (E/O 231). In other words while she seems to have chosen the absolute, the essential, herself in her eternal validity, she has not yet completed the choice. How so? To choose yourself is ultimately to choose freedom, and freedom (in the special way that Kierkegaard uses it) is always *responsible* freedom. It is not freedom from but freedom for, not negative freedom but positive freedom. Responsible for what? Responsive, in the first place, to the reality that is my concrete temporal life. Freedom is not simply the self-transcending capacity of the "I" to distance itself from the world (my specific particularity included), but the capacity to relate to this particularity, for I am also a creature living in concrete temporal conditions. Kierkegaard never tires of insisting that I am an *existing* cognitive spirit. Choosing only the abstract infinite self is to lose myself as a whole human being, to be less than integrated, to fail as a Kierkegaardian self. As the Judge says: "To choose oneself abstractly is not to choose oneself ethically. Not until a person has taken himself upon himself, has put on himself, has *totally interpenetrated himself so that every movement he makes is accompanied by a consciousness of responsibility for himself*—not until then has a person chosen himself ethically" (E/O 248, emphasis added). And by "putting on himself" the Judge means that the individual "becomes conscious as this specific individual," as the physical-psychic-social being that he has become and is becoming. It is clear that there is not finally an opposition between the ethical and esthetic, the esthetic is taken up—into the ethical—or at least that is the ideal aspiration.

Another way Kierkegaard has Judge William express this core of the ideal of personhood, the infinite ethical requirement, is in terms of duty. The idea of duty suggests a Kantian ethic, and Kierkegaard's vision is deeply, although not totally, Kantian. One's duty as the Judge refers to it appears not simply as the requirements of practical reason or as something required that is ultimately alien to us as human beings. Rather our duty is the fulfillment of our being as creatures who have an interest in how our lives are going and who can critically evaluate and shape our lives, who are predisposed toward the freedom of personhood. I think Kierkegaard assimilates the later Kant, the Kant of *Religion within the Limits of Reason Alone.* Here Kant (1793) speaks of a "predisposition to personality" that lies at the heart of the human being and provides an incentive for adopting the moral law within us. This "un-Kantian" idea is expressed by Kant thus: "The predisposition to personality is the capacity for simple respect for the moral law [*Wille*] as *in itself a sufficient incentive of the will* [*Wilkur*]. This capacity for simply respect for the moral law within us would be moral feeling" (1793, 22–23). I am *interested* in the moral law, in myself as an ethical person, in personhood, because of what Kant calls this "subjective ground" or "predisposition" that inclines me toward personhood. The "capacity for simple respect for the moral law within us" is nothing other than spirit as responsive freedom, as the ability to rationally and responsibly engage life. For the later Kant there seems to be an "ought" at the heart of the human being; an ought that compels my will (*Wilkur*) to adopt *Wille,* the considerations of practical reason, and thereby leads me into the freedom of personhood. Judge William agrees and puts it this way: "Duty is not something laid upon but something that lies upon" and is the expression of a person's "innermost being." Indeed, says the Judge, if the ethical did not have this "much deeper connection with the personality it would always be very difficult to champion it against the aesthetic" (E/O 254). This suggests that the ethical is deeply tied into the nature of the human being, and if a person does not come to understand themselves in this way they are not only making a cognitive shortfall about essential humanness but also missing out on a great good—the eradication of spiritual despair.

Conscience is another term that Kierkegaard uses to express the core of the ideal of personhood, and for many of us this clearly captures the responsive dimension of freedom, of spirit as responsible freedom. In *Concluding Unscientific Postscript* Climacus says that ethics has to do with the "eternal demands that conscience makes upon the individual" (CUP 346). In his *Journals* Kierkegaard is even more explicit: "Actually it is the conscience which constitutes personality [or personhood]. . . . The conscience may sleep, but the possibility of it is constitutive" (SKJP 3.483). I think Bishop Butler captures some of Kierkegaard's thoughts about conscience, when he says: "There is a principle of reflection in men, by which they distinguish between, approve and disapprove their own action. We are plainly constituted such sort of creatures as to reflect upon our own nature. The mind can take a view of what passes with itself, its propensions, aversion, passions, affections. . . . This principle in man which he approves or disapproves of his heart, temper, and actions, is conscience" (1727, 341). When Judge William says I am to be "transparent to myself" in "every movement" I make, I must "penetrate my whole concretion with consciousness," he is thinking of ethical duty as conscience, and he is thinking of it in a very strong sense. In this effort my overall goal is total and continual integration of myself throughout my praxis, for constancy and integrity of self as I engage the conditions of my concrete life: "The person who lives ethically expresses the universal in his life. He makes himself the universal human being, not by taking off his concretion, for then he becomes a complete nonentity, but by putting it on and interpenetrating it with the universal. . . . The task [for spirit] is to work the accidental and universal together into a whole" (E/O 256). This is a task that is not named by simply saying that I must engage life in evaluative terms, or that I should have a settled set of moral convictions and live within them, or that I am a person of "good conscience." It is far more strenuous than that.

Do the ideas of duty and conscience, more specifically moral notions, add anything substantive to spirit, or are they simply different ways of putting the same strenuous ideal? I do not think they add anything substantive, but they express more precisely the centrality of inwardness, of reflectivity and evaluative considerations for Kierkegaard's high ideal of personhood. Expressing spirit as duty and conscience accentuates spiritual life as a life of *evaluative strenuousness, a strong responsible freedom,* and not as a more romantic notion of self-expression, and not as a rationalistic notion of autonomy in opposition to the concretion that is my life. Kierkegaard's Judge William is clearly a radical defender of what Basil Mitchell calls "the traditional conscience" (1980, 78). A person who affirms the traditional conscience believes that moral demands are "not the expression simply of choices made by them or their society, but are in some important sense objective and categorical" (1980, 78). The rationale for the traditional conscience is usually tied to a "confidence in common human nature," and this confidence (often unknown to its defenders) is closely tied to a Christian theistic background. The Victorian confidence, says Mitchell, in "the importance and validity of conscience . . . derived from a Christian tradition" (1980, 84). In the final analysis, according to Mitchell, the defender of the traditional conscience cannot maintain strictly secular assumptions, for only a religious metaphysics of morals can provide the rationale needed. As early as Judge William, Kierkegaard affirms a similar answer to our interest in existential orientation; Judge William is a defender of an orthodox Christian humanism. But at this point I want to note how such an affirmation also clearly takes the Kierkegaardian vision closer to the normative ideal of personhood and further away from the minimal descriptive conditions necessary to be a human person. Let me explain.

Our coach is a person, and a person that is functioning relatively well. He does not suffer from an identity crisis; he is not in a state of identity diffusion; he is not in despair—at least by his own lights. He might be if he had not fastened onto and cultivated his talent for coaching after his playing career ended; he might be if he had not found the "esthetic" content of his life. He found a medium for self-expression and surmounted the despair that comes from the inability to settle into a "life." What he has, and it is what seems central to forestalling an identity crisis and the meaninglessness that goes with it, is a motivating and relatively coherent grouping of cares and identifications. As he is he is relatively well integrated: he is able to identify real possibilities and move to actualize them; and he is self-conscious about this. Spirit has ripened for the coach in the sense that he is self-consciously engaged with life but not swallowed by it; he loves basketball but he is not infatuated with it. Sure he has frustrations, for he is invested in definite finite activities. As Harry G. Frankfurt writes: "A person who cares about something is invested in it. He *identifies* himself with what he cares about in the sense that he makes himself vulnerable to losses and susceptible to benefits depending upon whether what he cares about is diminished or enhanced" (1988, 83). But these frustrations are not debilitating, for he does not expect to have a life without frustrations, for that would be a life without corresponding benefits; instead, he strives to surmount them as best he can, or he lives with them if he cannot. He is not defined by his capacity for responsible freedom, he is not a strong spiritual evaluator, he is not living a life of moral strenuousness, but does this leave him mentally wrecked, morally destitute, or even spiritually (in the sense of self-conscious satisfaction with his life-purposes) bankrupt? As I see it, it does not. He may have lost himself (or, better, never defined himself) as a strong spiritual evaluator, but he has not dissolved as a person in any normal sense. So why should he want to live as a strong spiritual evaluator?

Because the human being, as Kierkegaard sees it, is *essentially* responsible freedom. Spirit is not only an impersonal capacity to disengage, to continually take another step back, but *in relation to the self as existing and cognitive,* it is a capacity for and inclination to objective engagement or, better, to *objective reengagement*—a term I borrow from Thomas Nagel. This ideal of objective reengagement is another way of stating an ideal of personhood, and it arises naturally for human persons. As Nagel explains, given the basic structure of human existence, we have a strong aspiration to such integration. The critical question is just how far we need to, or should, take this project of integration, or (more normatively) what advantages, what benefits, can be gained from this ideal of selfhood as opposed to other ideals. As a first effort to explore this question, I turn to Thomas Nagel.

A View from Nowhere and Somewhere

At this point, in order to further clarify Kierkegaard's perspective as we have it in the Judge's mediation, it is worthwhile to briefly consider Nagel's contemporary perspective. Some of Nagel's views as they are developed in his *The View from Nowhere* are strikingly parallel to Kierkegaard's.[2] I turn to Nagel now because I think he captures in contemporary terms how, given the conditions of human existence, we can set for ourselves just the ideal of integration that Judge William has developed. The Judge presents his choice of responsible freedom, of spirit as spirit, as a necessary step for our well-being, as a humanly necessary path for the self if the "soul" is to flourish and not wither away. The critical question is just how strongly and comprehensively this ideal demands to be realized. I, with Nagel, think that we are naturally tempted to strive for the Kierkegaardian ideal of personhood, but that there must be limits to how strongly we require this, for at its ultimate the ideal seems impossible and we are faced either with adopting a more modest ideal or "believing" that somehow the conditions are provided for realizing (or at least accommodating) the ideal.

Nagel sees the human self in terms of two standpoints: the subjective and the objective; there is the internal perspective of the particular subject and the more external perspective of the thinker who transcends his or her particular circumstances and objectifies them. Or put another way, we are simultaneously engaged with our particular life and disengaged; we are both "inside" our life and "outside" it; both somewhere and nowhere. Nagel speaks of the problem of "how to combine the perspective of a particular person inside the world with an objective view of that same world, the person and his viewpoint included" (1986, 3). He sees the fundamental activity of life as balancing the internal and the external, or integrating the subjective, the contingencies of my life, with the detachment that our ability to objectify our life produces. Both poles have strong pull, and neither can be easily dropped.

Obviously these perspectives are part of each of us, but exhibit themselves to various degrees. Generally speaking what seems to happen for each of us as we mature is that our ability to objectify takes us further and further out of our particular limited perspectives and we naturally become less and less encased in our own small world and more comprehending of the wider world. We expand our cognitive and emotional horizons. And these horizons include ourselves; we objectify our personality; the ways we appear to ourselves come under the objective view. But as we take objectivity out further and become more detached from the particular contingencies of our life, Nagel notes that we face the "new problem of reintegration, the problem of how to incorporate these results into the life and self-knowledge of an ordinary human being. One has to be the creature whom one has subjected to detached examination" (1986, 9). We are, he notes, inclined to downplay one of these two poles. Perennially popular is the tendency to say that objectivity has it right and that we need to detach from our subjective standpoint as far as possible. But Nagel sees this as finally less than "objective" because "if we want to understand the whole world, we can't forget about those subjective starting points indefinitely; we and our personal perspectives belong to the world" (1986, 6). It is necessary, Nagel argues, "to combine the recognition of our contingency, our finitude, and our containment in the world with an ambition of transcendence, however limited may be our success in achieving it" (1986, 9). The really difficult issue is how to combine these two perspectives in our thought and lives; the basic dilemma creates multiple philosophical problems.

When Nagel considers the problem of freedom he argues that from the subjective perspective we see ourselves as autonomous agents, freely choosing courses of action, but then from the objective view our actions are part of the natural world and we see ourselves as a product of given conditions. Our first move is to take those conditions as they are revealed by the objective view and use them in our choices. We try to expand our autonomy. I consider the alternatives open to me and gather as much information as I can, then I choose. My choices are now more autonomous because they are not so influenced by factors I do not recognize. My freedom expands when I see how I am engaging the contours of temporality; I take more and more control. With this knowledge I can revise my course of action, set myself on a different course, one that is more of my own choosing. But as we push the objective view further we want to act in light of everything about our lives and the world in which we live. As Nagel says: "I wish to act not only in light of the external circumstances facing me and the possibilities that they leave open, but in light of the internal circumstances as well: my desires, beliefs, feelings and impulses. I wish to be able to subject my motives, principles, habits to critical examination, so that nothing moves me to action without my agreeing to it" (1986, 119). On Nagel's view, this is something that is natural to us as reflective human beings. The ethical posture, as a posture that tries to incorporate the objective standpoint into a particular subject's perspective and life, is one way of trying to bring our lives together. To quote Nagel again: "Ethics is one route to objective engagement because it supplies an alternative to pure observation of ourselves from outside. It permits the will [for Kierkegaard, the self-transcending spirit] to expand at least some way along the path of transcendence possible for the understanding" (1986, 136).

It is not hard to see Kierkegaard's view here. Kierkegaardian selfhood is not something above and beyond the relationship I have constructed in reflecting on my life. It is just that relation, or, better, it is the results of the aspiration for integration or for objective reengagement. And the path to integration that beckons is that of strong evaluative autonomy. The critical question is just how far can we take the ideal, just how deeply can an individual pursue objective reengagement? The Judge seems to say that it must be the single-minded core of one's self-identity, and therefore the soul must acknowledge that finite identifications cannot satisfy our infinite yearning or desire for an absolute standpoint: "Nothing that is finite, not even the whole world, can satisfy the soul of a person that feels the need of the eternal" (E/O 203). So it is not enough to take some steps toward integration, toward interpenetrating life with self-consciousness and living from the interpenetration; one must decisively and earnestly adopt that standpoint of personhood. The Judge sets up a strong ideal of complete objective reengagement, but can it be realized?

Strong Evaluative Identity and Moral Content

Before I consider this question, I want to consider in what sense the strong ethical/spiritual evaluator is a moral evaluator. I take it that there is a distinction between moral evaluation and a broader ethical or spiritual evaluative posture. Does the stance of the strong ethical/spiritual evaluator have any *moral* content, in the sense of perceiving and considering the interests of others in one's evaluative weighing? And what is that content if there is any? The decisive step for the Judge is to take upon one's self responsibility for one's whole concretion, all that one has become up until this point. What does this mean? One chooses to *accept* what one has become, the identifications that have shaped one, the capacities that are one's strengths, the limitations that are one's weaknesses, the whole actual identity formation as it has occurred. The Judge puts it well and gives us a hint about the next step: "The person who has ethically chosen and found himself possesses himself defined in his entire concretion. He possesses himself as an individual who has these capacities, these passions, these inclinations, these habits, who is subject to these external influences, who is influenced in one direction thus and in another thus. Here he then possesses himself as a task in such a way that it is chiefly to order, shape, temper, inflame, control—in short, to produce an evenness in the soul, a harmony, which is the fruit of the personal virtues" (E/O 262).

The task now is ethical self-identity; the conditions are set for genuine ethical existence, for becoming a Kierkegaardian person. From this point on the individual is engaged in an ethic of self-realization. In many respects, Kierkegaard's existential ethic has as much in common with classic Greek ethical attitudes, such as Aristotle, as with the altruistic orientation of modern Christian-influenced moral thought. Or at least this is true of Judge William's reflections. We are now involved in penetrating our actual full identity with the reflective ability to re-present this identity to ourselves, and this has the effect of giving us the ability to recast our full identity, to (in the Judge's words) transfigure ourselves. The first crucial point, a point that the Judge emphasizes, is that now I can load my own dice. As Flanagan writes: "Because self-representing is an activity internal to a complex but single system, it does not leave things unchanged. The activity of self-representation is partly constitutive of actual identity" (1991, 138). What was previously a process in which "I" had no oversight, now I am given the possibility of editorship or even, it seems, of sovereignty. And what the Judge told us in the beginning, "through the choice the personality submerges itself in that which is being chosen," is clarified; when it comes to the activity of self-representing identity, of becoming a person, what I fasten onto, what I shape and order, makes a deep difference from here on. But does this "choice" take us in a moral direction? If by moral we mean cultivating our existential identity as the core of the process of self-integration, it clearly does. If by moral we mean due consideration for the interests of others, it is harder to tell, but I think that, like classic Greek thought, the moral is central to the good human life for the Judge. And insofar as this is the case, some of the tension between the self's happiness and the well-being of others is overcome. Let me try to explain.

To get to the point where Kierkegaardian identity develops, the process of self-representing must expand so that self-representing identity *as normative* becomes central, becomes the full-time focus of the person. When I make this choice I make the choice not simply to care about who I am becoming, but to consider if I am becoming as I should. This activity becomes central to who I am. In this process I ethically engage my life, and my life, my full identity, my empirical me, is "a concrete self in living interaction with these specific surroundings, these life conditions, this order of things" (E/O 262). The Judge is well aware that social relations also constitute a person's full actual identity, and so, the Judge continues: "The self that is the objective [goal, *telos*] is not only a personal self but a social, a civic self" (262). So I am still an individual involved in various roles and relationships, institutions and ideals, but now I have the task of evaluating these, discerning the good, and willing it. I am accountable to this social dimension too. In this activity I come to appreciate the value of social or civic virtues. Doing my duty means, then, that I am ethically engaged in social life, that I consider life always in normative terms, trying to sort out the better from worse. More than that the Judge does not tell us because what exactly my duty is will be relative to me; that I have my duty to perform in becoming a person is the crucial point, for it is the universal. Doing my duty gives my life purpose and direction, but more than this since it gives it a purpose that is mine, for I am doing *my duty.* The exact moral content of my life, or the ethical self I am becoming, will be determined by my past, by the current conditions of my life, and by my growing practical wisdom. Judge William would agree with William James when James says that "there is but one unconditional commandment, which is that we should seek incessantly, with fear and trembling, so to vote and to act as to bring about the very largest total universe of good which we can see. Abstract rules can help; but they help the less in proportion as our intuitions are more piercing and our vocation is the stronger for the moral life" (1897, 209).

In pursuing the ethical life, the Judge suggests, one will work for a living (for all humans have a vocation, he says), one will marry and have a family, but these really seem just to be paradigmatic examples of what it means to be engaged in life as a self-conscious responsible project. For example, if I am born into a family as a female, I am a "daughter" and this designation carries with it certain familial, social, and cultural meanings, meanings that structure my point of departure as an ethical agent. I think that the ethical life has some particular moral content for the Judge because persons are always socially situated; they are defined in part by their social context. If I were to deny the interests and claims of others and be a strong egoist, I would not be taking responsibility for my full concretion. How deeply the ethical life will be a moral life remains unclear, because how my life goes next depends on how I work out the whole normative matter, how I negotiate the given of "daughter" and the possibilities for "this daughter" in the future.

The Judge (and Kierkegaard) does not think that we can say much more, for the empirical (which includes social context), while important, is not the core of the ethical. Indeed, the Judge (in one sense) is not really concerned about the specifics of the ethical life broadly conceived; the content question, the standards and principles for living are not foremost for him. The crucial point is that I engage my life as a strong spiritual evaluator. The point is that I consider (always consider) whether my life has any genuine worth, whether it realizes the good, whether my projects, my concerns, my identifications, are acceptable or should they be modified or even rejected. At one point Judge William says: "What is important in choosing is not so much to choose the right thing as the energy, the earnestness, and the pathos with which one chooses" (E/O 167). The greater the ethical earnestness, the more intense my spiritual passion, the more I am centered in spirit. I am striving, intensely and earnestly striving, to get it "right" but most important is that in so doing, I have got it right! It is almost as if, as Alasdair MacIntyre says, "the good life for man is the life spent in seeking for the good life for man" (1984, 219).

As we will see, this is a point that emerges even more clearly in *Con-*

cluding Unscientific Postscript, when Climacus declares that subjectivity, the orientation of the spirit and how I stand in relationship to my concretion, is the truth. Kierkegaard rarely discusses the content of ethical life; it is the *how* that is critical, not the *what.* As Gordon Marino mentions, Kierkegaard "fails to appreciate, let alone help us come to grips with, a fact that unsettles many a conscience and nearly every ethical theorist—the fact of moral diversity" (2001, 121). (And we might add religious diversity, for, as we will see, for Kierkegaard the religious is equally founded in the question of *how* I live in relation to what I understand.) That the Judge is not concerned with content, with normative standards, but with the inward intention to will the good, is clear when he imagines a moral skeptic who argues that moral codes are shifting and relative to social and historical context:

> Too often free thinkers have tried to confuse the concepts by pointing out how at times a people has pronounced something to be sacred and lawful that in the eyes of another people was abomination and evil. Here they have let themselves be blinded by the external, but with the ethical there is never a question of the external but of the internal. But however much the external is changed, the moral value of the action remains the same. It has been pointed out that whereas all civilized nations made it the children's duty to care for their parents, savages practiced the custom of putting their aged parents to death. This may very well be so, but still no headway is made thereby, because the question remains whether the savages intend to do something evil by this. The ethical always resides in this consciousness, whereas it is another question whether insufficient comprehension is responsible. (E/O 265)

The crucial point is to sincerely and honestly strive to be a fully engaged ethical agent, to put one's life together into a whole, to give it coherence and continuity, to make it all into *one's* self. This is a critical point for the Judge (and Kierkegaard): I am after a harmony of soul, a wholeness of character. *Ultimately this means that self-representing identity should be the constitutive basis of my full actual identity.* Full actual identity now has at its core the process of inspecting and evaluating full actual identity; I am defined by my activity of self-evaluating; or better, since this sounds too conceptual, I am living out of my activity of self-evaluation. It is easy to see that this is no simple matter, for my full actual identity is a result of the interaction between me (my thought, imaginings, emotions, etc.) and my empirical world, and the whole configuration is changing as my temporal scene changes. In addition, with spirit in the driver's seat, my full actual identity is also a result of how "I" respond to my full actual identity. Or better, my full actual identity should not be responding without me regulating the process: I am in the driver's seat; I am fully responsible, fully responsive to my life. *The empirical relations that constitute the self cannot serve as the constitutive ground for the self, only "I" can.* But can "I" provide a standard for ethical evaluation? Is it enough to sincerely intend the good? Kierkegaard sometimes seems to indicate that he thinks the question of the standard for engaging the world can be bypassed, but increasingly realizes that judging is the stuff of life, and judging means standards. If the empirical relations cannot constitute the self, what can? The "I" itself is nothing without relationship; relationship provides measures for engagement, but what relationships can ground a self-transcending self?

Judge William's Religious Psychology

If the personality is the absolute that has its *telos* in itself, where does the divine enter into the dynamics of the ideal of evaluative identity for the Judge? As I mentioned above, the Judge (like Climacus in *Concluding Unscientific Postscript*) finds the divine in the effort to penetrate one's concretion with ethical consciousness. In my effort to live as a strong evaluator, I encounter God; even though I may not choose the right thing. In the Judge's words: "Even though a person chose the wrong thing, . . . since the choice has been made with all the inwardness of his personality, his inner being is purified and he himself is brought into an *immediate relationship* with the eternal power that omnipresently pervades all existence" (E/O 167, emphasis added). The idea that in pursuing concrete freedom the individual is brought into a relationship to God is a theme more fully developed in later pseudonymous works. But it is clearly foreshadowed in the Judge's reflections. His is not simply an autonomous ethics in the Kantian sense, and by labeling his stance strong spiritual or evaluative autonomy, it should be clear that I do mean to say that his is a rationalistic ethic without connection to the other dimensions of humanness. The Judge's ethic is one of responsiveness and that includes, in the final analysis, responsiveness to God. As he puts it: "The ethical individual dares to employ the expression that he is his own editor, but he is also fully aware that he is responsible, responsible for himself personally, inasmuch as what he chooses will have a decisive influence on himself, responsible to the order of things in which he lives, [and] responsible to God" (260).

God, however, for the Judge (as in all of Kierkegaard's vision), is found within subjectivity; his is an inner theological journey. Realizing that one is spirit, that one holds in one's hands the capacity to achieve a self, to become a self-conscious unity of the universal and the accidental, is a most powerful experience; it is, the Judge declares, "The most inward and holy in a human being." Perhaps the most strikingly theological passage is when the Judge speaks of the ripening of the spirit as a moment when the self receives the gift of spiritual consciousness and knows itself in kinship with eternity:

> When around one everything has become silent, solemn as a clear starlit night, when the soul comes to be alone in the whole world, then before one appears, not an extraordinary human being, but *the eternal power itself,* then the heavens seem to open, and the I chooses itself or, more correctly, *receives itself.* Then the soul has seen the highest, which no mortal eye can see and which can never be forgotten; then the personality receives the accolade of knighthood that ennobles it for an eternity. (E/O 177, emphasis added)

We have here a sort of pietism, an experienced sense of being foundationally related to God, where the point of contact is the reality of self-transcending, self-constituting identity. I am not merely a "mortal"; I am related to eternity. Indeed, it is a fascinating passage, for the Judge suggests here that spiritual awakening is not so much something I do, as something that happens to me; I receive this infinite consciousness, this gift of spiritual freedom; the idea is parallel to that of "the ripening of the spirit." It is a point that both Climacus and Anti-Climacus return to.

Why then does the Judge go theological? For the Judge the self as spirit represents a point of orientation that is not merely empirical, but a secure standpoint in the flux of history, therefore it is the ultimate; he declares it divine. The spirit is not an empirical apprehension, it is an "inward" apprehension, and indeed it is inwardness itself. The Judge apprehends God within; Climacus expresses it this way: "God is in the creation, everywhere in the creation, but he is not there directly, and only when the single individual turns inward into himself (consequently only in the inwardness of self-activity) does he become aware and capable of seeing God" (CUP 243). The Judge does not spell out the epistemological status of this apprehension; he is not inclined to philosophical or epistemological reflections. This effort will await Climacus. Indeed, the full implications of the self as ultimately a "theological self" before God are not yet clear for the Judge. But what does seem clear for the Judge is that the human self, when it reaches toward ethical self-integration, comes to a point where it realizes that its project of strong evaluative identity is rooted in a power that provides spiritual grounding for an infinitely self-transcending self. The divine rooting provides no specific content for the self, it only increases the strenuousness of the task, it makes the task one that is divinely ordained. The ethical self is now a project that is "under an eternal responsibility" (E/O 270). To become ethically conscious is to become conscious of one's "eternal being" (271).

The Judge, it is sometimes argued, must be moving toward a theonomous ethic, where God is the source and ground of the evaluative stance of spiritual freedom. George Connell (1992) explores this "theonomous" dimension in Judge William's thought and argues that the Judge's theological convictions are related to motivational or practical concerns. He sees Judge William as claiming that "the self can only take responsibility for itself in an earnest, nonexperimental manner if this choice is taken before a higher authority able to hold the self to its choice" (1992, 65). In other words, "the unbounded self, the self that knows no higher authority than itself, is subject to its own whims and moods" (1992, 63). Connell also cites a late (1850, after the publication of *The Sickness unto Death*) journal entry that expresses Kierkegaard's view that a Kantian ethics of human autonomy is motivationally insufficient: "Kant was of the opinion that man is his own law (autonomy)—that is, he binds himself under the law which he himself gives himself. Actually, in a profounder sense, this is how lawlessness or experimentation is established. Constraint there must be if it is going to be in earnest. If I am bound by nothing higher than myself and I am to bind myself, where would I get the rigorousness as A, the binder, which I do not have as B, who is supposed to be bound, when A and B are the same self" (SKJP 1.76).

I do not see this divine motivational motif in the Judge's thought quite as much as Connell. He admits that he is looking at the letter Judge William writes entitled "The Aesthetic Validity of Marriage." I do think that this becomes a crucial point for Kierkegaard as his authorship progresses, hence the above journal entry. It is predominately the increasing sense of the exceeding strenuousness of the ideal that leads to the idea that only a divine mandate, one that holds my eternal blessedness at stake, will keep me engaging with an ideal that I sense is impossible for me. But I am not so sure the Judge understands things this way; he speaks of the ethical as my connection to the divine, and therefore, the ethical person has "an inner serenity and sense of security, for he does not have duty outside himself but within himself. When the ethical is viewed properly it makes the individual infinitely secure within himself" (E/O 254–55). The Judge does not need a higher authority to keep him engaged, he is no longer subject to whims and moods, he is secure in himself by virtue of his firm and absolute point of departure: personhood has its *telos* in itself.

In any event, as I see it, the Judge has very strong reasons, apart from any divine authority, to be responsive to the empirical world, for it is his relations to the world that enable him to become a concrete spiritual self. Without these relations a person is nothing, at least nothing in the ethical/psychological sense. If I have no self-represented identity, I am nobody for myself. And to lose myself as an ethical self results in depression; the spirit will not let itself be mocked, says the Judge. So there are strong psychological (or nontheological) reasons for engaging life as responsible freedom. And we can certainly note that many individuals seem to live lives that are ethically admirable, and they have no convictions about standing before a higher divine authority. So it is not an empirical truth about human moral psychology; it is, as we will explore later, a more normative truth that results from the very high ideal of Kierkegaardian selfhood. There is a need for a strong arm to twist me into continuing to pursue an ideal that leaves me with a contradictory and failing consciousness of selfhood.

Judging Judge William

In the Judge's reflections on the ethical we have the essentials of Kierkegaard's whole ideal of humanness; matters only get more intense as we move into what he calls Religiousness A (universal or immanent religiousness) and Religiousness B (Christianity). Although Christianity is arguably a qualitative transition, the essentials are in place for providing the Kierkegaardian justification for spiritual and finally Christian existence. The crucial point is that living within the ideal of personhood, it should be clear by now, is no simple task. But it is a task that is inescapable. The Judge sometimes suggests that it is a relatively straightforward task of making "the choice of one's self" and renewing it in the course of one's life. In the end the Judge seems confident that he can make the movement of infinity, that the infinite ethical requirement can be realized: the despair of life can be surmounted in the ethical victory over life's despair. Although I do not agree with Anthony Rudd (and other commentators), who argues that Judge William is finally just a reflection of the conventional mores of his society, it is clear that he thinks, as Rudd notes, that "one can succeed ethically. By willing to become a self, I can become a self—by ethical striving I can resolve the disharmonies of existence into a coherent unity" (1993, 142). But this is somewhat deceptive, for living as the Judge recommends means that I am simultaneously detached from all finite realities, I do not invest myself in them, *and* I am engaged in life or, better, reengaged with the finite world, with all the conditions that make up my concretion. I care about nothing in particular, for I despaired of life, but then I come back, I reaffirm everyday life, and thereby I achieve a highly reflective, inwardly active self. But maintaining such a self surely requires enormous effort to be both in life and out of it, to be both in the finite but not of it. Surely I will slip here or there, get emotionally bound up with a project, fall in love, care too deeply for my children, identify inordinately with my work, or even get caught up in a matter of (seemingly) great significance to my fellow human beings. Or, put another way, I will simply miss accurately tracking my full actual identity, and insofar as I fail at this I am not free. My ideal is to interpenetrate not only my world but also my internal self so that nothing moves me without the rational and responsible self consenting. Full evaluative selfhood, responsible spiritual freedom is lacking if there is a hard spot somewhere, an element of my history not yet mine. And this is true as I live forward and think backward and inspect my motives, my will, myself, for those finite relativities not yet infinitized.

Maybe this is why the Judge advocates choosing despair. But the implications of this choice were not clear to the Judge, at least in Climacus's opinion. The Judge realizes that no finite reality can serve as constitutive ground for unifying the self, and so he chooses himself as freedom. To do so in practice, in time as an existing person, means not having any finite aspect of life outside of the scope of consciousness; the ideal is transparency. As I pointed out above, this seems to mean at its highest reaches that I have to act from a God's-eye point of view, that I would have to be infinitely outside myself as I lived my particular life. This seems impossible. As Climacus says, in reviewing the work of the Judge: "The ethicist in *Either/Or* has saved himself by despairing, but in my opinion there was a discrepancy here. In despairing I use myself to despair, and therefore I can indeed despair of everything by myself, but if I do this I cannot come back by myself" (CUP 257–58). That is, I cannot come back to myself as full spiritual freedom because from what specific elements of myself, my world, do I live, where exactly do I stand, to what do I give my allegiance?

The Judge is now caught in the cul-de-sac of strong spiritual evaluation. He has found the point of transcendence outside the empirical and historical, it is himself as spirit, and he has touched the divine, but then he has to live in the empirical and the historical that is his concrete identity, for spirit is only relationship: it must have some content, or it is nothing. Rudd (1993) rightly suggests that one problem that shipwrecks the ethical stance is the question of the content of the ethical life: what specific projects does the ethicist commit to? But, of course, the problem really is that *all* content that is merely empirical, merely finite, either from considerations of human nature or our social context, is lacking. One sort of "content" is not merely empirical and that again is spirit, but as *existing* spirit I am inextricably bound up with the empirical world. And so it begins to look like my existence is bound up with (as Climacus will tell us) an irresolvable "contradiction." The Judge as adopting the strong ethical stance aspires to overcome the contradiction, to overcome the absurdity that comes from being a finite creature with an infinite task. But while the Judge has the ideal right, he has not yet seen that it is not possible, not possible at least without faith. In other words, Alastair Hannay's point is correct: Judge William has simply "underestimated the extent of the task of [Kierkegaardian] selfhood" (1998, 343).

Now Nagel's thought (as we looked at it above) suggests that the Judge is on the right track in holding together, in integrating, the reflective powers of objectifying *and* his particular actual identity through the ethical project of expanding inner horizons. This path of objective reengagement is a path of increased freedom. It seems clear that as a relational construct the self is just the activity of making self-consciousness the conditions of my life, identifying those cares and concerns that seem on reflection to be most acceptable, and then continuing to order, refine, and modify them. What is right in the Judge's view is that autonomy, as responsible freedom engaged with one's empirical world, the physical, psychical, and social concretion, is of great value. Humans find satisfaction in being able to successfully negotiate their life with their reflective abilities. There is clearly a link between engaged autonomy and human flourishing. The proof emerges in the praxis of integrating the two basic poles of myself. As John Stuart Mill put it, about the same time as Judge William:

> Where not the person's own character but the traditions or customs of other people are the rule of conduct, there is wanting one of the principle ingredients of human happiness. . . . The free development of individuality is one of the leading essentials of well-being. . . . To conform to custom merely as custom does not educate or develop in him any of the qualities which are the distinctive endowment of a human being. The human faculties of perception, judgment, discriminative feeling, mental activity, and even moral preference, are exercised only in making a choice. He who does anything because it is the custom makes no choice. He gains no practice in discerning or desiring what is best. (1859, 68–71)

This is not far from Judge William, and I think the Judge means to affirm just this link between autonomy, self-realization, and happiness. But the problem is that Kierkegaard aspires to more than this. Mill clearly realizes that autonomy, as bringing reflective consciousness to bear on life, is "one of the ingredients of human happiness." But Kierkegaard wants it to stand as nothing less than our whole and complete existential identity. Kierkegaard realizes, I think, that the self-transcending self is not satisfied with an approximate transcendence, with a few steps toward integration of the objective (or external) standpoint within my particular subjective life, that ethical autonomy provides; the spirit wants a vision that will, as Nagel puts it, "encompass ourselves completely, and thus become the absolute source of what we do" (1986, 118). In this passage I think Nagel captures exactly the aspiration that drives Kierkegaard's reflections:

> The external standpoint at once holds out the hope of genuine autonomy, and snatches it away. By increasing our objectivity and self-awareness, we seem to acquire increased control over what will influence our actions, and thus to take our lives into our own hands. Yet the logical goal of these ambitions is incoherent, for to be really free we would have to act from a standpoint completely outside ourselves, choosing everything about ourselves, including all our principles of choosing—creating ourselves from nothing, so to speak. (1986, 118)

Nagel concludes that while "we become dissatisfied with anything less than this," the "objective standpoint creates an appetite which it shows to be insatiable," and pursued to its conclusion it ends in incoherence: "We cannot assess and confirm our entire system of thought and judgment from outside, for we would have nothing to do it with" (1986, 118). He recommends, as I noted above, that we strive for a more modest autonomy, a posture of objective engagement and integration, and acknowledge that we can never fully achieve complete autonomy because our objective perspective is always incomplete. Kierkegaard (or Anti-Climacus), we might note, takes such objective reflections, and dissatisfactions, to show that there must be a "standpoint completely outside ourselves," since we have these ambitions and we cannot have been created "from nothing." The next step is a religious standpoint, a standpoint finally not our own.

Notes

1. As Alastair Hannay points out, the Judge claims that "the aesthetic life is by its very dependence on contingencies of nature prone to feelings of what the aesthete will himself call 'despair,' frustrations of all kinds . . . , what one might call 'everyday' despair. But despair of this piecemeal and random kind is 'finite' and partial, while what William seems to mean by the term is something that pervades a whole life" (1998, 336).

2. Edward Mooney artfully uses Nagel's thought to illuminate Kierkegaard. See his *Selves in Discord and Resolve* (1996).

2 *Johannes Climacus: Spiritual Existence Intensified by Reflection*

The ideal of personhood, of the strong spiritual evaluator, runs throughout Kierkegaard's authorship. I think that much of this ideal is found in the Judge's letter entitled "The Balance between the Esthetic and the Ethical in the Development of the Personality" examined in the last chapter; even the religious dimension of the ideal is found in nascent form in the Judge's writings. But the later pseudonymous authorship adds to the vision of selfhood by making it even more strenuous, and much of the increase is related to the role of reflection. At this point I want to consider Kierkegaard's thought as it unfolds in the reflections of Johannes Climacus, especially in *Concluding Unscientific Postscript.* Kierkegaard's pseudonym Johannes Climacus makes his first appearance in a recently translated and previously unpublished work that Kierkegaard probably worked on shortly after *Either/Or,* but before his major *Philosophical Fragments* and *Concluding Unscientific Postscript,* that bears the title *Johannes Climacus or De Omnibus Dubitandum Est* (Everything must be doubted).[1]

Kierkegaard's pseudonym Climacus is an intensely reflective yet existentially interested individual; his thinking is an effort to find spiritual meaning, existential identity. In the work *Johannes Climacus,* Kierkegaard tells the story of Johannes Climacus, a character somewhat similar to A in *Either/Or,* but more philosophical, more of a thinker, who takes to heart the thesis that everything must be doubted. Kierkegaard tells us in a note appended to a draft of the work that he intends to "strike a blow at philosophy" (JC xiii). He will portray Johannes Climacus, an individual who doubts everything, but "in order to hold on to this extreme position of doubting everything, he has engaged all his mental and spiritual powers. If he abandons this position he may very well arrive at something, but in doing that he would have also abandoned his doubt about everything" (xiii). And since he spent some time on the project, by the time he reaches the conclusion that doubting everything is impossible, his life is wasted: "Life does not acquire any meaning for him, and it is the fault of philosophy" (xiii).

There are obvious parallels to the position of "choosing despair" that finally shipwrecks the existential efforts of Judge William. Both doubt and despair are efforts to overcome the dichotomy of existence, but the purely reflective posture and the more advanced volitional position are flawed efforts to win through to spiritual meaning. Doubt, belief, skepticism, volition, and faith are crucial elements in the reflections of Climacus. Climacus, as we encounter him in *Concluding Unscientific Postscript* is also a doubter, but with an interest in existence: "The youth is an existing doubter; continually suspended in doubt, he grasps for the truth—so that he can exist in it" (CUP 310). Much of modern philosophy, especially the Hegelian speculative effort, positively confuses things for the existing doubter, for the question is always, How do I come to actualize the truth, that is, to live within it?

The *Concluding Unscientific Postscript* is a meditation on human existence framed by a conviction that Christianity will make little sense if the issue of becoming a person, or ethically engaging life as the Judge has posed the matter, is not foremost for the individual. Christianity is an "existence-communication"; it is for subjectivity and not a doctrine about objective matters external to the person. Rather than becoming a self, Climacus refers to becoming subjective and asserts that "subjectivity is the truth." In less than 40 pages the effort to approach Christianity from the "objective" side is disposed of, and part 2 begins, "The Subjective Issue," and continues for the next 550 pages. The subjective issue is nothing other than the issue of becoming a Kierkegaardian self, of becoming a strong spiritual evaluator who craves existence in the truth, where truth means bringing himself together, becoming a unity of subject and object. The objective issue approaches existential matters from either the historical-critical approximation process or the "speculative" theological effort to bring God to light objectively. Both efforts, if seen as efforts to establish ethical attitudes, religious faith, or Christian commitment—matters of spiritual identity—are misguided. They are fine as scholarship, but the existing person is concerned, anxiously concerned, about truths that orient him in life, about matters of meaning. There is, however, on Kierkegaard's terms, an unbridgeable gap between empirical historical inquiry and normative spiritual inquiry; the former is an objective matter, and the subject needs to be abstracted from her own subjectivity, but the latter is a subjective matter and the subject must be oriented toward her own subjectivity, toward the state of her soul, if she is to pursue normative matters.

Climacus examines this subjective orientation in a more consistently philosophical manner than the Judge. The *Concluding Unscientific Postscript* contains Kierkegaard's most sustained discussion of epistemological views and a comprehensive portrait of the dynamics of ethical-religious existence. But I want to begin by showing how Climacus's views parallel the Judge's yet go beyond his by emphasizing many points that the Judge left philosophically vague. Next, we will examine the epistemological orientation of Climacus, an orientation that clarifies for Kierkegaard how existence can be thought, and finally how he understands the transition to religious consciousness. All along I will continue to expand my critical perspective on the Kierkegaardian vision.

From Ethical Judge to Religious Philosopher

In the last chapter I pointed out that the Judge's admonition to his young friend to become a strong ethical evaluator, to choose himself as strong responsible freedom, is an ideal that is so high that one is in danger of never being able to get started. Yet like the Judge, Climacus affirms the ethical as the highest: "The ethical as the absolute is infinitely valid in itself" (CUP 142); "the ethical is and remains the highest task assigned to every human being" (151).[2] But Climacus emphasizes two points that the Judge did not stress, points that Climacus clearly sees as undermining the Judge's confidence, his feeling that he had surmounted despair: (1) the temporal character of life that makes existing a never-finished process: epistemologically speaking it makes my life uncertain; existentially it means that I can never fully get myself fully together but must always be striving to unify and (2) the fact that as a reflective (cognitive) spirit, I can grasp existence (with one notable exception) only through concepts which are inescapably general and framed as possibility never as actuality; this too means that life is uncertain and that ultimate integration eludes me. Together this makes it very hard to fully realize objective reengagement; indeed, I will argue that it makes it impossible. The fact is, however, that these objections are overstated, and objective reengagement modestly stated has much to commend it.

Although Climacus reaffirms the human self as a polarity developed in freedom, his advance on the Judge is to accentuate the fact that living as a human being is an infinite striving and a never arriving, for the human being is an *existing* infinite spirit: "What is existence? It is that child who is begotten by the infinite and the finite, the eternal and the temporal, and is therefore continually striving" (CUP 92). For Climacus a crucial difficulty, a difficulty not stressed by the Judge, is temporality, the becoming of life-in-time for an existing person. The Judge saw the temptation to try to stand outside of time, to transcend it in the infinite reflection, and insisted that what must happen is that we return to the activities and projects of our temporal life. But Climacus sees time as a serious difficulty for the existing individual who would strive to realize the ideal of personhood, who tries to think and act in existence, who seeks to live as strong spiritual evaluator. In a passage that clearly resonates with the Judge he says: "But truly to exist, that is, to permeate one's existence with consciousness, simultaneously to be eternal, far beyond it, as it were, and nevertheless present in it, and nevertheless in a process of becoming—that is truly difficult" (308).

In addition, equally early on in his reflections, Climacus accentuates the difficulties in thinking existence: "The thoroughly educated and developed individuality is known by how dialectical the thinking is in which he has his daily life. To have his daily life in the decisive dialectic of the infinite, and yet to go on living—that is the art. *To have the dialectic of the infinite for daily use and to exist in it is, of course, the greatest strenuousness. . . . And that is the way it is with a spiritual existence intensified by reflection*" (CUP 86n, emphasis added). Spiritual existence intensified by reflection captures the strenuousness of the ideal; it captures a crucial element for Climacus: the deep difficulties for cognition in relation to practice. Reflection is more of a problem for the individual who would become a strong spiritual evaluator than the Judge realized; indeed, the Judge seems somewhat deficient in his reflective capacity, somewhat dialectically flatfooted. But Climacus's rich reflections have to do with *just how existence can be thought;* Climacus's reflections are an effort to philosophically clarify what the Judge affirms but did not adequately think through. In so doing Climacus goes into even deeper water than the Judge. Moving beyond (but never dropping) the ethical, he delves further into the *meaning* of truth, of certainty, of faith, into God-consciousness and the God-relationship, and finally into Christianity.

Much of Climacus's reflections, seemingly epistemological, have direct existential import. In this passage the existential conundrum for the

Judge can been seen peering through the issue of just how we capture reality in thought:

> If being is understood as empirical being, then truth itself is transformed into a desideratum and everything is placed in the process of becoming, because the empirical object is not finished, and the existing knowing spirit is itself in the process of becoming. Thus truth is an approximation whose beginning cannot be established absolutely. . . . On the other hand, every beginning, when it is *made* (if it is not arbitrariness by not being conscious of this), does not occur by virtue of immanental thinking but is *made* by virtue of a resolution, essentially by virtue of faith. (CUP 189)

This passage begins the now-famous section on subjectivity as truth, and it has to do with becoming subjective, becoming a Kierkegaardian self, achieving the ideal of personhood. But what should be clear after our examination of Judge William's views is that this refers to my situation as a strong evaluator trying to put myself together. I am an empirical object, a concretion, and I have as my task to penetrate myself with consciousness, to bring the infinite evaluative reflection into the finite. But as an empirical being, as existing, I am in a process of becoming, and therefore my unity and integration is "transformed into a desideratum." Truth, for me as existing, is an approximation, a continual striving and a never arriving; I cannot find my absolute beginning because (to recall the Judge) if the empirical is the only road allotted to me it is arbitrary to remain standing at any particular point. How do I get started putting myself together? Not, claims Climacus, by virtue of any immanental thinking, not simply or only by reflection, but by virtue of faith. For, as we will see, Climacus finds no point of "positive" or substantive certainty adequate as my point of existential departure.

Existential Epistemology

Climacus's reflections on the epistemological situation of humans are difficult to sort out. He takes numerous passes at framing this situation throughout *Concluding Unscientific Postscript*. To start it seems that he is clearly very skeptical of our ability to achieve knowledge. In the initial reflection on the German dramatist Lessing, Climacus asserts that what is called "positive knowledge" (knowledge that makes some substantive claim about the nature of things), is not really knowledge: "Sensate certainty is a delusion (see Greek skepticism and the entire presentation in modern philosophy, from which a great deal can be learned); historical knowledge is an illusion (since it is approximation-knowledge) and the speculative result is a phantom" (CUP 81). (Climacus repeats an almost identical claim later in CUP 316.) Where can our poor existential thinker find a sure point of departure? And note well that Climacus is after just such a strong foundation. Every subject, Climacus continues, "is an existing subject, and therefore this must be essentially expressed in all his knowing, and must be expressed by keeping his knowing from an illusory termination in sensate certainty, historical knowledge or illusory results" (81). Well, at least one thing seems certain, namely that nothing is certain. This, claims Climacus, is the "advantage" of the "negative thinkers"; "they have something positive, namely they are aware of the negative; the positive thinkers have nothing whatever, they are deluded" (81). But another certainty is available to the existing infinite spirit, and that is that he exists: "Nothing historical can become infinitely certain to me except this: that I exist" (81). This sounds like Descartes's *cogito,* but it is really more than consciousness, it is how I stand, really stand, in relation to what I grasp in consciousness; it is the self-constituting power of spirit. The inward relationship I can sustain to the content of my thought by decisively identifying with it, this I can know with certainty. This is my ethical actuality or myself from the subjective perspective. I return to this certainty below.

So Climacus seems of the view that knowledge, knowledge as certainty, is hard to come by. If our standard for knowledge is certainty, we know only two things: that externalities, empirical realities, are always beyond our comprehension, and that the internal self-reflexive relationship I sustain to myself is within my grasp. To understand Climacus's radical rejection of knowledge one needs to see that he has a very strong epistemic standard in mind. In fact it seems to be a standard that, by his construal of our epistemic situation, could not possibly be met. A crucial point here is Climacus's view of how the mind grasps reality.

Reality, in the sense of the concrete empirical particulars, the subject of scientific and historical study, is always at a distance from the knowing subject, for knowledge is a matter of grasping the particular in terms of the general. How does this occur? The mind operates in terms of what Climacus (in *Johannes Climacus*) calls ideality, the mediacy of concepts, of linguistic expression. Before we have language and concepts, we simply have "immediacy" (which is an "indeterminateness"), but then we do not have any questions about truth and falsity or about doubt and belief. When we develop and acquire our language, we can grasp reality or, better, a conception of reality as it is mediated in consciousness. Hence humans "have" reality only through the mediation of concepts; they do not have the existing particular, they have an abstraction. To paraphrase Climacus, in the act of cognition, mediacy "cancels" immediacy by the word, abstraction "annuls" the particular existent, "but that which is given expression is always *presupposed*" (JC 168). The last phrase indicates that Climacus is a realist, although given his strong sense of the role of language and concepts in knowing, one wonders on what basis he makes this affirmation. It also suggests how consciousness is the space where reality and ideality come together; consciousness always has objects (really, thought-objects), and while they are abstractions from reality, they nevertheless presuppose the reality. Hence, if we mean by knowledge the certainty of direct immediate contact with reality we will not have it; knowledge is abstraction from reality; for consciousness, positive knowledge, is always a possibility, a hypothesis.

Much of this appears in the reflections of Climacus in the recently published *Johannes Climacus.* But it also clearly appears in *Concluding Unscientific Postscript:* "What actuality is cannot be rendered in the language of abstraction. Actuality is an *inter-esse* between thinking and being in the hypothetical unity of abstraction. Abstraction deals with possibility and actuality, but its conception of actuality is a false rendition, since the medium is not actuality but possibility" (CUP 314). All knowledge about actuality (save our ethical identity) is possibility, is hypothetical; it might be just the truth about things, but it might not be, it is conjectural. So reality, in the sense of actuality or existing particulars, really cannot be thought anywhere; thinking annuls it. Existence cannot be thought because when the mind grasps reality it does so in terms of concepts and the relationship of conception to reality is always one of possibility; reality is always mediated by concepts. Still Climacus wants knowledge in the strong sense, wants to make contact with actuality. And he thinks we can inwardly do this; the true rendition can be had subjectively.

Abstract thinking, in its objectifying effort, disregards the particular, hence it disregards me: "The way of objective reflection turns the subjective individual into something accidental, and thereby turns existence into an indifferent vanishing something" (CUP 193). Looking at myself objectively is to look at myself from the outside, and from the "external perspective" I appear as a brief historical moment, an arbitrary mix of forces outside of me. Looking at life from the external standpoint is, at the maximum, to try to look at it from a God's-eye point of view: "Precisely because abstract thinking is *sub specie aeterni,* it disregards the concrete, the temporal, the becoming of existence, and the difficult situation of the existing person because of his being composed of the eternal and the temporal situated in existence" (301). So how do I grasp my life? I am after all a thinker, and the task is to think existence, but existence is always some concrete particular, not the general: "Existence is a very difficult matter to handle. If I think it, I cancel it, and then I do not think it. It would seem correct to say that there is something which cannot be thought—namely existing. But again there is the difficulty that existence puts it together in this way: the one who is thinking is existing" (309).

I should note that while Climacus is clearly skeptical about abstract thought's ability to provide knowledge, or objective certainty, he favors it over "pure thought"—a recent lunatic invention, in his view. Abstract thought, while disregarding existence, "still maintains a relation to it" (CUP 313). Abstract thought abstracts from actuality, it goes from the particular to the general. So while abstract thought is unable to penetrate to the actual, it can provide possibilities, and possibilities are critical for the process of becoming a self.

This takes us to Climacus's discussion of doubt and belief. We have seen that Climacus leans toward critical realism; he inclines toward the position that there is a reality and that truth is just the agreement of thinking with being. But he is no naive realist, since he is fully aware that humans know reality only through concepts. This, however, makes knowledge a vanishing subject, if it is asserted, to borrow Kant's language, that thought grasps reality as it is in itself. Knowledge requires thought-constructs, which means reality as it appears to us, possibilities. The best that "objective" knowing can achieve is an approximation; empirical inquiry is always open-ended, never conclusive and final. This strikingly contemporary passage is worth quoting, if only because it also shows how Climacus is not satisfied by the more or less of empirical understanding; he wants firm knowledge, not merely well-founded opinion:

> The world-historical material is endless, and consequently the limit must in one way or another be arbitrary. Although the world-historical is something past, as material for cognitive observation it is incomplete; it continually comes into existence through ever-new observations and research, which discover more and more or makes rectifying discoveries. Just as the number of discoveries in the natural sciences is augmented by sharpening the instruments, so also in the world-historical when the critical quality of observation is sharpened. (CUP 150)

From this Climacus draws the conclusion that if I could avoid drawing conclusions about the truth-status of the concepts with which I grasp the world, then I would never be deceived. The skeptic keeps in mind that she is mediating reality, and thereby always says to herself: "These are just thought-constructs, I will not conclude that they are true knowledge, that reality is revealed." Of course, as we saw when looking at the self-constituting acts of the spirit in the last chapter, this individual will never become anything; she will lose herself as an "ethical actuality"; she will remain a possibility. Skepticism is not objectively wrong; in fact, in many respects, it is just the correct attitude for someone who desires objective certainty. But practically, existentially, it is a disaster; it is a recipe for bankrupting one's soul; it is subjectively wrong. To become ethically actual, and this is the only actuality I can really reach, I will need to decide that just such and such seems to be the case and live within that conviction.

Ethical Actuality as Certainty

Recall that the Judge settled on the personality, the self-constituting power of spirit, as the absolute. The personality at its core is just the capacity for agency, for sustaining a relationship to my empirical concretion. It is, following Flanagan, what we called the agent's capacity for self-representing identity. But like the Judge, Climacus identifies spirit as fundamentally concerned about how it stands with my life; spirit is an evaluative interest in measuring how I am related to myself. Climacus, again like the Judge, sees it as our Archimedean point, our certain grounding in the shifting sands of the empirical. Throughout *Concluding Unscientific Postscript* Climacus takes several passes at stating this core claim: "The ethical is the only certainty, to concentrate upon this the only knowledge that does not change into a hypothesis at the last moment, to be in it the only secure knowledge" (CUP 152). Further on Climacus returns to this point: "The only actuality concerning which a person has more than knowledge about is his own actuality, that he exists, . . . the only actuality there is for an existing person is his own ethical actuality" (316). In grasping my own "ethical actuality," I have "more than knowledge"; I do not simply have a thought-possibility; I have actuality. It should be clear that Climacus wants to draw a distinction between actuality in the empirical sense and actuality in the inward sense, and he is favoring the latter: "The actuality is not the external action but an interiority in which the individual annuls possibility and identifies himself with what is thought in order to exist in it. This is action" (339). I may not have the empirical right, indeed, I can never get objective certainty, but I cannot be mistaken about the relationship I sustain to the empirical. In Kantian fashion, Climacus states: "That my intention was this and that, I can in all eternity know absolutely, because this is an expression of the eternal within me, is myself, but the historical externality in the next moment can be reached only *approximando*" (575). I can have subjective certainty.

Such a position seems odd. Is Climacus claiming that the relationship I can sustain to myself is not a knowledge relationship, does not employ concepts? He sees it as the most secure knowledge; and he refers to it as "essential knowledge." He seems to think it is of a different order, a different kind of knowledge than straightforward empirical "positive" knowledge, which is really belief. But still, essential knowing must employ concepts to grasp the actuality that is just myself; after all, how else do I know things? Even Kierkegaard admits this. If that is the case, how is the problem of the gap between thought and reality really overcome? When I turn to the method of the subjective thinker we will look more closely at this issue. For now I want to stress how deeply Climacus is seduced by the lure of the objectivist urge, an urge that lives from (to use Richard Bernstein's phrase) the "Cartesian anxiety" (1985, 16–20).[3]

I think it is clear that Climacus denies that we can have knowledge of reality in any strong sense; a search for "objective" certainty will end without any spoil save my own subjectivity. What is the standard for knowledge in this strong sense? Some substantive claim that is beyond all possible doubt, that can be seen as a final, permanent, ahistorical framework or ground that I can appeal to in building all my other claims to know. As Bernstein puts it, "The objectivist maintains that unless we can ground philosophy, knowledge, or language in a rigorous manner we cannot avoid radical skepticism" (1985, 8). Kierkegaard finds his ground in subjectivity; inward knowledge is secure. Without this the only option is skepticism. While existing realities are beyond our grasp as they are in themselves, we can grasp the internal self-reflexive relationship we sustain to thought-possibilities; we can know ourselves just as we are. After all, what am I as a self but just the relation I sustain to my thought? Ethically speaking the possibilities I live in are my existential actualities. To quote Climacus once more: "The ethical can be carried out only by the individual subject, who then is able to know what lives within him—the only actuality that does not become a possibility by being known and cannot be known only by being thought, since it is his own actuality, which he knew as possibility, before it became actuality" (CUP 320).

C. Stephen Evans, however, proposes that "one must recognize that Kierkegaard uses the term 'knowledge' in two different ways" (1998, 165). One sense is that knowledge requires a certainty that classical foundationalism thought was required to say that we know. This is the epistemic objectivist sense that we have just reviewed. The other way is to use knowledge in a looser sense where there are many "things that in everyday life are regarded as known" (1998, 165). Evans claims that the issue comes down to "the demand for objective certainty present in the classical epistemologies. If one accepts this demand, Kierkegaard argues, nothing can be known except the individual's own ethical reality. Kierkegaard himself, however, is not committed to this ideal and seeks to undermine it by showing that much of what we accept as knowledge in ordinary life does not meet it" (1998, 165). I think this is to misconstrue how seriously Climacus (and I think Kierkegaard) bought into the epistemic standards of modern classical foundationalism. In particular, I think he was influenced by Descartes's, Kant's, and Hegel's efforts to satisfy our desire for ultimate constraints; he wants, as Bernstein says, "a stable and reliable rock to secure our thought and action" (1985, 19). (I want to note, even here, that despite himself Kierkegaard moves away from these objectivist concerns toward a more hermeneutical posture when it comes to defending his vision of the normatively human.) At this juncture, however, I want to stress how Climacus feels compelled, because of the high standards of epistemic certainty he holds, to advocate a conception of human understanding that rests on the (presumably) more secure basis of the subject's own self-reflexivity than on our interpretations of empirical reality.

The crucial distinction in Climacus's conception of human understanding is the difference between subjective and objective standpoints, what he later calls the "absolute distinction": "In order to clarify the divergence of objective and subjective reflection, I shall now *describe* subjective reflection in its search backward and inward into inwardness" (CUP 198–99, emphasis added). We know how objective reflection goes: its search for external certainty ends in possibilities, hypotheses, and an infinite never-ending approximation process. But when we turn reflection to the subject and ask about truth, we are asking about how the subject stands in relation to what he may know: *"If only the how of this relation is in the truth, the individual is in truth, even if he in this way were to relate himself to untruth"* (199). Now we know that we can never be sure if we are relating to the truth when it comes to objective reality, the "what" is a matter of possibility. But no matter, for the really critical point, the point where we can be certain, is in the *how* relationship. But what does it mean to say that this how relation is in the truth? Climacus takes knowledge of God as his example, and we will return to this point, but let us first take a somewhat less controversial example: knowledge of another person.

Climacus says that I need to relate myself to God in such a way that my relation is in truth a "God-relation." But we will substitute "person-relation" for "God-relation" and follow Climacus's line of thought. What is the result? If I was to approach the other person objectively I would inquire into her as an empirical reality, I would enter "upon all approximating deliberation intended to bring forth" this person objectively. Of course, I could not be sure that I had grasped her just as she is, for presumably getting to know someone is sort of like historical scientific inquiry, never certain, never final. This could take some time to get to know who the other is, but presumably I could get to know her more and more. Still I might say to myself, I cannot be sure that I have grasped her in the whole truth and nothing but the truth; I might be missing something. I begin to get concerned, since this person is my lover, and I really need to know just who she really is. I need to know her dispositions, her tendencies, even her inner character, for my well-being depends on it. My anxiety increases, and I strongly desire to be certain that I know her; it is not too much to say that it occupies my attention full time, that I begin to be just the person who desires knowledge of my love. If we are talking about God, just now, in this anxious concern to know God, in this infinite concern, I am closer to the truth, closer to God than if I would dispassionately seek God out objectively—or so we will see Climacus argue. But with regard to my lover this seems altogether wrongheaded if it is meant to bring her, another reality, to light. I would do better to continue to observe her behavior and talk with her about her beliefs and values. But notice, it does tell me something about myself. I have become just that person who is identified with getting to know my lover. I can know this truth.

Where does this leave us? This much is clear: when it comes to understanding who I am as a subject I can ask how I stand in relation to what I think I grasp as the facts about myself. But this does not seem to be very helpful in coming to understand the world around me, or even me as an empirical reality, as the concretion that I am. And I thought this was the critical issue. How can I get myself together if only the subjective is securely within my grasp? Above, Climacus was working to clarify subjective reflection, and for subjectivity "this 'how' is the passion of the infinite, and the passion of the infinite is the very truth." But then, on the very same page, he reminds us (as he always does) that the subject is existing: "The existing person is in the temporal realm and the subjective 'how' is transformed into a striving that is motivated and repeatedly refreshed by the decisive passion of the infinite, but it is nevertheless a striving" (CUP 203). So subjectivity as truth now seems displaced; it is the case that I can know my subjectivity but that is only half of the matter: the objective is just as important, if the goal is to put myself together, to exist in the truth.

This being the case, we must, says Climacus, put both the subjective and the objective perspective together when we decide on a definition of truth. Truth now is used in the more commonsense way: as just the way things really are, as (to use our earlier example) what is the case about my lover's disposition. Say I come to the conclusion, because the evidence I have gathered supports it, that my lover is a kind and generous person. What do I have? "An objective uncertainty, held fast through appropriation with the most passionate inwardness" (CUP 203). This, Climacus tells us, is the highest truth for an existing person. It includes the objective effort, but it knows that finally my "knowledge" is a belief, a decisive step of faith. This definition of truth, Climacus continues, "is a paraphrasing of faith." When we take Climacus's road we end in a position where we must acknowledge that any substantive steps we take are really finally deciding that such and such is the case, we are willing to believe. It goes like this: I want to live my life in the truth, to be an identity of subject and object. But that is possible only for God. The best I can get is an objective uncertainty. Truth for an existing person is a "desideratum," an ideal toward which we are always striving but at which we never finally arrive.

As Anthony Rudd rightly notes, some contemporary philosophers, such as Hilary Putnam, argue for a conception of truth as an ideal toward which we strive in our thinking (1993, 34). But Climacus, Rudd continues, while seeing truth for humans as an ideal, thinks that there is indeed a truth about things and that God has that truth. What Rudd fails to see (at least at this point in his analysis) is that Climacus yearns for the truth, he desires truth in a strong objectivist sense; he desires to put subject and object together, to get a God's-eye view, while noting continually that such an aspiration cannot be realized, at least not on strictly human terms. As Climacus says, "It is not forgotten that the subject is existing, and that existing is a becoming, and that truth as the identity of thought and being is therefore a chimera of abstraction and truly only a longing of creation, not because truth is not an identity, but because the knower is an existing person, and thus truth cannot be an identity for him as long as he exists" (CUP 196). There is clearly a sense in which Climacus aspires to truth in a strong sense, to a God's-eye view. As Rudd repeatedly points out, throughout Kierkegaard's whole authorship one sees the "desire for the absolute, the infinite longing," and driving the whole spiritual trajectory is a desire to achieve "ultimate integration and coherence in our lives" (1993, 139–40). On Kierkegaard's terms, continues Rudd, "someone who is searching for absolute values, for firm foundations for his moral life will not be satisfied" with merely human approximations, limited and incomplete perspectives on life (1993, 134). This is basically right; Climacus is a strong objectivist, satisfied with nothing less than the firm foundation and absolute values, with nothing less than the truth, which alas cannot be had for the poor existing subject. This is the deep and pervasive tension in Kierkegaard's authorship.

But unlike Climacus, I will conclude (with Putnam and more pragmatic thinkers) that while human objectivity is intimately intertwined with our human psychology, culture, and biology, and so is not the metaphysical objectivity of a God's-eye view, it is "objectivity for us."

So for Climacus I end up staking my beliefs on an objective uncertainty held fast inwardly; my knowing is in fact a venture of faith. But so too is my very self a venture of faith, for becoming a self is also just a bringing together of the empirical concrete conditions of my life *and* consciousness and will sustained by spirit, sustained in faith. But is there such a great difference between these steps of faith and a more modest reasonableness, a perspective on human understanding that is fallibilistic yet not relativistic, that simply rejects the high conditions of the objectivist in favor of practical and pragmatic employment of reason? As long as we do not start making leaps of faith without any credence, but consider relative reasonableness, I see little difference. And this, I will argue, is just the sort of epistemological stance that Kierkegaard approaches in framing his existential anthropology, his vision of the normatively human. But that is to say that his very foundationalist aspirations give way to a pragmatic edifying hermeneutics and thereby to a philosophical position that is relatively adequate or (negatively) not the essential truth about the human condition.

If I read him rightly, Evans's construal seems a little strained to me. What Climacus is saying is that we do not have knowledge, for knowledge is just what we have when we are able to surmount the gap between ideality and reality, to bring thinking into identity with being; and this is something that Climacus clearly believes can be done only when it comes to my own ethical actuality. Now, when it comes to so-called substantive knowledge, we always have a subjective step, a venture of faith, and those who think they have knowledge are fooling themselves. The positive thinkers are deluded; they are in fact making a subjective commitment—but are unaware that this is the case. If I say that this is knowledge too, that knowledge is just the everyday beliefs that we tend to settle on, then we are in danger of removing the whole tension of the infinite longing for firm foundations, for absolute worth, and the clash with our finite limitations within the temporality of existence. Once we begin down the path of disengagement from our everyday beliefs and subject them to critical consciousness and ethical evaluation, the ground is forever moved from under our feet. We are, Kierkegaard believes, either swimming in faith, swimming "out on 70,000 fathoms of water," or we have deceived ourselves and slid back into the delusions of the positive thinkers.

The best way to keep Climacus's point straight is to see all substantive knowledge (save subjectivity) as dissolved in doubt, and the only alternative is belief. Belief of course does not need be blind and without considerations of evidence and reason. But truth for finite humans is educated guesses, relatively informed beliefs, rough approximations. What makes one belief more plausible than another, what makes one opinion more cogent than another? This seems a critical issue to me, but all this is the stuff of relative knowing, a more or less of approximation, and it is something that Climacus does not dwell on. Ethically we have the business of the casuist, and that business is not of concern for the individual looking for nothing less than firm foundations and absolute values. Kierkegaard never dwells on the conditions of relative knowing. His point is that we really do not have knowledge, that objective positive thought's security is a delusion and not an answer to the Cartesian anxiety about firm foundations and fixed points of departure. The answer lies down the subjective path. And so the important point is that for Kierkegaard a *major* subjective decision can never really be denied: either one is a skeptic displaced from life, or one acknowledges that one is reengaging everyday life, striving but never arriving, constantly placing the displacement of the infinite into the task of everyday living. Making these movements is the health of faith; failing it is despair. And of course, most of us (all of us?) fail here, since we so easily become "positive thinkers," not acknowledging the continual discontinuity that the infinite reflective powers create in our lives, the constant contradiction between being a finite existing being and having to do with the infinite. This is the tension, the contradiction, of human existence, and it is a tension that I argue Kierkegaard overstates.

The Subjective Thinker: Formulating an Existential Anthropology

Although we have reached the point where it is clear how reflective consciousness gives way to willed resolution in the effort to realize personhood, Climacus has much more to say about the cognitive side of becoming subjective. I want to take some time to examine the line of thought here. It is very important to my conclusion about the merit of Kierkegaard's project. I want to consider just how Kierkegaard formulates his beliefs about humans and their existential condition, and my argument is that he is swimming with the rest of us and so his whole existential vision is a more or less of relative knowing. Kierkegaard has turned our attention to subjectivity. Why turn attention in this direction? One reason (I think a central reason for Kierkegaard) is because it is here that he thinks we can have the most secure point of epistemological departure when it comes to ethical and religious issues, when it comes to framing the question of how we shall live. I trust that by now I have established there is good evidence in at least two of Kierkegaard's main works that this is the case. Another reason is that ethical and religious issues are really first-person issues for Kierkegaard. Matters of meaning are subjective matters, and they involve our well-being. But my claim is that this turn to the subject is no more epistemologically secure than any other empirical knowledge.

After turning attention in this direction, Kierkegaard becomes increasingly confident that he can think existence in more general terms. By the time we reach *The Sickness unto Death,* we have a very rich analysis of the conditions of human existence—although concretely exemplified, it is nevertheless also a very abstract analysis. But nowhere is Kierkegaard very clear about how he has developed his vision of the human person. *I am asking about the epistemic status of the whole existential framework, the vision of the normatively human.* My general sense is that he did not work this out. I think that Kierkegaard's approach is best seen as hermeneutical, where hermeneutics means, in Richard Rorty's terms, the "attempt to make sense of what is going on at a stage where we are still to unsure about it to describe it and thereby to begin an epistemological account of it" (1979, 320). Kierkegaard is attempting to make sense of subjectivity and to articulate its concerns as these are encountered in the actual process of lived-experience. And such an existential psychology was not, in his day, well thought out. Although we have not yet examined Anti-Climacus's analysis of our situation, and in many respects it is here that Kierkegaard is most explicit about the complete structure and rich dynamics of human existence, we find Climacus reflecting on just how we think existence. Although Climacus's reflection has to do with how *each person* can understand himself or herself in existence, there are also some clues about how he, as existential anthropologist, has developed his understanding of human existence, of subjectivity in general.

I have already mentioned how Climacus tells us that he will "*describe* subjective reflection in its search backward and inward into inwardness," where description involves us in objectifying our subjectivity. In the same section on subjectivity he speaks of "essential knowing as pertaining to existence"; objectivity, as we know, is (from the subjective perspective) "accidental knowing." Subjective knowing, however, is seen as essential knowing; as Climacus puts it: "Only the knowing whose relation to existence is essential is essential knowing. Essentially viewed, the knowing that does not inwardly in the reflection of inwardness pertain to existence is accidental knowing, and its degree and scope essentially viewed, is a matter of indifference" (CUP 197). But, continues Climacus, essential knowing "does not signify the above mentioned abstract identity between thinking and being, nor does it signify that the knowledge is objectively related to something existent as its object, but it means that the knowledge is related to the knower" (197). He concludes that "only ethical and ethical-religious knowing is essential knowing" (198).

Presumably essential knowledge still employs abstractions; the difference is that this knowledge concerns also the individual's ethical and spiritual identity. There is a cognitive relationship in "essentially knowing"; it is who I am, or what I have identified as the substance of myself. Evidently, we are talking about those ideas, those possibilities to which I sustain a relationship and so call mine. Do these perceptions of identity escape the dialectic of doubt and belief? As we noted earlier, Climacus's claim is that in knowing myself, what he calls my ethical actuality, my moral and spiritual character, I am grasping more than knowledge, this apprehension is "secure," it is a knowing that does not slip into a hypothesis, an idealized possibility. What I know as a subjective thinker are those identifications that constitute myself; they are not an externality, but do they escape the limits of empirical knowing? We are talking about the "interiority in which the individual annuls possibility and identifies himself with what is thought in order to exist in it" (CUP 339). As we mentioned above, Kierkegaard is referring to our intentions, our autonomous decisions, our thoughts about our state of mind as they are captured in our reflexive ability: "That my intention is so and so I can know; I can in all eternity know absolutely" (575).

I am convinced that Kierkegaard came to believe that the mind is (or can be) directly luminous to itself. But I think that while we have an access to our own mental states and activities that others do not, our construals of these states are really no more certain than anything else, than any other empirical construals. Further on, in a section entitled "The Subjective Thinker," Climacus provides an even clearer sense of how we are to think existence. I quote him at some length here, because he begins to realize that "essential knowing" shares elements with human understanding generally; it too employs our powers of objectifying but in the service of existential orientation and the practical moral negotiation of life. This approach has more in common with the reasonableness of practical reasoning than the high-minded rationality of theoretical reasoning.

"The subjective thinker's task is to *understand himself in existence.* True enough, abstract thinking does indeed speak about contradiction and about the immanental forward thrust of contradiction, although by disregarding existence and existing it cancels difficulty and contradiction. But the subjective thinker is an existing person, and yet he is a thinking person" (CUP 351). This is an interesting passage because earlier Climacus seemed to deny that abstract thinking could even approach the problem of the existing person. I quote that passage: "Abstraction disregards this definite something [the existing individual] but the difficulty lies in joining this definite something and the ideality of thinking by willing to think it. Abstraction simply cannot concern itself with such a contradiction, since abstraction expressly prevents it" (302). But is not Climacus's whole reflection just such a concern with the issue? Admittedly abstraction might "disregard" the difficulty of how I can think existence, but still the subjective thinker is trying to *understand* something. Climacus tries to clarify.

"Instead of having the task of understanding the concrete abstractly, as abstract thinking has, the subjective thinker has the opposite task of understanding the abstract concretely. Abstract thinking turns from concrete human beings to humankind in general; the subjective thinker understands the abstract concept to be the concrete human being, to be this individual existing human being" (CUP 352). What is it to *understand* the abstract concretely? As an understanding it must be some sort of employment of concepts. It must be to consider how a general idea relates to a particular case, a matter of *application.* If it is that, we need first a general idea to apply, but we need more, we need practical wisdom in applying it. And if for the subjective thinker the "abstract concept is the concrete human being" then the problem is not so much abstraction, as the general idea of *how this idea relates to the particular case, to a particular somebody's life.* Climacus, I submit, is talking about practical rationality, *phronesis,* and at one point he notes that "the existing person continually has a *telos* and it is of this *telos* that Aristotle speaks when he says that theoretical thought is different from practical thought in its end" (313). Climacus affirms the primacy of practical reason.

Finally, in this critical passage, Climacus seems to allow that abstraction is not the issue; the issue is the direction of thought, and the issue is that application is crucial: "In a certain sense the subjective thinker speaks just as abstractly as the abstract thinker, because the latter speaks about humanity in general, subjectivity in general, the other about the one human being (*unum noris, omnes* [if you know one, you know all])" (CUP 353). This is a striking passage. It makes explicit the way to an existential anthropology; a portrait of the structure and dynamics of human existence can be painted in the striving to apply, to live, what is understood about existence; the actual engagement provides a fuller, far more accurate, picture of human existence. The gap between the abstract thinker who speaks "about subjectivity in general" and the subjective thinker who understands particularity has narrowed. In some fashion, of course, this is what Kierkegaard has been up to all along, but I think this is one of the clearest explicit indications of how it is possible. Notice the bridge between abstraction and concreteness; this is the key move, and the way is open for capturing the movement of ethical actuality, of subjectivity, and framing a more adequate conception of humanness.

These passages in *Concluding Unscientific Postscript,* I suggest, prepare the methodological way for the move to fully develop the anthropological contemplation as we find it in *The Sickness unto Death.* In *The Sickness unto Death* Kierkegaard is clearly speaking about "subjectivity in general." In the supplements to *The Sickness unto Death,* Kierkegaard says of his "psychological exposition" that section C, "The Forms of Despair," is "a psychological description of the forms of despair as these appear in actuality, in actual persons, whereas in [section] A ["Despair Is the Sickness unto Death"] despair was treated abstractly, as if it were not the despair of any person, and in [section] B ["The Universality of This Sickness"] despair was developed in terms of consciousness as decisive in the definition of despair" (SUD 151). Kierkegaard admits to providing an abstract general analysis of the *human* condition of despair. In his journals, he goes even further: "Even though I achieve nothing else, I nevertheless hope to leave very accurate and experientially based observations concerning the conditions of existence. I am convinced above all that these conditions are always essentially the same" (SKJP 1.455).

Still, there is no doubt that Climacus (even before Anti-Climacus writes his psychological exposition) goes a long way forward with discerning the conditions of human existence. But what I am concerned to point out is that he has revealed the terms of *how* to think existence, and these terms are finally tied closely to the individual thinker himself or herself. The abstractions of the subjective thinker, the individual striving to interpenetrate existence with consciousness and to will the conditions discerned, are abstractions "about the one human being," and we grasp the universal in the particular—"if you know one you know all." I may be making too much of this passage, but I think that for Kierkegaard a good deal of epistemic weight is carried by introspection.[4] Surely Kierkegaard knew and enjoyed the literary expressions of human subjects in their existential conditions, but when he says that section C of *The Sickness unto Death* is a "psychological description of the forms of despair as these appear in *actuality,*" does he refer to ethical actuality or empirical actuality?

If the former, then Kierkegaard (as first-person explorer) is the only one who can (on his terms) have any confidence in grasping what is his own ethical actuality, and it ends in solipsism. But if the latter (and as existential anthropologist, it would have to be the latter), then we enter into the whole dialectic of doubt and belief, into the approximation process of empirical knowing. I am inclined to think that Kierkegaard's "ethical actuality" finally reduces to a broadening of the scope of empirical actuality; perhaps a radically empirical Jamesian approach best captures Kierkegaard's approach. When he says that he hopes "to leave very accurate and experientially based observations concerning the conditions of existence," whose experience is being observed? Whose psyche is being described? Primarily, I would argue, his own psyche; his is an introspective analysis.

Existential Sources: A Historical Interlude

Charles Taylor, in his discussion of the sources of modern identity, helps us see how Kierkegaard with his introspective analysis of interiority, his "radical reflexivity," stands squarely within the Western construction of the self (1989). Taylor argues that many distinct strands constitute our modern existential identity. Kierkegaard, I will argue, stands at a critical juncture in the construction of the Western identity, and his response is an effort to integrate these important strands. The primary strand of Western consciousness is the inwardness emphasized by Augustine. In Taylor's words, "It was Augustine who introduced the inwardness of radical reflexivity and bequeathed it to Western tradition of thought" (1989, 131). Augustine calls us to look within, to make our own psychic activity the object of our consciousness, to sustain a relation to the relation that constitutes us as a self. And he does so primarily because he believes that this is how we know the truth of our condition and that truth finally is God as the source of human consciousness. As we saw in the Judge's thoughts as well as in Climacus, the foundational certainty is just my capacity to grasp myself. As Taylor says, "Augustine makes the fateful proto-Cartesian move: he shows his interlocutor that he cannot doubt his own existence" (1989, 132). In doing so Augustine is answering the skeptic, but more importantly he is establishing the first-person standpoint as "a certainty *for me;* I am certain of *my* existence" (Taylor 1989, 133). Clearly, we are firmly in Kierkegaard's territory.

Another crucial Augustinian notion that influences Western Christian (and Kierkegaard's) thinking about the proper existential orientation is the doctrine of the will. The idea that the person can "give or withhold assent," can make a moral choice, is more critical than the ability to rationally objectify. But will is more than simply making a decision, it also identifies a person's disposition, the orientation of his or her character. So it is the making of a strong commitment to who I will become; this is not just knowing what I should do, it refers to how I orient how I stand in relationship to the goods that I recognize; the goods that come to constitute me. This idea of *my* moral orientation becomes crucial in later Christian moral sensibility; foreshadowing Kierkegaard, the idea grows, as Taylor says, that "moral perfection requires personal adhesion to the good, a full commitment of the will" (1989, 137). Finally, while there is a *telos* toward the good for Augustine (as for Kierkegaard), it is not an inevitable *telos,* but one that I must attend to, that I must participate in. My "will" (now intertwined with myself) must be a "good will," but my attention tends to falter and my will slides from the ideal of the strong moral and spiritual evaluator. In short, I discover that I cannot extricate myself from my deep attachment to the particularities of my world, to my concerns and my particular life. Kierkegaard explores the psychological dynamics of these constraints on, and supposed perversities of, the will most fully in *The Sickness unto Death.*

After Augustine, on Taylor's narrative, we get two distinct trajectories: Descartes and Montaigne. On the whole I see Kierkegaard working to restore the classic Augustinian vision of the self, but with many new dimensions, the most pronounced of which is his affirmation of both Descartes's disengaged consciousness and (to use Taylor's phase) Montaigne's "recognized particularity." Taylor himself inserts Kierkegaard into his historical narrative as a theistically rooted imaginative transformation of ordinary reality and everyday life in the face of the "postromantic" crisis of self-affirmation. This is achieved by the decisive choice of the self, a movement we chartered in Judge William's letter. On my reading, Kierkegaard's efforts to weave together fading Christian visions with newer romantic affirmations leads to what I earlier identified as the ideal of objective reengagement; at its extreme, it is the ideal of the strong spiritual evaluator, who (in Taylor's words) chooses himself "in the light of infinity" (1989, 449). My point now is that when it comes to the framing of his vision of the dynamics and structure of human existence, to thinking existence, Kierkegaard is clearly following a path already charted by Montaigne. Kierkegaard's relationship to Montaigne's perspective is clearly complex, for much of it he rejects. But in the above delineation of the epistemological approach of the subjective thinker, he affirms, I will argue, Michel Montaigne's approach.[5]

Descartes, on Taylor's story, radically secularizes Augustine's vision by locating the moral sources within us. While Augustine engaged in the radical reflexivity of interiority, he finally did so as a means to locating the true source of the self, a source not ourselves, but the power which constitutes us. Descartes, however important God was for him, ended with "an inwardness of self-sufficiency" (Taylor 1989, 158). For Kierkegaard this is finally an empty self-sufficiency because of his more deeply relational view of the self, but also because of his deep constitutive grounding in Augustinian Christianity. But my concern here is to look closer at Taylor's delineation of a lesser-studied early modern figure. With Taylor, I think that Montaigne's perspective is extremely important for an adequate understanding of our contemporary situation; he foreshadows an expressive naturalism that Kierkegaard knew well from the German romantics. But I also think that while both Kierkegaard and Montaigne share an epistemological orientation and an affirmation of human particularity, Montaigne offers the beginning of an alternative to Kierkegaard's vision.

Montaigne's posture is one of radical reflexivity, but his efforts to disclose the self are not efforts to disengage and objectify, but efforts to explore the rich concrete conditions of particularity. Montaigne's inward turn discovers a complex and multifaceted unique web of contingencies; the self is more a particularity that individuates and less of a universality that connects. If we are oriented toward the universal we are in the grip of a theoretical approach that tends to falsify the concrete empirical actualities of life. Although he may have had a yearning for discovering foundations and secure points of practical departure, Montaigne increasingly leans toward the view that aspirations such as these are best set aside. In the final analysis he justifies his descriptive self-exploration with the claim that this is the best way to grasp the "human condition." As Taylor puts it, quoting Montaigne, "This life, however 'base et sans lustre,' will reveal as much as any other, because 'every man beareth the whole stampe of humane condition'" (1989, 179).

What is striking is that Montaigne is doing just what Climacus proposes: in considering my own ethical actuality (read now: radical empirical actuality that includes inwardness), I am afforded a more adequate understanding of selfhood, of the dynamics of human existence, than I would if I started from abstractions and tried to mold myself to them. The subjective thinker's task, remember, is to *understand himself in existence:* "The subjective thinker understands the abstract concept to be the concrete human being, to be this individual existing human being" (CUP 352). Kierkegaard, like Montaigne, seeks to know himself as a particular individuality, shaped by these particular passions and this particular environment. This theme of my concretion harkens back to the Judge, but Climacus, I argue, is working to clarify how the Judge's ideal of objective reengagement is epistemologically formulated. The epistemological approach is not really the disengaged rational consciousness of Descartes, but, as Kierkegaard puts it, "accurate and experientially based observations concerning the conditions of existence." Kierkegaard has a much stronger sense than Montaigne of a demand for moral perfection, a demand that Montaigne rejects, but Kierkegaard does seem to think that his ideal issues from an effort to negotiate practical life. The person who strives to interpenetrate his or her concrete existence with consciousness and agency will come to Kierkegaard's vision of human existence. But that Montaigne did not come to the same realization already casts doubt on Kierkegaard's existential vision.

An Edifying Hermeneutical Philosopher

But more exactly how does Kierkegaard proceed to frame his vision of the normatively human? Following what we have seen in Climacus's reflections of the subjective thinker, I think that we see Kierkegaard's strategy rightly when we see it as one of practical reason, as an effort to interpret himself in his own efforts to get some practical orientation in life, to find a coherent and effective posture from which to live. He is (as Rorty suggests) an edifying hermeneutical philosopher (1979).

Much of what guides Kierkegaard in his effort to think existence, to live through the question "how should I live?," is what he refers to as the upbuilding or edifying. I think that Kierkegaard was pursuing a project of awakening and upbuilding, a pragmatic project that has as its center our need to be edified and educated, to advance our self-understanding, to live meaningful lives. In his journals he refers to the edifying as "a side of cognition": "It is strange what hate, conspicuous everywhere, Hegel has for the up-building or edifying, but that which builds up is not an opiate which lulls to sleep; it is the Amen of the finite spirit and is an aspect of [essential] knowledge which ought not to be ignored" (SKJP 2.214). Louis Pojman translates this last phrase as *"it is the side of cognition which ought not to be overlooked"* (1984, 10). What guides Kierkegaard's analysis of human existence is what satisfies the need for "adequate" praxis. This is what he considers to be the only reliable guide as we negotiate existence; the felt tensions, the lived experiences, the joys and sorrows of life are our guides, and they are Kierkegaard's guides as he charts the conditions of existential identity. The edifying hermeneutical philosopher tacks back and forth between thought and action; he aims always to frame his view from within reflective praxis. The reflective practitioner of life discovers what a particular existential stance involves, how it feels in lived experience. Reflection on the consequences in terms of their felt-adequacy for negotiating life leads one to consider possible revisions in light of unforeseen existential conditions. The revisions are then tested in the individual's praxis, and new unforeseen existential horizons arise as one holds fast in praxis, leading to still further reflections and further adjustments. So what we have is a progressive movement beginning in reflective praxis, holding fast in appropriation, registering feedback in self-reflection, in the actuality of subjectivity, and adjusting in light of what edifies the self, what educates (where educates means "brings forth") and illuminates our practical lives. Kierkegaard's genius is his ability to translate the results of his particular efforts to do just this into a more general vision of the human self as it orients itself in moral and spiritual space.

But experience does not carry its own significance; it must be captured in nets of meanings, in conceptual schemes. Even the inner experience of my own state of mind, my own construals of who I am, my self-represented identity, is an interpretive construction. As a post-Kantian, well read in Hegel, Climacus realizes that concepts are our inescapable vehicle for grasping reality, and so reality is really always outside our grasp. Except, however, when it comes to my own ethical/psychological actuality, for although conceptual it is also who I am as relationship to empirical possibilities and so (Climacus concludes) not an approximation process to externality, but a more direct apprehension of interiority. The apprehensions take place as I strive to apply my objectifying efforts to my own life and consider the feedback, the lived experiences. But this too is conceptualized, an interpreted experience, and so does not escape the dialectic of doubt and belief. Experience, or at least experience that means anything for us, is always interpreted experience.

The issue here is one that Marilyn Piety takes up in her essay entitled "Kierkegaard on Rationality" (2001). In considering just how Kierkegaard thinks about the transitions from one existence-sphere to another, she argues that his moves are not just irrational leaps, but rest on felt incoherences in the course of negotiating life, especially our experience of suffering. In order to get some critical leverage, she argues that Kierkegaard made the important distinction "that experience is distinguished from the various interpretations which may be supplied to it. The medium of experience, according to Kierkegaard, is *actuality,* while the medium of such interpretations is *ideality.* That is, the interpretations represent clusters of concepts and the medium of concepts is abstract, in contrast to the medium of experience which is concrete" (2001, 69). We have seen, however, that there is only one place where Climacus (and Piety quotes Climacus in *Concluding Unscientific Postscript* as her main source) thinks we have direct access to actuality, and this is our own ethical actuality. And even here the ethical actuality, while just my concrete experience, is not without conceptual dimensions; even Climacus seems to admit this. Piety herself admits that experience does not always "incline one toward a *particular* interpretation of existence" (2001, 69). But that is to say that experience is fairly plastic, and this is just the problem in my judgment. Can Kierkegaard really build his case for his vision of human existence on experience, where experience is separate from his interpretation of it, or does ideality (or in our terms, the conceptual presuppositions and cognitive schemes that he brings to his experience to constitute it) seep in around the edges?

Piety adds a footnote that opens up the crucial role of concepts in constituting experience: "It is important to acknowledge, however, that the conceptual framework to which an individual subscribes helps to define his experience" (2001, 73). And she judges that Kierkegaard understood this, but she adds, on his terms "an individual's experience must still . . . be assumed to be substantially independent of the framework which helps to define it, or else it cannot have the role in transition from one framework [stage of existence] to another that it is described by him as having" (2001, 73). To bolster this distinction she cites Thomas Nagel's claim that we ascribe psychic states, such as suffering, to creatures that do not employ concepts. Nagel's point is true, but limited; suffering can be an extremely rudimentary sense of experience, and we need to be careful with the term *experience.* To use a different example, the specific sort of suffering that we label despair is something that we would not ascribe to creatures that lack linguistic capacity and rich resources of sentience. But more important, I think we should rather say that experience could serve as a lever to push the individual to adopt a different interpretive perspective, without experience being distinct from linguistic and conceptual packaging; it would just be that the packaging is not explicit for the individual, that from his or her first-person perspective it is not well thematized. And then the situation is better characterized as one where a current conceptual scheme of living is not cohering with an alternative experience-near, but as yet inarticulate, conceptual scheme. In Kierkegaard's own case we do not, after all, think that he came to the different existence-spheres solely on the basis of his felt-experience; he had extensive knowledge (specific sorts of knowledge we might add) about estheticism, ethical consciousness, and (most crucially) Christianity long before he had knowledge by acquaintance or knowledge by experience.

Indeed, I would argue that he could not have had such specific experiences without the prior schooling in these larger meaning-giving constructs.

Piety argues finally that Kierkegaard is not an irrationalist in the way that some philosophers charge. And on this score she is surely right. But my question is whether Kierkegaard finally is to be read as thinking that he anchored his vision in the sort of inward certainty that Climacus believes we can each have when it comes to our identity, or whether he is willing to see it as founded in the relative adequacy of human knowledge, a vision subject to the dialectic of doubt and belief, to the usual constraints of human inquiry. Kierkegaard's confidences run very deep here I think. The insistence on the pervasiveness of despair, and on the necessity of adopting religious and finally Christian stances in the face of despair, suggest that he thought he had gotten the conditions of human existence firmly in his grasp. It is, I admit, difficult to determine from his writings his final epistemic views, but I think there is at least some reason to think that he was a sort of early existential phenomenologist, a radical empiricist of a pragmatic variety.

But if Kierkegaard's vision rests on such a pragmatic and radically empirical stance, his confidences run too high. A thoroughgoing edifying hermeneutics involves a crucial element not acknowledged by Kierkegaard. There is the feedback of lived-experience that is evaluated in light of the upbuilding or existentially helpful. But this does not mean that one's stock of understandings, one's conceptual heritage, is bypassed. As Rorty writes: "Abnormal and 'existential' discourse is always parasitic upon normal discourse, edification always employs materials provided by the culture of the day" (1979, 365–66). That may put it a little too narrowly, but even existential discourse must use some terms from available cultural resources, and Kierkegaard (in my judgment) is rediscovering and reformulating a traditional Western Christian vision of the normatively human. A careful analysis of Kierkegaard's vision of the normatively human reveals that it reflects the effective history of Western Christian culture. Taylor puts Kierkegaard's problem well when he says: "When a given constellation of self, moral sources, and localization is *ours,* that means it is the one from *within* which we experience and deliberate about our moral situation. It cannot but come to *feel* fixed and unchallengeable, whatever our knowledge of history and cultural variation may lead us to believe" (1989, 111–12). It is not (as Kierkegaard would seem to have it) simply that the existential analysis supports Christian existence; it is also that the Christian convictions structure and influence the existential analysis. Despite his inward efforts, one can bypass neither cultural context nor explicit metaphysics when it comes to ethical and religious thought.

This means, finally, that Kierkegaard's anxiously concerned existential earnestness, his picture of life as a strenuous contradiction without rest save a paradoxical Christianity, is an overstatement. While human persons deeply desire integration of self, the relatively well-integrated self is cause for despair only if the ideal of full and complete integration is taken to be what is required. But in fact, empirically, individuals are not existentially demolished, not psychologically debilitated, when they self-consciously live with their lives invested in activities and beliefs that they know are relative to their particular life and times. The high requirement issues from an assumption that nothing less than a standpoint outside of existence will do, but this we see cannot be had while still within existence. Despite the fact that this is seen as a contradiction, even an impossibility, it is held out as the ideal by Kierkegaard. Such an ideal can live only from a faith that the ideal is required by sources beyond the conditions of existence. So how does Kierkegaard get beyond existence from a radically empirical attention to existence?

God-Consciousness as an Existential Necessity

What is pervasive in Climacus's reflections is the inability of the individual to achieve himself or herself as a unity of finite and infinite. I can never really or fully get the two sides of my being together. This is what I refer to as the cul-de-sac of strong spiritual identity. Climacus is much more aware of the contradictions, the comedy, and the absurdities of human existence as a polarity, than the Judge, who accentuated the passion and earnestness needed for existence in the ethical. As Climacus puts it: "Existence itself, existing, is a striving and it is just as pathos-filled as it is comic: pathos-filled because the striving is infinite, that is directed towards the infinite, is a process of infinitizing, which is the highest pathos; comic because *the striving is a self-contradiction.* From a pathos-filled perspective one second has infinite value; from a comic perspective, ten thousand years are but a prank, like yesterday, and yet the time the existing individual is in does consist of such parts" (CUP 92, emphasis added).

In the reflections of Climacus, Kierkegaard reaffirms the basic terms of the human being as a combination of (to use Nagel's language) the internal subjective perspective and the external objectifying standpoint. But being oriented in this way creates a situation that is at one and the same time interested and comic: I am concerned about how I stand in relation to what I grasp with my powers of objectifying, how my subjective life measures up, yet I perceive that from this objectifying perspective, my life is arbitrary, it is shot through with contingency, and I am just a drop in the ocean, a seemingly meaningless moment. To quote Nagel again: "Finding my life objectively insignificant, I am nevertheless unable to extricate myself from an unqualified commitment to it—to my aspirations and ambitions, my wishes for fulfillment, recognition, understanding, and so forth. The sense of the absurd is the result of this juxtaposition" (1986, 218). Kierkegaard knows the "humorous"; he knows how the juxtaposition of the infinite and finite creates a sense of the comic: where "there is life there is contradiction, and wherever there is contradiction, the comic is present" (CUP 514). But he also knows what he calls a tragic interpretation of the contradiction, a perspective that sees the contradiction and despairs over a way out (516). And the tragic perspective clearly carries the day as Kierkegaard's thought develops, for this perspective is pervasive in *The Sickness unto Death.* Why does this perspective win out, why does Kierkegaard not settle for a relatively adequate grasp of life and a relatively coherent actual identity, a relatively integrated self—with a dash of irony thrown in?

On Climacus's reading, the effort to negotiate life, to achieve the continuity of selfhood, is most strenuous; *it even seems impossible:* "The difficulty for the existing person is to give existence the continuity without which everything disappears. An abstract continuity is no continuity, and *the existing of the existing person essentially prevents continuity,* whereas passion is the momentary continuity that simultaneously has a constraining effect and is the impetus of motion" (CUP 312, emphasis added). Can an existing person put things together for more than a moment? It would seem that his very existence is the stumbling block: "For an existing person the goal of motion is decision and repetition. The eternal is the continuity of motion, but abstract eternity is outside motion, and a concrete eternity in the existing person is the maximum of passion" (312). In passion, in the infinite concern for my ethical actuality, myself, I am as close to realizing myself as I can get. When I hold the tension between the finite and infinite in consciousness, I acknowledge that I am taking a step, my step, forward back into myself. Such decisive inward steps are possible because I have the capacity for continuity, the eternal, but temporality is always displacing my continuity; to maintain myself the inward resolve always must be redone. *I am constantly arriving only to depart.* The arriving is the maximum of my passion, and my stance is holding the contradiction together as I move, and insofar as I have any continuity, really become a self, I do so by virtue of spiritual freedom. In becoming a self, I am becoming a concrete eternity. My self-formative activity is now understood by Climacus as a religious activity. In this moment, when the infinite ethical passion of achieving the highest good of the self as a unified synthesis of infinite and finite, of living in the spirit, is at its height, the self knows God; the reality of God is manifest.

In the Judge's letter it becomes clear that Kierkegaard is inclined to construe the ethical as very closely related to the religious. In fact he says very little about a specifically atheistic secular ethical stance; the atheist almost seems by definition amoral or, at least, minimally moral since the impression of infinity is lacking. In describing the ethical posture of the strong evaluator, the Judge utilizes religious language. Or put more existentially, in pursuing the inward effort to interpenetrate my existence with consciousness, I experience the divine. Climacus makes that exact same point this way: "In fables and fairy tales there is a lamp called the wonderful lamp; when it is rubbed, the spirit appears. Jest! But freedom, that is the wonderful lamp. When a person rubs it with ethical passion, God comes into existence for him" (CUP 138). As I pursue the goal of ultimate integration, practice spiritual freedom, I come to realize that I am the problem. So I put myself out of the way, I adopt the stance that Climacus calls "infinite resignation." This is the first expression of my holding fast to the infinite within the finite: "In immediacy the individual is firmly rooted in the finite; when resignation is convinced that the individual has the absolute orientation toward the absolute *telos,* everything is changed, the roots are cut. He lives in the finite but does not have his life in it" (410). But then, continues Climacus, "the task is to gain proficiency in repeating the impassioned choice and existing, to express it in existence." And this means that the individual continually declares that the things of this world are of relative value in comparison to his or her efforts to orient to the absolute end of becoming subjective or realizing the infinite ethical requirement. But this renunciation is suffering for an existing individual since, as existing, he or she is inextricably tied into the world. And then it is not just suffering; it is guilt, since the individual is ethically responsible for his or her failure to achieve the task set for human existence.

I discover that I am bound to the finite in ways that cannot be overcome; as Nagel says, I cannot extricate myself from my involvement in my particularity. Despite the fact that I long to transcend my particular engagements or, better, to live within the particular as a universal human being, I cannot. I yearn for the absolute relationship, for the God-relationship, for an eternal happiness, yet I live in relative contexts. The Judge was concerned to return to the particularities of life on the terms of spiritual freedom, but Climacus sees that the return is always flawed, and so the victory of spiritual freedom recedes, and the task looks even more difficult.

Climacus speaks of an existential pathos that maintains an orientation to the absolute *telos,* the highest good for an existing individual. Put another way, this ultimate goal is nothing other than existing in the truth, where the truth is defined as a unity of subject and object, and truth (recall) is not something I as an existing person can realize. Truth is for God alone. I have objective uncertainties held fast in inwardness. But nevertheless truth exists, and since I am linked to the eternal, my *telos,* my subjective aim, is to transform myself into a concrete eternity: "To become subjective should be the highest task assigned to every human being, just as the highest reward, an eternal happiness, exists only for the subjective person or, more correctly, comes into existence for the one who becomes subjective" (CUP 163). But walking the knife edge that is existence, a joining of a polarity that is a contradiction, is a most strenuous project, admits Climacus: "The practice of the absolute distinction makes life *absolutely strenuous,* especially when one must also remain in the finite and simultaneously relate oneself absolutely to the absolute *telos* and relatively to relative ends" (422, emphasis added).

How does walking the tightrope of existence go for the existing individual? First I must die to immediacy; I practice renunciation of all finite involvement. In this effort I must inspect my life to insure that I am not tied to any finite interest in a way that preempts my interest in the absolute *telos,* in the infinite ethical requirement to realize personhood. But all that the inspection shows is that I am hopelessly enmeshed in the world, that I cannot get completely free of the finite or, better, that I cannot freely engage the finite while keeping my sights on the infinite. Again, my task is impossible, and so I suffer. But since my task is my duty, not only do I suffer, but I agonize in guilt. Guilt-consciousness is now my state, as I realize that I am not orientated toward the eternal either. While I suffer because I cannot fully renounce the finite, I am guilty because in my inability to put myself together I am equally removed from the infinite. So once again at the height of existential pathos, I am strung between the two sides of myself, but (says Climacus) I have the relationship to God that is expressed in the pervasive misrelation. As Climacus puts in a passage that clearly foreshadows the analysis in *The Sickness unto Death:* "The essential consciousness of guilt is the greatest possible immersion in existence, and it also expresses that an existing person relates himself to an eternal happiness, . . . expresses the relation by expressing the misrelation. Yet even though the consciousness is ever so decisive, *it still is always the relation that carries the misrelation,* except that the existing person cannot get firmly hold of the relation because the misrelation continually places itself in between as the expression for the relation" (CUP 531–32, emphasis added).

This then is Climacus's analysis of the religious consciousness. Coming into relationship with God is becoming even more subjective, but it is also a deeper alienation from the ultimate goal of human existential integration. The deeper alienation is seen in the suffering and guilt of the individual, but this is a sign that the individual is oriented in the correct direction, toward the absolute *telos* and *eo ipso* toward God (CUP 413). So in this agonizing stance, squarely in the contradiction that constitutes the ideal, is a certain comfort (560). Although I do not have what I yearn for, there is a reward even now: "There is nevertheless a tranquility and restfulness in all this strenuousness, because it is not contradiction to relate oneself absolutely to the absolute *telos,* that is, with all one's might and in renunciation of everything else, but it is the absolute reciprocity in like for like" (422). So when I put myself out of the way, there might seem to be nothing, but in fact, on Climacus's reading, when I do so I am taking the next step toward selfhood, for I am oriented toward the eternal, and so I am "refreshed" in my passion for the infinite (203). When I postulate God as the ultimate horizon of my existence, I can again maintain the strenuousness of the strong spiritual evaluator. My "refreshment" is my inwardness where I know myself as spirit, as a self-transcending self, that *must* have an absolute *telos, must* have God, if I am to find spiritual harmony. Kierkegaard believes that spiritual despair cannot be the end of life's story, there must be an infinite self-sustaining spiritual ground. This obviously harkens back to St. Augustine's famous confession that we are restless until we (self-consciously) rest in Thee. Kierkegaard's religious conviction, that there must be an infinite self-sustaining spiritual ground, is founded in the inner experience of being dissatisfied with anything less than complete transparency, with anything less than the absolute source of who we are and what we do. Since the urge for such a God's-eye view is not easily discarded, the only alternative is to posit God as just the source of this longing. This argument for God is further clarified in *The Sickness unto Death.*

Just as the Judge did not much care about the specifics of the ethical life, the important thing being to pursue it with the utmost earnestness, to strive for a good will, so too does Climacus not care much about theological speculations, the important point being to grasp what the notion of God means for me as an existing cognitive spirit: the existential import of God. And that import is that God is the absolute horizon in which my striving can find its true home. God is the answer to my infinite longing for grounding as existing cognitive spirit. In comparing the objective path to God with the subjective, Climacus says that there is more truth on the subjective, "on the side of the person who is infinitely concerned that he in truth relate himself to God with the infinite passion of need" (CUP 201). And in the longing, the need for God, I discover God as an existential necessity. Recall how the Judge suggested that the striving for the good was (in fact) the good, so too with religion—*the striving for God is God:* "At its maximum, the 'how' is the passion of the infinite, and the passionate of the infinite is the very truth. But the passion of the infinite is precisely subjectivity, and thus subjectivity is truth" (203). Again what is crucial is the passion, the infinite longing, the urge to complete transcendence, an urge which we cannot achieve, but which remains, and the remainder must be God.

What are we to make of such a claim about the locus of God's reality? We should first note that the need is not merely a psychological need; it is more of an existential or spiritual postulate given the aspirations for objectifying our world and ourselves so thoroughly that we have a vantage point from which we can understand and act without the normal constraints of finitude. We strongly desire an absolute *telos,* and our need compels us to postulate God. In this fascinating footnote Climacus sounds more like Anti-Climacus as he explains the necessity for God: "God is indeed a postulate, but not in the loose sense in which it is ordinarily taken. Instead, it becomes clear that this is the only way an existing person enters into a relationship with God: when the dialectical contradiction brings passion to despair and assists him in grasping God with 'the category of despair' (faith), so that the postulate, far from being the arbitrary, is in fact *necessary* defense, self-defense; in this way God is not a postulate, but the existing person's postulating of him is—a necessity" (CUP 200).

But then the theological claim rests on the analysis of the human condition. That analysis has brought the self to an existential condition that is (to put it lightly) desperate. But is Kierkegaard's analysis correct? We are again driven back to the question of the epistemological status of the whole existential anthropology. And that, I have already argued, is a radically empirical and pragmatic analysis of the conditions of human existence. Climacus speaks of the certainty an individual human being can achieve if he or she turns attention to the inward relationship that constitutes his or her self-represented identity. But we have already seen that this locus for certainty is doubtful; the apprehensions of how we stand are equally subject to self-deception, misconstrual, and the general theoretical schemes that we bring to frame our self-represented identity. Now Climacus tells us that there is a refreshment, a rest and tranquility, in the strenuous resignation, suffering and guilt of Religiousness A. In an extensive note, he elaborates on just how the religion of immanence is upbuilding (edifying) for the individual, since in it he finds God, his *terra firma*. Since this passage also relates to my comments about Kierkegaard as edifying philosopher who uses the pragmatic, the morally helpful, as a criterion to determine his stance, it is worth quoting in its entirety:

> Wherever the relationship with God is found by the existing person in the inwardness of subjectivity, there is the upbuilding. . . . The totality of the guilt-consciousness is the most upbuilding element in Religiousness A. The upbuilding element in the sphere of Religiousness A is immanence, is the annihilation in which the individual sets himself aside in order to find God, since it is the individual himself who is the hindrance. Here the upbuilding is quite properly distinguishable by the negative, by the self-annihilation that finds the relationship with God within itself, that suffering-through sinks into the relationship with God, finds its ground in it, because God is in the ground only when everything that is in the way is cleared out, every finitude, and first and foremost the individual himself in his finitude, in his caviling against God. Esthetically, *the sacred resting place of the upbuilding* is outside the individual; he seeks that place. In the ethical-religious sphere, the individual himself is the [sacred resting] place [of the upbuilding], if the individual has annihilated himself. (CUP 560–61, emphasis added)

This passage captures a lot of the ground that we have already covered. The upbuilding is the sense of grounding that comes from shattering the finite self for the infinite abstract self. It is a sacred resting place. Even in Judge William's letter we encounter the move to distance one's self from all possible content, to dwell in the abstract infinite self. The Judge, however, declares this move a disaster and a course headed for suicide because the individual would become nothing; he did not see it as the route to God. Yet for the Judge the divine is encountered when spiritual freedom is pursued, and insofar as the Judge's efforts were also oriented toward becoming a Kierkegaardian self, bringing the polarities of selfhood together in praxis, the Judge touched on Climacus's religion of inwardness, of immanence. What he lacks is a clear sense that while faith provided the refreshment to return to the battle, the reengagement is always a suffering struggle to hold together what can never be brought fully together. The Judge shares something of the delusions of the positive thinkers.

Kierkegaard brings us to the brink where we need God. But how did we get there? We got there because the ideal was so very high. Indeed it was an ideal that we came to realize as nigh impossible for us as humans. *The very cognitive capacities that drive the aspiration for transcendence reveal it to be impossible;* this Climacus knows, indeed it seems to be his final stumbling block. Ethically speaking, the epistemological craving for firm foundations, for total transcendence, is translated into the desire to find a secure point of departure for praxis, to find something that is not arbitrary and open ended. This point appeared to the Judge to be just himself as self-transcending spirit and the task of self-conscious responsible reengagement with life. But then Climacus argues that while this is the ethical task, and whether we are engaged can be grasped with certainty, the fact is that we discover our failure only to fully engage. The constant stumbling blocks are the temporality of our finite existence and the inability of the self-transcending self to displace any and all substantive positions, to reign in the finite attachments to the world. Keeping these stumbling blocks clearly in mind is the height of my religious pathos; it generates a suffering guilt consciousness that signifies God. We are beings, says Climacus, that are "eternally structured" (CUP 422), and so we have a potentiality for a God-relationship, a potentiality realized in keeping the guilt that signifies the relationship to God. So God, while an existential necessity for us, the assured ground of our infinite longing, is a mixed blessing, since God-consciousness also seems to up the ante even higher. On the one hand, without the enabling sustenance of God, we would flounder in a never-ending approximation process; we could never get started and would be subject to the temptations, the self-deceptions of the positive thinkers. But with God we are refreshed and can again move, move in the faith, that while we are swimming with no ground to ever stand on, God is our buoyancy. Here faith is more of a sort of general human ability to engage life, to become a self, despite the fact that the self at this point knows that the steps are risks, ventures without certainty. As I noted earlier, this sort of faith does not look too different from a general confidence that our deliberations, widely informed and well thought through, are as good as it gets; while not God's view they are better than nothing; they are not absolutely and finally the way and the truth, but they are relatively adequate for creatures such as ourselves to negotiate life with some confidence. Why this "faith" should entail a divine reality, much less lead to Christian convictions, will occupy us fully in the final chapter.

For Climacus the height of existential identity on purely human terms is found in a self that displaces itself, that sustains the misrelation, and so is sustained by a relationship to God. Religiousness A, says Climacus, "has only universal human nature as its presupposition" (CUP 559). While the state of my existence is a despairing contradiction, a suffering guilt consciousness, at the same time (in this most agonizing state) it retains a glimmer of the ultimate satisfaction, of a peace (we might say) that surpasses understanding—experiences that supposedly point to God.

I am "refreshed" as I maintain myself in the absolute relation to the absolute *telos* and a relative relationship to the relative. But while Climacus himself portrays Religiousness A as a still more intense posture of spiritual existence, a posture that surpasses Judge William's and is even truer to the contradictory conditions of human existence, it is still not yet the assured spiritual rest of Christianity. To get there even the understanding must be given up.

If I have discovered God, one might think that I am no longer spiritually restless, but that is just not the case for Kierkegaard. What makes Christianity compelling for me is that with God clearly in my sights I now see that the high standard cannot be renounced, for it is just God's standard; I am more than simply a finite creature with an infinite task; I am a finite creature before God. And to live up to that standard I will need extrahuman assistance. But extrahuman assistance for a human being looks nonsensical, especially for one who has come so far in existential understanding. I need an opening to achieve (or to accommodate) the impossible, and the impossible is me in my contradictory condition of trying to get together that which cannot be joined; I come to see that before God I cannot really go on. My praxis is always truncated by the fact that I really do not have what I ultimately need to surmount the cleavage in myself: a perspective outside existence yet within existence. So existence before God makes the strenuous task of personhood just more accentuated, the urgency of wholeness is more pressing. I am willing to give up everything for it, even my mind.

Climacus is an existential seeker, and he thinks that Christianity offers a unique, "higher," or more adequate existential orientation than Religiousness A. It is, however, only from the vantage point of Religiousness A that Christianity can be understood, existentially understood. Although, interestingly, Climacus says that "Religiousness A is so strenuous for a human being that there is always a sufficient task in it" (CUP 557), he also claims that when in the state of Religiousness A, a most strenuous passion, eventually it will "give rise to a passion that is even higher" (560). This is the passion for Christianity. And it is a passion with great difficulty, for as Climacus admits: It is my intention "to make it difficult to become a Christian, yet not more difficult that it is," but, he says, it is difficult for a human being "to relinquish his understanding and his thinking and to concentrate his soul on the absurd" (557).

While Climacus has a good deal to say about Christianity, I am going to let Anti-Climacus bring us to Christian existence. But my coverage of Christian existence will not be extensive even in the next chapter. This is because my conviction is that the vision of the normatively human is what compels the Kierkegaardian self toward a specific sort of Christianity. But if the analysis of human existence and the ideal intertwined with it are in question or, better, overstated, then the dire need for the paradoxical religiousness that Kierkegaard knows as Christianity is itself in question. Ultimately Kierkegaard's reading of Christianity and Christ is deeply influenced by what he comes to think humans finally must have to resolve the dire straits they are in: a point of transcendence of existence within existence. But if humans are not in such dire straits the radical solution is not needed. In other words, ratchet down the ideal, and the air goes out of existential pathos, and the rationale for adopting the Kierkegaardian form of Christian existence evaporates. And, of course, it is just my argument that this is the case.

Notes

1. See the Hongs' introduction to *Philosophical Fragments* and *Johannes Climacus* (1985, x).

2. Although *Fear and Trembling* draws a sharp distinction between the ethical and religious faith, such a distinction is not embraced by Climacus, and I think that it represents a view that Kierkegaard came to increasingly disavow. Kierkegaard's Religiousness A, what he calls natural human religious consciousness, and his specific Christian Religiousness B make sense only against the horizon of a demand for moral transcendence, for full Kierkegaardian self-realization.

3. In Bernstein's analysis of Descartes's efforts as a spiritual search for existential grounding, we see a striking parallel to Kierkegaard. Descartes's *Meditations,* says Bernstein, "portray a journal of the soul, a meditative reflection on human finitude through which we gradually deepen our understanding of what it means to be limited, finite creatures who are completely dependent on an all-powerful, beneficent, perfect, and infinite God. If we practice these spiritual exercises earnestly, as Descartes urges us to do, if we follow the precarious stages of this journey without losing our way, then we will discover that this is a journey that is at once terrifying and liberating, culminating in the calm reassurance that although we are eminently fallible and subject to all sorts of contingencies, *we can rest secure in the deepened self-knowledge that we are creatures of a beneficent God who created us in his image*" (1985, 17, emphasis added).

4. Reidar Thomte's historical introduction to *The Concept of Anxiety* concurs with this reading of Kierkegaard's epistemic approach: "Kierkegaard's method is keyed to the principle *unum noris omes,* which actually expresses the same as the Socratic dictum 'know yourself,' provided that the *unum* is understood to be the observer himself, who does not look for an *omes* but determinedly holds fast to himself, the one who actually is all. Thus every human being possesses, or is within himself, a complete expression of humanness, whose essential meaning cannot be gained from scientific studies. That is, neither rational speculation nor natural science will disclose to the existing individual his essential nature and purpose. Self-knowledge is attained by man in existing" (CA xv).

5. Kierkegaard has a couple references to Montaigne in his journals, but as the Hongs point out, while he owned a German edition of Montaigne's writing there is only one direct reference to him in his published works; in *Christian Discourses* he refers to Montaigne as a "wise man." The Hongs estimate that he probably started reading Montaigne after 1847, which would be after *Concluding Unscientific Postscript* was written but before *Sickness unto Death* (SKJP 4.824).

3 *Anti-Climacus: Theological Selfhood and the Dialectics of Despair*

When it comes to Kierkegaard's mature existential vision, *The Sickness unto Death* is perhaps his clearest statement. It is also, interestingly enough, given Kierkegaard's aversion to systems, his most systematic statement about the conditions of human existence. As I indicated in the last chapter, it is my belief that the epistemological reflections in *Concluding Unscientific Postscript* clarified for Kierkegaard just how existence could be thought. The sometimes dizzying reflections of Climacus give way to a more serious analytic earnestness of a religious psychologist with a well thought out message; it is, as Kierkegaard himself says, almost "too dialectical" for an edifying work (SUD xiv). Anti-Climacus seems to have more existential confidence than Climacus. And in this respect he is closer to Judge William's efforts to state just how one can integrate the accidental with the universal and become a whole and coherent self. Indeed, a strong case can be made, as John Davenport (2001) suggests, that much of the Judge's convictions carry through to Kierkegaard's later writings such as *Works of Love* and *The Sickness unto Death.* The Judge's convictions about human existence, about the ripening of spirit and the repression of spirit leading to depression, are parallel to Anti-Climacus's claims that the self as spirit is the condition for the self as despair. They share a similar understanding of the structure and dynamics of human existence and (to a lesser extent) of the perils of despair and the possibilities for existential identity.[1]

Still, Anti-Climacus extends Judge William's divinely grounded reengagement with life, clearly finding our situation even more fraught with snares than the Judge. The Judge, I argue, with his choosing despair and then striving for continuity, stands at "the thoroughfare to faith." In Anti-Climacus's words: "The despair that is the thoroughfare to faith comes also through the aid of the eternal; through the aid of the eternal the self has the courage to lose itself in order to win itself" (SUD 67). Has the Judge won himself? Has Climacus? As I have suggested, Judge William approaches the general religious faith that Climacus affirms as Religiousness A. He has despaired, has given up the finite self, but then his return is too easy (at least for Climacus); he too readily participates in social and cultural life; the spell of transcendence does not captivate or debilitate. But maybe that is as it should be. As for Climacus, he could see a way through the "contradictions of human existence," but he was unable, or unwilling, to take the step, the final step of relinquishing the last tie to finitude—his own intelligence, his yearning to see life whole, to live in the truth, to achieve the transcendent perspective. Kierkegaard's Anti-Climacus is firmly in the ethical-religious existence-sphere, and while he delineates the promises and pitfalls of this stance, he finally engages life on the terms of the higher passion identified by Climacus, the passion beyond Religiousness A, the passion of paradoxical Christianity. Anti-Climacus takes the step to live from the assured rest of a spiritual consciousness that knows that it is absolutely dependent on God and then trusts that God has provided the terms for us to accommodate our dire circumstances. Considered substantively, Kierkegaard believes, the terms of this faith are unintelligible, but they are existentially compelling. So Anti-Climacus takes the matter even further by going beyond the human religiousness that Climacus held to and expressing a specific sort of Christian faith, a faith that the God's-eye view is revealed in the gift of transcendence of existence within existence, in Christ.

One central point that distinguishes Anti-Climacus's perspective is his discussion of the transcendent standard for the self: that the self must know itself as "before God." This is an explicitly theological standard, and it is (Anti-Climacus tells us) really an *"aggravated condition,"* not a substantive change in the structure of human existence. Nevertheless, it is a very significant advance for the individual self insofar as the individual is now self-conscious about this divine criterion of selfhood. (This is the aggravation.) The self from the beginning is in fact a self that is created and demanded by God: a "theological self" as Anti-Climacus says. Kierkegaard's anthropology is finally a theological anthropology with a standard for the self that is given by the very structure of the self as a relational reality finally not self-constituted. The self *as a relational reality* is not created by the self but discovered by the self; I discover that I am "a derived established relation"; this is not something that I have established. I suggest that we already saw the beginning of such a natural-law view of the moral and spiritual trajectory for humans in Judge William's writings.

In Anti-Climacus's hands the claim is that in the course of striving for existential identity, for spiritual selfhood, the individual comes to the experiential realization that strong evaluative identity cannot find its identity with itself, but it needs a source greater than itself, it must have a power not itself in relation to which it can find a transcendent home. That Kierkegaard understands selfhood as having a skeletal structure not of our choosing was clear when the Judge spoke of the ripening of the spirit and the receiving of the gift of the eternal power to which he is finally responsible. And in Climacus's reflections it is also clear, perhaps best seen, when he says that Religiousness A, the immanent God-relationship, has only human nature as its presupposition. Anti-Climacus reaffirms this analysis of the human as God-constituted; his analysis of the self in part 1 is nothing other than Religiousness A in a more systematic tone; it too issues from universal human nature. Once perceived, however, the God-relationship only accentuates the strenuousness of the self's task as directly before a divine standard and compels a search for further relief, relief at any cost. And so enters Kierkegaard's reading of Christianity as the absurd and paradoxical good news.

Besides further development of the critical points mentioned in the previous chapters, I have two additional points to develop in this one. My first point is that despite the tone of pervasive failure to ever achieve selfhood, despite the overwhelming strenuousness of the ideal of personhood, in *The Sickness unto Death* Kierkegaard provides an understanding of the dynamics of existential identity formation that enable us to see just how an individual can increasingly solidify existential identity and so increasingly surmount the spiritual despair that issues from efforts to evade the task of existential identity. I see it this way: as an individual expands self-conscious engagement with the world, with others, with culture, with the meanings these others "carry," his or her horizon of meaning and significance expands, and so despair will lessen. Davenport suggests this view when he writes: "Kierkegaard's aim is to show that the natural tendency or 'teleology' of human selfhood (or maturation of the spirit) *is* toward choices that involve commitments to substantive social roles, engagement in practices, and the cultivation of human relationships" (2001, 290). I extend this line of thinking with the claim that human selfhood matures fully when it lives self-consciously, rationally, and responsibly within broad frames of cultural significance.

Kierkegaard's notion of the self as a relation that relates itself to itself, and becomes in relation, provides an understanding of how others constitute us and provide evaluative measures for selfhood, for our first-person identity. Although Anti-Climacus refers primarily to a divine other, I will argue that the self, as a relational construct, is shot through and through with others on his view. Others for the self are not simply concrete persons, but are more importantly the social roles, character ideals, and institutionally embedded forms of life; finally, they are the living traditions of religions, philosophies, and other frames of cultural significance that can serve as existential points of reference. From this perspective, I will conclude that the religious identity that knows spiritual rest and feels that despair has lifted is finally the consciousness of an individual that is self-consciously engaged in the resources of living social and cultural traditions. This more Hegelian reading is disputed by other commentators, but I argue that in the final analysis it is the most plausible analysis of Kierkegaardian selfhood. Here I draw most heavily on MacIntyre's thought as it was developed in *After Virtue*. The final conclusion I draw, however, is similar to Jeffrey Stout's.[2]

As we noted in chapter 1, Kierkegaard's construal of the human being (like Nagel's) suggests that we do have a strong tendency to use our cognitive abilities to transcend our particularity, and practically speaking that means that we expand our horizon of understanding to expand the range of our free action. Anti-Climacus shares this construal. But it is one that can tempt us to an excessively high standard of existential integration, a standard that while conceivable is in fact impossible. If this is so why does Kierkegaard insist on the posture of the strong evaluator? Is it needed for human well-being? On the one hand, such a posture seems a recipe for permanent and unyielding dissatisfaction, for a pervasive spiritual despair, but to deny ethical evaluation any role in our lives is also unsatisfactory. I argue (and this is my second main point) that Kierkegaard insists on nothing less than ultimate and complete integration, on nothing less than the infinite ideal, the posture of the strong evaluator, because he started with, or assumed from the beginning, religious commitments. While Kierkegaard has Climacus suggest, and later Anti-Climacus argue, that the individual in the course of struggling for existential orientation discovers the reality of God, I claim that this argument is flawed. I will argue that the argument presupposes the God that it intends to establish.

Structures of Human Existence

The Sickness unto Death clearly continues the basic vision of the normatively human found in Judge William's letter and Climacus's reflections. Although Climacus only occasionally uses the term *despair,* no argument is needed to establish that the contradictions that constitute the sufferings of the existentially anxious human consciousness that Climacus knows are just the advancing conditions of despair that Anti-Climacus masterfully delineates. We already saw that Climacus speaks of the person as cognitive existing spirit, as a child of the finite and the infinite, or temporality and eternity. When Anti-Climacus begins *The Sickness unto Death* he begins with a strikingly similar abstract framing of the human self: "A human being is a synthesis of the infinite and the finite, of the temporal and the eternal, of freedom and necessity, in short, a synthesis" (SUD 13).

This description already expresses a tripartite structure for the human person. As we noted in clarifying Judge William's views, the person is a polarity of given contingent conditions and an ability to objectify those conditions; human persons just do engage this polarity, they become selves in the course of their life. But we also learned in the Judge's reflections that there is more to Kierkegaardian selfhood than becoming a personality, where that means gaining some sort of actual identity; there is the ability to *achieve* a self. This achievement is afforded by what Anti-Climacus consistently refers to as spirit. It is the self in its capacity to relate to itself as a relation between empirically given conditions and its cognitive perception and representation of those self-constituting relations. In the terms I adopted from Flanagan, selves have a capacity for self-represented identity when the self is self-consciously framing who it is and where it is going next. The self is a thoroughly relational construct for Anti-Climacus; the self is a web of relations that can and should be spun by itself: "The self is a relation that relates itself to itself or is the relation's relating itself to itself in the relation; the self is not the relation but is the relation's relating itself to itself" (SUD 13). It is clear that when Anti-Climacus says that "the self is . . . the relation's relating itself to itself" that the self he is concerned with is self-represented identity and not simply the empirical me as a third party might observe me and construct a representation of me.

The self, Anti-Climacus tells us, can also be referred to as a synthesis between necessity and possibility or between given empirical conditions and cognitive imaginative objectifications, but it is one that relates it to itself, that has the ability, by virtue of being "spirit," to further objectify and review itself and form its own self-representation. So strictly speaking, the individual who simply has a certain settled disposition, a personality, as a result of the conditions under which he or she was "synthesized," but who has very little self-reflexivity and does very little editing of his or her given actual identity, is not a self in Kierkegaard's normative sense, not a self-conscious spiritual self. The distinction between actual identity and self-represented identity helps us see how someone can be a human being with a personality, a relatively settled set of dispositions, tendencies, and values, and still not be a self in Kierkegaard's use of the term. Such an individual is not really a self, or such an individual fails to self-actualize the synthesis, fails to live out of the relational dynamic that constitutes selfhood.

A well-developed, even hyper, self-consciousness, Anti-Climacus tells us, is decisive when it comes to selfhood. As he puts it: "Generally speaking, *consciousness—that is, self-consciousness—is decisive with regard to the self.* The more consciousness, the more self; the more consciousness, the more will; the more will, the more self. A person who has no will at all is not a self; but the more will he has the more self-consciousness he has also" (SUD 29, emphasis added). This passage makes it clear that when Kierkegaard speaks of the self he is speaking of a conceptual and volitional achievement by the individual: the individual's ability to conceptualize and then to commit to, or at least sustain a self-conscious relation to, a specific image of who he or she is. To become a Kierkegaardian self it is necessary first to be *conscious* of the synthesis between given finite conditions and our perceptual and cognitive grasp of these conditions, a synthesis that occurs for us all in the course of our maturing toward adulthood. To do that is to be self-conscious, to maintain a relation to what we called our full actual identity, the conditions of which are ever changing. Only in maintaining this relationship do I achieve selfhood; Kierkegaard's view of the self is best seen, as C. Stephen Evans rightly claims, as "a relational achievement theory of self" (1997, 2). On this view it is not possible, as Evans says, "to be a self apart from a relation to something outside the self from which the self derives its identity" (1997, 9). Of course, outside does not simply or only mean external to the psychophysiological individual; all it means is that the something is not the self in its spiritual capacity to "stand in relation" and so become "ethically actual" or gain a definite existential identity. So it could be a talent or a passion, it could be another's image of who one is or should be, it could be a social ideal or a cultural construct, in relation to which the self defines itself.

Given Kierkegaard's view of the self as a relational achievement it is not hard to see how despair comes into the picture. Despair is, says Anti-

Climacus, "the misrelation in the relation of a synthesis that relates itself to itself" (SUD 15). In the first place those who do not come to any clarity about themselves, who do not seriously engage in the activity of self-representing, are, on Anti-Climacus's view, failing to realize the essential aspect of humanness. This failure is the most basic and common form of despair. So the first form of the failed self is to be completely unaware that one is even in despair, that one is failing, that one is unconscious of or, better, is not well focused on one's own self-reflexive capacities for self-representation, and that who one is and who one is going to become is in one's own hands. In Judge William's language, such a person has spirit but it is immediate spirit; the person lives esthetically, and the ethical self has not yet emerged. Anti-Climacus says much the same thing: "The *man of immediacy* is only psychically qualified (in so far as there can really be immediacy without any reflection at all); his self is an accompanying something within the dimensions of temporality and secularity, in immediate connection with 'the other'" (51). Such a person has an "actual identity" constituted by various past identifications, tendencies, and beliefs, but they do not engage in much self-reflection or make much effort to take their lives into their own hands. Such a person has a misrelation in the relationship that constitutes the self and does not even realize it. Such a person has little capacity for living *for* himself, and this, Anti-Climacus says, is because he is not conscious of himself as spirit. We already learned about this condition from Judge William; to deny the spirit, to deny that one can engage life in evaluative terms and structure who one is according to self-chosen plans and projects, is a recipe for depression and deep dissatisfaction. Of course, we also learned that more than even self-consciousness about my plans and projects is needed for the individual to surmount the deeper despair, spiritual despair.

Although Anti-Climacus claims that "most people virtually never advance beyond what they were in their childhood and youth: immediacy with the admixture of a dash of reflection," he also notes at one point that many people have a dim awareness of the despair that defines their state (SUD 57–58). Very often, he says, "the person in despair probably has a dim idea of his own state; to some degree, he is aware of being in despair, . . . he may try to keep himself in the dark about this state through diversions and in other ways, for example through work and business as diversionary means, yet in such a way that he does not yet entirely realize why he is doing it, that it is to keep himself in the dark" (48). I dwell on this point, for I think that Kierkegaard is careful not to paint the adult person as without any self-consciousness, for, as Flanagan rightly argues, minimal persons "possess some sort of self-representation. But this self-representation can be extremely dim and inchoate" (1991, 63). We noted this point when we reviewed Judge William's thought. The esthetic person is not simply a wanton, but more often is a person that is self-conscious, or can be more self-conscious and does not want to be. Rather than a relation unto himself or herself, such a person wants to be defined directly by a relation to something or someone else. Even at that point in his authorship Kierkegaard understood that for most of us it is our very self-consciousness, and the anxiety that comes with having to live our own lives, that leads us to despair.

The next advance in despair comes with an advance in self-consciousness. How so? In general, spiritual despair comes into the picture only when the self recognizes itself as a relation and then as a misrelation or as a failed relationship, a relation not yet achieved. As Anti-Climacus says, when we consider that the self as synthesis "is a relation between two . . . a human being is still not a self" (SUD 13). Once one has consciousness of one's self as spirit, as a relation for one's self, then one also has some consciousness of themselves as a task, of the gap between what is given and what might be. There is now a distance within: there are the actual conditions that have made one who one is, and there are the possibilities for the future. The individual now faces the issue of self-represented identity: she faces the question of self-definition. And with this question she faces the evaluative question of a measure for the self: the goal or *telos* will be the measure of every step. Who am I going to become leads finally to the question against what standard will I determine who I am becoming. Only when this issue is clearly before the self can Kierkegaardian spiritual despair come before the self. But before we examine the two fundamental forms of despair in Anti-Climacus's view, further examination of the "constituents of the synthesis" that provide the necessary conditions under which despair is defined and under which it emerges for concrete individuals is in order.

In my view one of the best statements of the full dynamic relational structure of the human being considered psychologically is found in part 1, section C of *The Sickness unto Death*. It is also clear in this section, as it is for Climacus, that the human being has a spiritual task—namely to become a self, but not simply an ethical self or even a spiritual self "intensified by reflection," but a theological self—intensified by God. In Anti-Climacus's words, "The self is the conscious synthesis of infinitude and finitude that relates itself to itself, whose task is to become itself, which can be done only through the relationship to God. To become oneself is to become concrete. But to become concrete is neither to become finite nor to become infinite, for that which is to become concrete is indeed a synthesis. Consequently the progress of the becoming must be an infinite moving away from itself in the infinitizing process, and infinite coming back to itself in the finitizing process" (SUD 30).

We have already noted that central to Kierkegaard's vision of personhood is a task of integration; this means that human beings are at their essence *ideals for themselves.* Personhood is given, but only potentially; personhood is not something that happens as a matter of course. We must achieve ourselves, and that means we are a freedom that must be responsive to ourselves, putting together, synthesizing, the two fundamental sides of ourselves: our finite particularity and our reflective and volitional capacities. Now, for Anti-Climacus, there is clearly a third party to the relationship that is selfhood: spirit, that agency of relationality, must sustain a relation to "that which established the self as a relation." The final horizon for the self, the ultimate relationship, the criterion for measuring selfhood is finally that which is not the self, but is the power that constituted it. But what exactly is this power? And why do I need a relationship to it? We will return to Anti-Climacus's important arguments for seeing the human self as gaining spiritual peace and psychic equilibrium only when it stands in relationship to a supreme other that transcends its particular temporal relations and provides an "objective" point of departure for an "authentic" self. I want to conclude this section with a final characterization of the dynamic relational process of developing and sustaining an existential identity, turning next to a sustained examination of the snares along the way.

Anti-Climacus's use of the term *concreteness* as the goal for selfhood is somewhat confusing, for the concrete would seem to be the finite. A better term might be "actual," a term that Anti-Climacus uses when he considers the self as a dialectic of possibility and necessity with the task of "becoming actual." Kierkegaard's vision of the normatively human is focused on self-actualization, where actualization occurs as the self (as spirit) freely establishes responsive relationships to the social and biological world, to rules and roles, to tendencies and talents. Only in this way can a self gain reality, become actual. The self is the individual's representation of his or her *actual* identity *for* himself or herself. But since humans are temporal, becoming a self is moving, always moving, from a lack of awareness of the psychical-physical synthesis that I have become, and am becoming, to an increasing awareness of this synthesis that is me and which as spirit I help to constitute and ultimately should completely constitute. So becoming a self is always a *process* of conceptualizing my concrete situation and then determining a relationship to that situation; interpenetrating my concretion with consciousness enables me to see how I might stand, but then because I am a temporal creature, my contingency conditions change and I must again grasp myself for myself. In this way I am synthesizing, I am not just synthesized. To paraphrase Anti-Climacus, the progress of becoming a synthesis, of synthesizing an actual self, must be a continual moving away from contingency in the reflective process of conceptualizing my life and a continual coming back to reality by appropriating my construals in willed resolutions, in beliefs and commitments, in "holding fast" to my emerging actual "self."

Dialectics of Spiritual Despair

The notion that an essential task is set for every human being is central to Anti-Climacus's reflections. Every human, Anti-Climacus tells us, is "primitively intended to be a self" and to continually become a self (SUD 33). In general terms that task, as we learned already from the Judge, is to self-consciously integrate the finite with the infinite, to interpenetrate those ever-changing finite conditions with consciousness and will. The genius of Anti-Climacus is to delineate exactly how the self can fail to achieve this most strenuous task, can fail to balance the polarity, because (finally) it fails to achieve an adequate grounding for spirit and so ends in despair, that "sickness of the self." The problem with this perspective is that it makes it impossible for us to ever eradicate despair; despair (it seems) must be accepted and accommodated.

It is fascinating to see how much of the basic forms of spiritual failure were already relatively clear for Kierkegaard when he created Judge William's perspective. For example, when Anti-Climacus speaks of the despair that issues from an excess of infinitude and a lack of finitude or from an excess of possibility and a lack of necessity, he is expanding on the Judge's point about the dangers of being overwhelmed by the experience of the infinite self, the naked abstract spiritual I, and neglecting the concrete conditions that will afford definiteness of self. This is the self that knows no limits, that lacks self-conscious relations to the finite world and has lost itself in the infinite reflections of the imagination (SUD 31). Like the Judge, Anti-Climacus mentions the infinitizing of the God-relationship and notes (interestingly enough) that it can "so sweep a man off his feet that his state is simply an intoxication. To exist before God may seem unendurable to a man because he cannot come back to himself" (32).

In general terms, the problem with the self lost in possibility, the esthete intoxicated with imagination, or the mystic that is God-intoxicated is that such a person cannot "submit to the necessity in one's life, to what may be called one's limitations" (SUD 36). That human beings have a definite degree of concreteness seems central to Kierkegaard's theory of the human being. Just how much we are constrained and limited by it, and how much we can mold and rework, is not clear; we will return to this point. This concreteness, or the individual's concretion, is a product of both biological conditions and social relations. As Anti-Climacus says, a person's finitude is defined by his "concretion," it has "necessity and limitations, is this very specific being with these natural capacities, predispositions, etc., in this specific concretion of relations" (68). The point of departure for one's identity is one's "more essential contingency" (33)—an interesting phrase, again suggesting that some aspects of my given identity are irrevocable, and a contingency that I must accept.

Anti-Climacus declares that every individual is "destined to become himself, and as such every self certainly is angular, but that only means that it is to be ground into shape" (SUD 33). By this Anti-Climacus means the same thing that the Judge meant when he said that a person's task is to take his concretion as he finds it and "order, shape, temper, inflame, control—in short, to produce an evenness in the soul, a harmony, which is the fruit of the personal virtues" (E/O 262). Bishop Butler's reflections on the relations between my natural tendencies and "affections" and my capacity to evaluate my nature and determine how I should proceed capture Anti-Climacus's claims about how selfhood synthesizes temporal and eternal or natural conditions and reflective capacities. A parent, says Butler, "has the affection of love to his children: this leads him to take care of, to educate, to make due provision for them; the natural affection leads to this: but the reflection that it is his proper business, what belongs to him, that it is right and commendable to do so; this added to the affections becomes a much more settled principle, and carries him on through more labour and difficulties for the sake of his children, than he would undergo from that affection alone" (1727, 341–42). In Kierkegaard's language a spiritual self works with the material on hand, the tendencies and affections, the full finite concretion, to form an ethical self, to craft an existential identity, a responsive synthesis of freedom and necessity.

So the self is both discovered and constructed, and overall my proper role is ethical editor, or perhaps an artist who works with the materials and their limitations to create a work, a self. But then there is the opposite problem of a lack of infinitude or possibility and an excess of finitude or necessity. Anti-Climacus puts the *whole* dialectic within which every self moves this way: "Possibility and necessity are equally essential to becoming (and the self has the task of becoming itself in freedom). Possibility and necessity belong to self just as do infinitude and finitude. A self that has no possibility is in despair, and likewise a self that has no necessity" (SUD 35). To lack possibility is to lack the reflective skills of the ethical editor or to lack moral imagination, for it is to let the conditions of finitude shape the self so that one just is (or becomes) more or less whatever the natural and social conditions foisted on one. Here the self's biggest temptation is that it *"permits itself to be tricked out of its self by 'the others'"* (33, emphasis added). It seems clear that this is the more common sort of loss of spiritual selfhood, and this loss of selfhood, Anti-Climacus says, "goes practically unnoticed in the world" (34). Indeed it appears to be a distinct advantage when it comes to keeping the social wheels running smoothly not to complicate things with one's particularity or deliberate matters deeply or feel that things are not as everyone expects them to be.

Anti-Climacus is far more positive than the Judge about the need for infinitizing reflection and imagination. He has less worry that individuals will get lost in possibility and a stronger sense that what most individuals really need is more imagination. As Stephen Crites notes, possibility and our relation to the infinite get the nod over necessity, and the relation to the finite, in Anti-Climacus's reflections. Crites writes, "For despair is above all the 'no exit' situation, the refusal of possibility and therefore the denial of God" (1992, 155). There is a clear preference for imagination and reflection, for the infinite reflection, for limitless possibility, and then an essential link between this side of humanness and God in Kierkegaard's mature reflections. This is so for two crucial reasons: the centrality of "spiritual freedom" and the identification of eternity with the self's capacity for radical self-transcendence. This creates a context in which a deep spiritual despair is pervasive and impossible to eradicate.

Because the self is not simply a relation between the physical and the psychical, but is a relation for itself, and the "for itself" is identified as spirit, the heightened sense of consciousnesses that is self-consciousness is paramount. Recall that for the Judge there is immediate spirit, but then the spirit "ripens" and spirit knows itself *as* spirit. The self is then freedom or can identify itself as freedom. The distinction between consciousness functioning to unself-consciously grasp the world and the state of mind once self-consciousness is firmly in place, once I know myself as free, is one that *in either case rests with the psychic reflective side of the human being that projects possibility.* All told, reflection, objectifying, imagination, conceptualizing—all add up to the spiritual side of the human self on Kierkegaard's construal, and it is the spiritual side that creates all the trouble, but which Kierkegaard believes is essential to surmounting despair and finding the peace that surpasses understanding. Only with possibility is there salvation, and so Anti-Climacus says, "When someone wants to despair, then the word is: Get possibility, get possibility, possibility is the only salvation" (SUD 38–39).

Second, Anti-Climacus clearly connects the self's capacity for reflection and imagination, its capacity to be for itself, its volitional and attending abilities, to the eternal; spirit is our kinship with eternity. This was already clear for Kierkegaard in Judge William's letters. The human being, Anti-Climacus says, is a synthesis "of the temporal and the eternal" (SUD 13), and on the side of eternity are those abilities that enable us to be more than simply a one-dimensional response of the contingent finite conditions that make up human life: "Despair is a qualification of the spirit and relates to the eternal in man." And, he continues, *a person "cannot rid himself of the eternal.* . . . He cannot throw it away once and for all, nothing is more impossible; at any moment that he does not have it he must have thrown it or is throwing it away" (17, emphasis added). But by this Anti-Climacus means nothing other than that it is impossible to rid one's self of the knowledge and abilities our reflective and volitional capacities afford, namely self-knowledge and self-relationship or freedom. And so he concludes with the parallel point: "A person *cannot rid himself of the relation to himself* any more than he can rid himself of this self, which, after all, is one and the same thing" (17, emphasis added). Our final question will be whether this identification of the self's psychic capacities for self-conscious relationality with the eternal, with God, can be made good.

Many of these reflections on the basic outlines of the dynamics of human selfhood, and the negative consequences of losing the dynamic, seem right to me. Individuals need to be able to maintain a working relationship with the finite world, themselves included; the finite world, we might say, is their foremost medium. The narrative that is their self-identity has to track the real world to some degree. But apprehending and appropriating their world entails projecting possibilities into the future, and not simply possibilities for action but possibilities for thought, conjectures about just how things stand. In a basic sense, to become a self seems (minimally) a matter of not getting lost in the imagination with possibilities outrunning actual self constituting attending and committing, or not getting stuck in identifying one's self with necessities that stifle the self's ability to move creatively into the future. This seems well established and widely acknowledged. Even MacIntyre, in his most recent *Dependent Rational Animals,* argues that we human creatures must, in order to become "independent practical reasoners," be able to both "imagine alternative possibilities" for the future and to recognize "limits upon our choices" (1999, 76). While difficult, this does not seem excessively difficult, much less impossible. What seems wrong to me is how exceedingly strenuous, even impossible, this path becomes in Kierkegaard's hands. This occurs because of Kierkegaard's claim that while engaging life a person must be clearly objectifying and attending to the springs of his action; the beliefs, values, and motives that are constituting his identity should, every step of the way, be transparent to him so that he is radically responsible for himself. In this activity are the self-constituting efforts of a *radically* self-transcending self. Here, in the cul-de-sac of the strong spiritual evaluator, we have a recipe for radical despair. But even without such an extremely strenuous demand in place, we can follow Kierkegaard down the road toward more modest forms of existential despair, to the painfully *conscious* forms of despair, and begin with weakness of will.

The first snare for me as a self-conscious self is simply to try to ignore the fact that I have a life that I can take responsibility for, to remain in the dark about this side of myself. As I mentioned earlier, I think few adults directly live from their actual identity without some minimal degree of a subjective perspective; every adult has some self-consciousness, and although most people do not identify themselves with the self-transcending self, the spirit, they still have enough distance to be held accountable and responsible for their actions. Normally, it seems to me, all individuals realize, by the time they reach adulthood, not only that they are a particular self but that their decisions shape their lives, they discover that they *have* a life. As Flanagan says, "Normal persons, regardless of social arrangements, develop an awareness of themselves as spatiotemporal particulars with a subjective life that has a certain sort of unity and continuity; and they care how their lives go" (1991, 61–62). Why would one want to try to ignore or minimize the attention paid to the capacity for self-consciousness, to one's self as responsible freedom?

A first reason involves what one discovers, or thinks one discovers, about one's actual identity, the self one has become or is becoming given social and biological contingencies. Such a discovery presupposes some self-reflection, presupposes that a person does not live directly from one's identity-constituting conditions. Such a discovery about the finite conditions of life Anti-Climacus calls "despair over the earthly or something earthly." Why should this be cause for despair? If a person has very little self-reflection, then despair can be occasioned by the loss of whatever it is that they stand in relation to, whatever defines them directly; in this case despair would be like an accident that befell them. But if there is a somewhat greater degree of self-reflection, then the condition of despair begins like this, according to Anti-Climacus: "When the self with a certain degree of reflection in itself wills to be responsible for the self, it may come up against some difficulty or other in the structure of the self, in the self's necessity" (SUD 54). I perceive my tendency to respond with hidden pleasure when I surpass my friends, or I realize that the social conditions that shaped me left their mark on me, and I tend to react in ways that disturb me and can cause me regret. In short, I find that certain elements in the concretion that is me, in my full actual identity as it has been synthesized, are beyond my capacity to alter or reverse, and so there is a part of me that I do not own. I am free but for that part of me. But with the spirit taking the wheel, this self realizes that "there is much that he can lose without losing the self," for such an individual has to a certain degree "separated his self from externalities" (55). This self now understands that identity is not directly dependent on concrete conditions, but is a matter of willed attending, a matter of what I stand in relation to. But there is this part of my actual identity, my particularity that I cannot get free of, cannot stand over against, cannot will through, cannot therefore transcend. It has me rather than I having it! What must occur for such a self is that he must venture way out, make a total break with finitude: "The difficulty he has run up against requires a total break with immediacy, and he does not have the self-reflection or the ethical reflection for that" (55). What he lacks, says Anti-Climacus, is "a consciousness of a self that is won by infinite abstraction from every externality, this naked abstract self, which is the first form of the infinite self, and the advancing impetus in the whole process by which a self infinitely becomes responsible for its actual self with all its difficulties and advantages" (55).

If a self remains here it is a despair of weakness; he suffers through and tries to resign himself to his inability to achieve radically responsible selfhood. What is it that this self cannot do that causes him to suffer? He cannot get completely detached from all the particular contingencies that make up his life. He mourns the loss of his son, the son who meant so much, but who died in an accident, or he cries over his inability to continue to feel deep attachment to his wife, or he despises himself for his ambitions at work, ambitions that mean ignoring other's difficulties. Or, conversely, and more positively, he remains tied to pleasures of writing fiction, time with his imagination that means much, or he senses that could not do without his bicycle rides soaking in the sights of the country. In short, he is not a radically self-transcending self; he is just a "relatively adequate" self-transcending self. He is still tied to finitude, he is not freely and totally synthesizing, he discovers that he is getting synthesized. Whether one should, in the final analysis, despair over this depends on how one thinks about one's self, about the standards against which one evaluates their life and their expectations for flourishing.

So this is a spiritual despair, a despair over the power that earthly things have, occasioned when one senses that the earthly might not be, should not be, the measure for the self, that there is, as Anti-Climacus repeatedly says, "something eternal in the self" (SUD 47). Such despair comes about not by a loss of an earthly condition, not by a change in circumstances, but by reflection itself, by the self itself. When the self grasps that despair is occasioned not by the loss of something or someone, but the self's deep attachment to finite identity-constituting relations, self-consciousness has advanced, says Kierkegaard. If I am not defined by the other, but essentially by my self-willed relation to the other, it is in myself that despair resides. With this insight, the self might advance one step further, to a condition that Anti-Climacus labels "despair over weakness"; this is not merely despairing over the earthly, but over myself as so deeply tied to the earthly; it is really a "despair over the eternal" (60), over not engaging the eternal, over my inability to live *as* spirit. Anti-Climacus says that this remains a despair of weakness, for rather than making an effort to push deeper the spiritual passion, rather than transcending these attachments, denying them power over selfhood, one just suffers through, hoping maybe these conditions will "go away" if ignored. But what is needful, in Anti-Climacus's opinion, is a "metamorphosis in which consciousness of the eternal in the self breaks through so that the battle can begin that either intensifies the despair in a still higher form or leads to faith" (60). Construing the self as eternally structured compels us to more intense reflective strenuousness (one clearly delineated by Climacus) or makes us break with understanding altogether and believe.

This self now perceives that it is the earthly *as such* that is the problem; it is not only particular contingencies, but also temporality as such that is the snare. But as Kierkegaard never tires of telling us, we are *existing* temporal creatures, and so the despair lies with us as part of our essential structure. While we are existing temporal creatures, we are also creatures with capacities to stand over against these conditions, and so we see our earthly involvements with a tinge of irony. How can someone invest so much worth in things that moth and rust corrupt? It is, as Climacus noted, a bit comical; it is absurd to be an existing cognitive spirit. But Anti-Climacus is too earnest to laugh for long; he sees only a suffering person yearning for transcendence. Often a person at this stage of consciousness has a hidden inwardness; he "plays" for a time at being "someone in the world." This self despairs because she cannot find a way to win through to, or to live from, the eternal—and so she suffers over her inability to resolve her despairing condition. In other words, this self has partially transcended finitude, but cannot find rest because she yearns for an ultimate standpoint outside the vicissitudes of finite life. She really is not seriously engaged as a strong spiritual evaluator, she is hiding behind a persona; she is not steeping out into a spiritual venture, because she cannot find a way forward, and so her identity is defined (falsely she often feels) by various socially constituted roles and concerns—and yet she is "outside" them, not finally defined by them. Anti-Climacus puts it this way: there is a "carefully closed door, and behind it sits the self, so to speak, watching itself, preoccupied with or filling up time with not willing to be itself and yet being self enough to love itself. This is called inclosing reserve. [It] is the very opposite of immediacy and in terms of thought, has great contempt for it" (SUD 63).

By not willing to be himself, Anti-Climacus means that such a person will not identify with himself as a strong evaluator. It is, then, not the social roles and concerns that are the problem, but *how* he is engaged within them or, better, how he cannot really reengage in them. As Anti-Climacus says: "Outwardly he looks every bit 'a real man.' He is a university graduate, a husband, father, even an exceptionally competent public office holder, a respectable father, pleasant company, very gentle to his wife, solicitude personified to his children. And Christian?—Well, yes he is that, too, but prefers not to talk about it" (SUD 63–64). But he cannot take a steady diet of this "real world," he often longs for solitude, needs to refresh himself with his sense that he is not defined by the earthly, that he transcends this, but he lacks the confidence and courage to take the matter any farther. What a self must finally do is conceive itself as a creature before God, a creature that stands finally in relation to God, and then in this faith he will be sustained by God as he steps out. But what is the thought and will of this God? What is the content of the God's-eye perspective? Anti-Climacus, of course, finally stakes his faith on Christianity, that the God's-eye perspective is revealed in Christ. But given our deeply and inescapably pluralistic world, why think that this alone is God's perspective? We will return to this critical point.

Even at this point we have reached a despair that Anti-Climacus tells us is "quite rare in the world" (SUD 65). But there is a still further advance, an advance that is presumably rarer still. If the self firmly grasps that the condition of despair is a result of the eternal, a result, that is, of the self in its capacity to imaginatively transcend the world and the earthly conditions that captivate it, then such a self might muster the will to say that these concerns for the concrete world are really inconsequential; they are not really me. Nothing really defines me, so I define myself!

The self now begins to use the "eternal within the self," the spirit, to will to be a specific self, a self that the self itself determines is best for it. Rather than saying that nothing ultimately defines me and giving it up and putting faith in the power that transcends it, this self says I will define myself, I will set the bar for my life, I will determine the criterion for measuring myself.

Such a self, says Anti-Climacus, wills to be itself *in defiance,* in defiance, it seems, of the conditions of an existing temporal creature, but more significantly in defiance of a power which constituted the whole self and which sets its *telos.* Such a self remains in despair, a despair of defiance. Anti-Climacus puts the matter this way: Such a self has "a consciousness of the infinite self. And it is this self that a person in despair wills to be, severing the self from any relation to a power that has established it, or severing it from the idea that there is such a power. With the help of this infinite form, the self in despair wants to be master of itself, to create itself, to make his self into the self he wants to be, to determine what he will have and not have in his concrete self" (SUD 68). This is despair because such a self does not acknowledge that it cannot really get going on these terms. Why? Because at this stage it really knows that these efforts are truncated by the very infinite self that makes them. The self cannot reengage the finite world when it knows that it is not defined by it. Why? Because it is engaging the world in terms that it has, in the final analysis, arbitrarily chosen: "In the whole dialectic within which it acts there is nothing steadfast, that is, nothing *eternally steadfast*" (69, emphasis added). Such a self, Anti-Climacus believes, can "quite arbitrarily start all over again, and no matter how long one idea is pursued, the entire action is within a hypothesis" (69). Such a self is its own master, absolutely its own master, but this too is despair, for this self and the selfhood it constructs, the existential identity it has developed, lacks "infinite interest and significance" (69). And since such a self "recognizes no power over itself, it basically lacks earnestness and can conjure forth only an appearance of earnestness" (68). In this portrayal of the self, at the very height of despair it is very clear how deep a role that the desire for totality, for ultimate finality, plays in Kierkegaard's vision.

Sometimes the despair of defiance is a despair of resignation, a stance very close to Climacus's Religiousness A. Here the self is willing to be itself but by way of not identifying with anything. But such an infinite resignation is also an evasion of the essential task. Infinite resignation loses the self, for it refuses responsibility for the self's full concretion, with all its drawbacks and deficits. Such a self is not active, not willful enough to fashion a self, but it uses the distancing power of the self to displace finite conditions that cause it discomfort and suffering. Indeed, such an advanced despairer understands that it is just himself as a concrete creature with certain limitations and necessities that he wills not to acknowledge. Finally, if a self cannot get free of some element of his concretion, he might begin to define himself as just a self that is ruined by existence. The self he wills to be is the self that constantly drags him down. It is an active despair, a protest against existence within existence. He has, for example, a penchant for gambling and while he despises this side of himself, he has been unable to disengage this element, and so he has been synthesized against his better judgment—he has become a gambler. Instead of taking responsibility for this element, instead of transcending it, he identifies with it and uses it against the idea that he might ever be able to get spiritual rest.

So in the final height of despair, using the infinite self, the "eternal side of the self," I am either going to just "let things go," try to resign myself to them, or I am going to move forward without them, disowning them as I create a self as I would like it, either in a positive creativity or spiteful willfulness. But even if I do my best to reengage with the world, to interpenetrate the temporal with the spirit, to live in the world as a strong spiritual evaluator, I will fail. The critical Kierkegaardian dilemma reappears every time: I cannot identity myself with any finite condition, my identity cannot finally be defined by any psychic conditions, any natural tendency, any particular social relation or institution; my measure for selfhood, the goal of my striving, must be a transcendent standard. Somehow I need the confidence and courage to stand naked in existence and yet to engage, to go forward with nothing supporting me—nothing finite at least. The only way a self can do this, the only way I can become the self I am essentially intended to become, is, claims Kierkegaard, to stand in a conscious and free relationship to my creator, to God. I will fail unless I am willing to lose myself as I would have it and will myself as God would have it. But *how* would God have it?

Kierkegaardian Selfhood and Social Relations

Before we move to Anti-Climacus's discussion of theological selfhood, I want to examine Kierkegaard on the role of the other in constituting the self. Usually Kierkegaard sees the other as a pervasive snare in the effort to secure existential identity. The social pathology of the herd mentality, the peer pressure that while particularly evident in adolescence remains a pervasive feature of human life. I want to take some care to explore the social dimension of the human situation, for as I have indicated

I think that Kierkegaard underestimates the role of others in the flourishing of selves, as well as just how deep these social relations constitute us. At several points he seems aware of how critical others are for our lives, but in the final analysis he seems to think that social relations are usually only a diversion, and at best preliminary, to becoming a strong spiritual evaluator. Despite the fact that Kierkegaard clearly understands how selves are constituted through their relations, he is finally critical of remaining within the social and cultural practices prevalent in one's times. He clearly sees that the particular social relations within which one discerns one's actual identity naturally supply a normative guide for how to live; the social ethos provides a moral horizon. Why is this so bad?

Individuals, he believes, escape the conditions of spiritual self-reflection through immersing themselves in the beliefs, values, and general chatter of "the others." Anti-Climacus heaps scorn on this in a way that would astound the Judge, for the Judge seemed most wary of the individual dissipating himself in possibility, even in a religious intoxication of infinite consciousness. Anti-Climacus, however, satirizes those "superficial nonpersons and group people [who] feel such a meager need for solitude that, like lovebirds, they promptly die the moment they have to be alone. Just as a little child has to be lulled to sleep, so these people need the soothing lullaby of social life in order to be able to eat, drink, sleep, fall in love, etc." (SUD 64). It is clear that Anti-Climacus sees one of the most pervasive and deepest traps for the spiritual self in sociality. Many a person seeks to evade the task of selfhood, says Anti-Climacus, through social diversions: "Surrounded by hordes of men, absorbed in all sorts of secular matters, more and more shrewd about the ways of the world—such a person forgets himself, forgets his name divinely understood, does not dare to believe in himself, finds it too hazardous to be himself and far easier and safer to be like the others, to become a copy, a number, a mass man" (33–34).

I want to argue that Anti-Climacus overstates his case here. I concur with Stephen Crites (1992, 150) when he says that "the mass man is a social pathology not inherent in sociality as such." The social dimension of human life does not need to defeat our interest in personhood, *so long as this interest is not seen as so strong that nothing short of moral transcendence will do.* If it is the case that finitude and necessity are essential to becoming a self, then social relations would seem to be an unavoidable part of the dialectic of selfhood, and the self that eschews all social relatedness is a self that fails to actualize and is in despair. On the other hand, if the problem is that all possible relations to finitude will in the final analysis fail the self, then it seems that nothing short of a transcendent standpoint is needed. If the problem goes this deep then, even a radically antisocial, solitary, spiritually passionate philosopher (a Nietzsche) is in as much trouble as the immediate person radically defined by others; the problem is our deep entwinement with our essential contingency.

Maybe the critical point is really more a matter of *how* one lives in the finite world, of how one lives in relation to others. Does the self just naturally take the other as her standard and point for negotiating life; does she adopt their "world" uncritically and unself-consciously? Or does she take others as providing a significant portion of her "essential contingency," a portion that can (to a greater or lesser degree) be interpenetrated with consciousness and will in the ongoing dynamic process of moral personhood? If the latter is the case, then the self might seem to have some capacity to more or less successfully negotiate the world and achieve a solid and effective existential identity. But it also might seem that if the self has transcended these relations she faces the question of a basis for their affirmation; a basis, it would seem, that cannot be derived from just those social relations. But how deep do these relations to the other go? If these contingent social and cultural relations have constituted her not simply by their developmental influence but by providing a context for normative thought and evaluation, then the transcendental aspirations of the self may be impossible. If these relations are embedded in the language and institutions of the society and culture in which she was synthesized, they cannot be escaped or completely transcended for they set the terms for all possible interpretative construals of life. It might then be wiser to take a more modest approach and understand that transcending one's self is a matter of degree, a more or less affair that is to be judged by how well it serves human flourishing. This, of course, is less than Kierkegaard would claim, but it is I suspect where we are. We might also point out that the web of relations that constitutes the self is not easily revoked once spun; the engagements of the self shape it to the very core, they mold and shape the plastic nervous system into patterns and process that we can not simply renounce and say, "That is not me," for now it is. Willed revolution in the self is not as simple as Anti-Climacus suggests; we are shaped by our willed past for the future. We will return to these topics in the concluding chapter.

One point that comes clearly to the fore in *The Sickness unto Death* is that the self receives its normative content by the relations within which it stands. With the Judge we choose our self, and our existential identity is shaped by our past, by the current conditions of our life, and by our growing practical wisdom. For Anti-Climacus it is much the same, but it is clear that where the relations that form the standards for the self are the various finite relations in which a person stands, we are never beyond a humanly, worldly measure for the self. But this will not do for a strong spiritual self. To transcend that situation the Judge had to fasten on to himself as spiritual freedom, but since he had to become someone, to be an actual self, he had to reengage the world. The terms of his life were then the particular relations of his life, his concretion as he could best interpenetrate it with consciousness and will. Throughout Kierkegaard's authorship he claims that a person's concretion is made up of relations, biological and social. As we noted earlier, Anti-Climacus says that a person's finitude is defined by his "concretion," it has "necessity and limitations, is this very specific being with these natural capacities, predispositions, etc., in this specific concretion of relations" (SUD 68). In short, what the person has for determining who he or she is to become are set by the finite conditions, the web of relations that constitute his or her world. While I have the spirit as my point of transcendence, this does not provide a transcendental standard or criterion for measuring life. My criterion remains an immanental criterion, but Kierkegaard claims that I yearn for more.

More than any other student of Kierkegaard, C. Stephen Evans has explored the relational dynamics of the selfhood and the implications of the idea of a relational self for Kierkegaard. Evans rightly points out that one crucial point of departure for this discussion is chapter 1 in part 2 of *The Sickness unto Death,* and I will follow Evans's careful analysis up to a point in my reading. Evans argues that the relational character of the self makes it clear that social relations are deeply constitutive of the self as Kierkegaard portrays it. In fact, I argue that they are so deeply constitutive that where Kierkegaard speaks of the power that constitutes the self as God, the divine other, I argue that this power within which the self "rests transparently" is a cultural other that provides the soil for thought and action; the power or powers that "establish" a person's self-represented identity at the "spiritual" level are frames of cultural significance or forms of life. Can we say more? Not unless we get into the messy job of a full-blown metaphysics.

Anti-Climacus clearly tells us that selves get their evaluative reality, their existential standard, their measure for their identity, through the relations that provide criteria or goals for them. Anti-Climacus begins section 2 by telling us that the first part of his psychological exposition was one where he considered "the category of the human self, or the self whose criterion is man" (SUD 79). Or, as he says a bit further on, "the pagan and the natural man have the merely human self as their criterion" (81). And now he wishes to examine how things stand when the self is "directly before God." But the critical point for us now is how Anti-Climacus explains that whatever the self "stands directly before" provides its measure and thereby its goal and then its ethical actuality or its self-represented identity. Anti-Climacus puts it this way:

> What infinite reality the self gains by being conscious of existing before God, by becoming a human self whose criterion is God. A cattleman who (if this were possible) is a self directly before his cattle is a very low self, and, similarly, a master who is a self directly before his slaves is actually no self—for in both cases a criterion is lacking. The child who previously has had only his parents as a criterion becomes a self as an adult by getting the state as a criterion, but what an infinite accent falls on the self by having God as the criterion! (SUD 79)

Anti-Climacus only barely suggests, with these quick examples, what might be possible in the way of a social and cultural standard for the self if we developed his line of thought. He follows this with a more abstract analysis: "The criterion for the self is always: that directly before which it is a self, but this in turn is the definition of 'criterion.' Everything is qualitatively that by which it is measured, and that which is its qualitative criterion is ethically its goal; the criterion and the goal are what define something, what it is" (SUD 79). While a child has a personality, a constellation of beliefs and values, these are just a reflection of the parents; adolescents often measure themselves, define who they are, against their peer group, and this might even be dimly self-conscious. And so too adults become selves, at least selves of a sort, says Anti-Climacus, when they define themselves before a more abstract social reality, the state. If this is the standard for the self, then such a self understands itself only in the terms defined by the society in which he or she participates, or so Anti-Climacus seems to suggest.

Evans reads Anti-Climacus this way: "What makes the self a self is a 'criterion,' a goal or end by which it measures itself. However, that criterion, that sense of an 'ideal self' is given in and through relations with others" (1997, 11). In the final analysis, argues Evans, becoming a self is "fundamentally a matter of coming to understand for oneself the ideals of selfhood that are embedded in the language and institutions of a society, so that one can consciously pursue those ideals for oneself" (1997, 11). These ideals of selfhood, he continues, "are embedded in those relations by which humans are socialized and become parts of concrete communities" (1997, 11). It seems clear that if Evans is right about this point (and I think he is) then there is no necessity in the self's relations to others being ethically debilitating or spiritually bankrupt, as Anti-Climacus repeatedly suggests. In fact, it seems clear that others play a major role in enabling human beings to become selves. So a woman might be a college professor at an American university and deeply identify with the aims and interests of higher education in America. But she need not be uncritically involved with this measure, but will think of herself as self-consciously pursuing this ideal, a goal that largely defines who she is. Her life as a college professor will be a critical engagement with the ideals and aspirations of the professorate in America and not a parroting of the line of the "other professors" or even the AAUP.

Evans argues that for Kierkegaard persons who are engaged in self-conscious and critical relations to others, or more specifically, to ideals of selfhood embedded in the language and social practices of a culture, have a self and furthermore often have a life that is "rich and meaningful" (1997, 12). To live directly or even largely within the confines of the social rules and roles, the plans and projects of the times, is not the same as living rationally and responsibly in relation to the social practices and institutions that constitute human community and connectedness and ultimately constitute selves. The latter affords greater selfhood, a psychically richer more meaningful life, and not an impoverished and psychically empty life, and presumably a life with less despair. But Evans still thinks that Kierkegaard is right; that such a self remains spiritually deficient and to some extent in despair. Such a person, our professor above or the coach in chapter 1, is not an "authentic" and "genuine" self. In an earlier article Evans (1995, 85) puts the Kierkegaardian point this way: "Kierkegaard recognizes that actual human selves are formed relationally, but he thinks that a self which *only* has other human beings as its measure, even the 'adult' who takes the 'official' standards certified by the state as his measure, can never be *secure.* Genuine selfhood requires that the self stand consciously before God." It seems that the problem, as Evans sees it, is not so much finite social relations as such, but a question of the final measure for the self and thereby a question of existential security. If the self is to be ultimately secure, this final measure can never be simply the social and cultural relations within which it lives.

But let us look more carefully at what such a self is said to lack and hence what makes it insecure. Evans sometimes seems to suggest that any individual who does not exercise "responsible choice," who does not know the "call of conscience," is not an authentic Kierkegaardian self. Conversely, to exercise rational and responsible freedom is to be a Kierkegaardian self. Evans puts it this way: "It is in adolescence that the individual discovers that he or she must choose and affirm—or reject—what has been handed down to him or her by culture. Such a call to responsible choice is at the same time a discovery that choices matter—that one is called to choose responsibly. In Kierkegaard's language it is the discovery that human persons are spirit, and Kierkegaard interprets this encounter as God's call to individuals to become what God has created them to become" (1995, 91). But this alone is too weak; it does not name the Kierkegaardian ideal. While Kierkegaard mentions conscience as central to his view, we must remember that finally it is conscience as moral transcendence and final spiritual grounding and not simply the self as rational and responsible actor. What has to happen, as I have said before, is that rational and responsible freedom has to have such a commanding place in the individual's psychological economy that nothing less than moral transcendence will do, nothing less than God's perspective will provide security. It is one thing to be an "effective deliberator" or even a modest spiritual evaluator and quite another to be a *strong* spiritual evaluator. Against the standards of the strong spiritual evaluator, everything I am about begins to pale; my concerns and my social relations are merely relative, just contingent and arbitrary, and I despair. This, as I have already suggested, sets the bar so high that it is insurmountable, but of course we cannot live that way, and so even when we think we have surmounted it we are still here on earth with our fallible construals. Our measures are inevitably mediated to us through our finite social relations; we are dependent on socially and culturally created meanings.

Other commentators, such as Anthony Rudd (1993) and Merold Westphal (1987), seem to suggest that anything short of God-consciousness can only be a crowd-consciousness, and this is a similar Kierkegaardian-inspired mistake. The idea that anything less than transcendence is utter failure and leaves us at the mercy of the current social forces seems seriously overstated to me. As Westphal puts it: "From the ethical point of view, it is the social order that is the self's ground, the 'power that established it.' Such a view treats one's fellow humans as the primary other to whom one relates. Since a right relation to this power [the social order] that has established the self constitutes the self's health, the result is that each 'seeks to be like the others, to become a copy, a number, a mass man'" (1987, 46). Besides the fact that this divides the ethical even more sharply from the religious than Kierkegaard would have, why can I not have a relationship to others that is existentially enriching and yet critical? Furthermore, in a diverse and pluralistic world can the social order even provide an unambiguous reference for me; *which* others do I seek to be like? To say that without the ultimate God-relation I am just a "mass man," seems premised on a need for nothing short of ultimate orientation, before which all other orientations are merely starter relations, not sufficient places from which to live a meaningful life. I am inclined to think, as Evans suggests, that the person with such social relations can have a meaningful and significant life; it is surely the case that there is no necessity in this person being just a number, a "mass man," a copy of the others.

Rudd puts the matter this way: "For Kierkegaard, individuality and commitment to self formative projects can only be held together at the religious level. The esthete neglects the latter and his soul is dissipated into multiplicity. The ethicist neglects the former and he vanishes into the mass of the conventionally respectable" (1993, 121–22). When Rudd says that the esthete makes no commitment to self-formative projects, we need to remember that Kierkegaard's bar is finally so high that only God's project will really confer ultimate coherence and security, for all other projects are merely finite. As Rudd himself says, "If we are to achieve that ultimate coherence and integration of our lives, the desire for which Kierkegaard posits as the force driving us on through the spheres of existence, we must turn from spiritual self-sufficiency in order to relate ourselves to God" (1993, 140). The trouble is that then all of us begin to look like failed esthetes, for does anyone really get clear access to God's project, or does the finite seep in around the edges? Furthermore, surely there is an important difference between someone who has never come to any degree of critical self-consciousness and someone who has developed considerable clarity about who they are and what they are doing, although not transparency. Or conversely, when the Judge is accused of a lack of individuality, just what is needed for Kierkegaardian individuality? If my projects are immanental, related to others or to social and institutional practices, I am not necessarily just a "mass man." In the final analysis, does anyone really transcend, completely transcend, social practices and cultural frames and chart their own unique way? We all, to various degrees, constitute ourselves out of the social and cultural resources available. But then we are in a pluralistic situation and we have lost ultimate integration. Rudd says that this is a problem for a secular ethics: "A nonreligious ethic remains pluralistic" (1993, 134). But is the "plague" of pluralism escaped at the religious level, is there not a problem with religious pluralism too? It seems clear that there is.

Our choice is not simply either "mass man" or strong spiritual evaluator. Both these sorts of similar responses seem to me to pose false alternatives. No doubt many people just follow the populace and never really come to much clarity about themselves and what they are doing, but surely many other individuals live lives of genuine integrity, of moral and spiritual import, but they are not strong spiritual evaluators in Kierkegaard's sense. I see the lives they are living best characterized as lives of *modest* ethical/spiritual evaluation. I take it that my coach in chapter 1 is just such a person: he is not an egotist, he lives his life in a wide circle of meaningful relations; he pursues the development of his talents and his life-project; he sees his limits yet works to improve himself against standards that are socially, biologically, and culturally constituted; he is not by his own lights in spiritual despair. If he took up the demands of strong evaluation he might be. But why should he do that? Will his life be further enriched? Will he escape the plague of pluralism?

As I have already suggested, I think humans can flourish when they live out of an existential identity that they know is not ultimate; my additional point here is that Kierkegaard's own existential construals and commitments are also bound by such conditions. Indeed, given how deeply Evans argues that ideals of selfhood are embedded in the language and institutions of a society, it seems natural enough to wonder how he thinks that Kierkegaard's own thought about and experience with ideals of selfhood managed to escape this condition. Relations to others shaped Kierkegaard too: in particular, an especially impressive and passionate father—"I owe everything to my father" (JSK #773)—and Kierkegaard's own serious study of ideals of selfhood, especially those of Western Christendom. Does his declaration that we cannot take the state as our normative measure, cannot take others as our final measure, that the final criterion cannot be finite contingencies, mean that he was not influenced by them? Can one be so confident that Kierkegaard has transcended these relations? I think a strong argument can be made that Kierkegaard himself was restoring an older inherited vision of human life that he found compelling as he read off the effective history of his own immersion in just those strands of moral and Christian culture. If I am correct that the argument for the strong evaluator who ends in paradoxical Christianity is unsuccessful, then this explanation beckons. This argument will be fully developed in the final chapter.

Despair's Demand: Anti-Climacus's Argument for God

As we noted earlier, the first part of *The Sickness unto Death* is not as explicitly theological as the second part, where despair is defined as sin when the self is before God. Yet it is also clear that the two parts are not discontinuous, for the self is, from the beginning, standing in relationship to God, whether conscious of this or not. In fact, already in the first part this is explicit; when Anti-Climacus moves into a discussion of "despair as defined by consciousness," he puts all his cards on the table:

> Every human existence that is not conscious of itself as spirit or *conscious of itself before God as spirit,* every human existence that does not rest transparently in God, but vaguely rests in or merges in some abstract universality (state, nation, etc.) or, in the dark about his self, regards his capacities merely as powers to produce without becoming deeply aware of their source, regards his self, if it is to have intrinsic meaning, as an indefinable something—every such existence, whatever it achieves, be it most amazing, whatever it explains, be it the whole of existence, however intensively it enjoys life esthetically—every such existence is despair. (SUD 46, emphasis added)

It is clear in this passage that Kierkegaard understands that human beings orient themselves in relation to others or, better, in relation to the reactions and responses of others—where the others are often social selves within me. These social selves can have their most potent exemplification in the ideas and ideals of various groups, communities, and nation-states: in all manner of human construal of our condition. It is also clear that a purely naturalistic view of the self is rejected; the self has a source that is not merely finite; the self is in kinship with God. So finally all others that the self might stand with, others that might provide my final measure for evaluating my life and deciding how I should orient my practice are inadequate.

But now the crucial point is that it makes every difference to be aware that one stands before God, that the final horizon of one's self-consciousness is God: "What infinite reality the self gains by being conscious of existing before God, by becoming a human self whose criterion is God . . . an infinite accent falls on the self by having God as the criterion!" (SUD 79). There is a final relation for the self and, Anti-Climacus tells us, it is the relation to that which established the entire relation. The finite free relational self must, Anti-Climacus asserts, "either have established itself or have been established by another" (13). And he is of the view that the human self is "a derived, established relation, a relation that relates itself to itself and relating itself to itself relates itself to another" (13–14). What is Anti-Climacus saying? Is there any question that the other is God? And how does he know this must be the case? Does he have an argument?

Given what we have said about the relational character of the self, Anti-Climacus might seem to be claiming that when I endeavor to represent who I currently am, to conceptualize myself, I must acknowledge that the content of myself, my commitments and identifications, are from outside of myself. I did not in the first place establish myself but *it was established for me* as I unself-consciously synthesized my world, and now

I take it over. The Judge seemed to claim just this when he said that we are to bring consciousness to bear on our concretion and that our concretion is related to our finite yet essential contingency. Furthermore, as I continue to chart my way, I am going to stand in relation to the world, that is, my actual identity as I constitute it must have a social dimension because being in the world is inescapably social. I will be shot through with social relationships and practices; and when it comes to spiritual matters, self-conscious relations to this world have constituted my central purposes and their significance for me. But it seems more than these finite conditions that happen to have constituted us, or even those relations that we self-consciously attend to, that Anti-Climacus refers to when he asserts that the self "relates itself to that which established the *entire* relation [that is, the self]" (SUD 13, emphasis added). I, however, argue that those social relations that established us are more of a pervasive presence than Anti-Climacus, or Kierkegaard, realize.

On one plausible reading, he seems to be saying that it is just the whole matter of being an existing cognitive spirit: this is what is given and what cannot simply be ignored or denied, but from which we must live. We cannot escape being a self; we cannot escape being a relation that relates itself to itself. And this is to say that we cannot escape being spirit, and spirit is nothing other than the eternal, our link to the divine. The self's psychic capacities for self-conscious relationality and transcendence are identified with the eternal, with God. This clearly seems Anti-Climacus's conclusion in the section entitled "The Possibility and the Actuality of Despair" (SUD 14–17), which we examined briefly earlier. There Anti-Climacus argued that a person cannot rid himself of the eternal, which is to say that he cannot rid himself of the relation to himself any more than he can rid himself of this self. This was evident in Climacus's reflections as examined in the last chapter. But then the theological dimension of the self seems to get a more explicitly social and relational reading in part 2. God has created existing cognitive spirits or finite yet free relational selves; as Anti-Climacus says, "God constituted man a relation." And then this is a relation that must finally stand in relationship to its creator. There is now more of a distance between self and God; God is more like another self, an internalized peer group, a social self, or even an *ideal Socius,* to use William James's idea, before which I measure my existential identity (1890, 316). While Climacus said that we find God by taking an inward journey, Anti-Climacus sees selves as finally relating to an infinite transcendent God. (There is a tension here between the self as in kinship with the divine as a creature with an eternal dimension and as separated from God by the very limitations of his or her finitude.) It is not just in the spiritual intensity of despair and guilt that I maintain the God-relation, it is not just the passion of the infinite, but it is in "standing before God"—a phrase that has more relational quality than we have yet heard from Judge William or Climacus. God has created us to stand in relation to him; without him we cannot ground our existential identity. And so, despite great efforts to "tear his self away from the power that established it, he cannot manage to do it; [because] that power is the stronger and forces him to be the self he does not want to be" (SUD 20). Of course, in a deeper sense, if Anti-Climacus is right, this is the self he really wants to be, he has just not realized it yet!

How does Anti-Climacus know this? His core argument is this passage in part 1 of *The Sickness unto Death:* "If a human self had established itself, then there could only be one form [of despair]: not to will to be oneself, to will to do away with oneself, but there could not be the form in despair to will to be oneself. This second formulation is specifically the expression for the complete dependence of the relation (of the self), the expression for the inability of the self to arrive at or to be in equilibrium and rest by itself, but only, in relating itself to itself, by relating it to that which has established the entire relation" (SUD 14). We have examined the forms of despair, and we know that Anti-Climacus refers to the despair of defiance here, an advanced form that uses infinitude, the self as spirit, to deny the *telos* of human existence. Such an individual, we learned, "wants to be master of itself, to create itself, to make his self into the self he wants to be" (68). This person does not suffer from lack of will, they are not weak in the usual sense, rather they refuse to acknowledge that *on their own* they can never really achieve what they really want: spiritual grounding, a meaning and purpose to life that is not just something they have created, something their social times have fashioned, or even something generations of practical human experiencers have settled on, but something that transcends all merely finite conditions. So this heroic effort of the infinite self fails: I still experience despair, I still simply have not found spiritual rest.

The argument is, as Louis Pojman points out, "a variation of the argument from contingency, although it substitutes dependency of the spirit for dependency of being" (1984, 15). On my own I cannot surmount spiritual despair, but only when I give up and lose myself, myself as I would have it, and give myself over to "that which established the entire relation" do I gain spiritual rest. Anti-Climacus's argument for the reality of God is closely related to his convictions about the conditions of human existence as despair. Anti-Climacus is clearly of the view that any life that does not finally relinquish itself to God, to the power that created it, will be unsatisfactory. It is the experience of despair that drives Kierkegaard to his conviction that there must be a God. Spiritual despair cannot be the final word; there must be a divine source for my yearnings, for only a transcendent standard can ground my aspirations as spirit. But whence this spiritual despair?

Despair is the core experience that establishes the empirical backing for the argument for God; but the despair issues from the religious aspiration: there must be a place out there for our high spiritual demands to rest since the moral and spiritual despair that would result if there were not is intolerable. The idea that we might just be contingent creatures, arbitrarily constituted, and unclear on our ultimate source (just like the Niger River) is not a serious option for Kierkegaard; the implications are evident: life would be nothing but despair. But this argument begs the question. This argument is premised on the idea that we are subject to such a high ethical and spiritual demand in the first place, and how was that established? Intense irresolvable spiritual despair is a consequence of the assumption that nothing less than ultimate integration, complete transparency, and total unity will do. Nothing less than a God's-eye perspective will do. Where does this assumption derive? For Kierkegaard it is an immoveable intuition, a core spiritual insight: there is a question about our whence and wherefore that cannot be answered adequately by us. In other words, for Kierkegaard, *the radically self-transcending self is always beyond itself* and so never able to secure its existential identity, but unable to function without an existential identity.

To settle on a relatively adequate existential identity given all I can best discern is not good enough for such a self. As early as the Judge's *Ultimatum,* ostensibly a letter from a pastor friend who concurs with his view and which he attaches to his letters to A, this point is clear: "So every more earnest doubt, every deeper care is not calmed by the words: One does what one can. If a person is sometimes right, sometimes in the wrong, to some degree in the right, to some degree in the wrong, who, then, is the one who makes that decision except the person himself, but in the decision may he not again be to some degree in the right and in to some degree in the wrong?" (E/O 346). To be in the more or less of human approximations, our best justified beliefs, is, in Kierkegaard's judgment, demoralizing and spiritually unsatisfactory. Such a state is intolerable; the only solution is beyond finite human wisdom and its conclusions. As the ultimatum letter puts it: When a person found time to deliberate "the examination gave him a more or less, an approximation, but never anything exhaustive. How could a person ever gauge his relationship with God by a more or a less, or by a specification of approximation? Thus he ascertained that this [common, practical] wisdom was a treacherous friend who under the guise of helping him entangled him in doubt, worried him in an unremitting cycle of confusion. What had been obscure to him previously but had not troubled him did not become any clearer now, but his mind became anguished and careworn in doubt. Only in an infinite relationship with God could the doubt be calmed; only in an infinitely free relationship with God could his care be turned to joy" (E/O 352). And so Kierkegaard sees it as humanly necessary to conclude that there must be a transcendent source of value and meaning, there must be a God. The idea that there just might not be such a source was not even an option; the consequences were too abysmal.

In *Fear and Trembling,* Kierkegaard has Johannes de Silentio declare: "If a human being did not have an eternal consciousness, if underlying everything there were only a wild, fermenting power that writhing in dark passions produced everything, be it significant or insignificant, if a vast, never appeased emptiness hid beneath everything, what would life be then but despair?" (FT 30). But Anti-Climacus later clarifies: despair would not really be a possibility if we did not have an eternal consciousness: "If there were nothing eternal in a man, he could not despair at all" (SUD 21). So it is not that we must posit eternity to save us from despair, but that the spiritual despair that we know is a consequence of the fact that we are creatures who are in kinship with the eternal or that *we are creatures construed as tied to the eternal,* and we are therefore creatures that desire the transcendental perspective, the Archimedean point, a grounding in God. Kierkegaard's existential argument for God rests squarely on his construal of the human being as a creature in kinship with the divine, as always already oriented toward God. This means, of course, that God is assumed in the very attempt to establish God.

As Charles Taylor points out, this is again the classic "Augustinian approach to proving the existence of God, which proceeds via a radical reflection on my own spiritual nature. My longing for perfection, coupled with my manifest imperfection, points to the higher being who implanted this aspiration in me" (1989, 311). My question is this: Can we really get this conclusion out of our own spiritual nature? What does our so-called spiritual nature come to? If our spiritual nature comes to our capacity to call into question, to doubt about, to wonder, to envision possibility; if it is the pervasive sense that there is more here than meets the eye, the capacity to ever push back the horizon of consciousness; or if it is particularly the capacity to reflect on our own thoughts and feelings, to envision who we are, to view ourselves from outside, so to speak, I doubt if we can get the strong metaphysics of eternity conclusion from either imagination or self-consciousness. Nagel (for one) argues that we can deny physical reduction of subjective states, maintain the irreducibility of subjective consciousness, and still not be compelled to postulate metaphysical souls and the like. We can maintain a connection between the physical and the mental, though we may not yet understand the details. There can be an exceedingly complex relationship between the mind, or the subjective perspectives of consciousness, and the organic structures and process that make up the brain, but we cannot deny, as Nagel says, that "the mind is after all a biological product" (1986, 31). This does not preclude rich conceptions of the human creature, but there is no logical necessity to declare the mental subjective features eternal or spiritual, that is, no reason to announce a spiritual self disconnected from nature.

Kierkegaard's point about the eternal side of the human is based in the experience of the subjective perspective as radically self-transcending, as Anti-Climacus put it, the perception of "a consciousness of a self that is won by infinite abstract from every externality, this naked, abstract self" (SUD 55). Kierkegaard's mistake comes, using Nagel's words, from the Cartesian assumption that the self's very nature is "fully revealed to introspection, and that our immediate subjective conception of the thing [the self] in our own case contains everything essential to it, if only we could extract it" (1986, 34). Further, there is the obvious point that for human creatures that are physically or mentally impaired these psychic capacities are severely limited. And the clear conclusion is that these capacities are part of our psychobiological structure; they are tied, in short, to our finitude. It seems plausible to see human organisms as something of a nature-spirit unity; we are to a large degree fitted for this finite world in which we find ourselves. We will do better to think of spirit as naturalized, as immanently intertwined with our nature.

Perhaps the most pointed question however is this: Do humans have a longing for moral perfection, for ultimate psychic integration, that if it goes underrequited will end in despair? Do humans find that they can live only as strong spiritual evaluators? My answer, as is clear from what has come so far, is no. While humans do have an interest in expanding their cognitive horizons, in bringing their objectifying capacities to bear on their praxis, this does not demand that anything less than complete and total unity is failure. Indeed such an impossibly high bar threatens to make the Kierkegaardian ideal nonsensical and life within it torturous. It seems to me that we do better to speak of degrees of achieving selfhood; indeed, if Kierkegaard is right about the self as a relational achievement, then (other things being equal) the more rational and responsible relations I have to the world, the more I establish myself and the less I am in despair. The person with minimal relations, with little investment in the world, is the person in despair: the greater the investment the larger the return. As William James says: "Sympathetic people proceed by the . . . way of expansion and inclusion. The outline of their self often gets uncertain enough, but for this the spread of its content more than atones" (1890, 313).

If the foregoing is right, then the argument for God falters on what turns out to be an unfounded (or at least not rationally required) premise about humans being subject to a goal of moral transcendence. The most that Kierkegaard can finally claim for his argument is that it is demoralizing not to believe in God, where God insures that moral concerns are in the grain of the universe; or, it is morally helpful to believe in God. Kierkegaard's core strategy, as I have already argued, is to see our concern with getting our proper life, with a meaningful and enriching self-understanding, with edification, as that which compels us toward the strenuous life of morally and spiritually strong evaluator and ultimately to posit God. Now while I do not think he can get as much leverage out of this pragmatic argument as he would like, some gain is afforded. What does the existential argument for God come to? Robert Merrihew Adams best states the gain that is afforded.

Adams argues that there is a "moral advantage in accepting theism," if we believe that "theism provides the most adequate theory of moral order in the universe" (1987, 151). Adams states the advantage in terms of defeating demoralization, whereas for Kierkegaard the similar advantage is in defeating despair. In Adams's words it is "demoralizing not to believe that there is a moral order of the universe, for then we would have to regard it as very likely that the history of the universe will not be good on the whole, no matter what we do" (1987, 151). This argument, Adams points out, has some limitations. First, one must admit that a theistic worldview is not the only metaphysical standpoint from which we can articulate a moral order of the universe. At least making the case for a theistic worldview is needed, and it is something that Kierkegaard seeks to bypass. Second, even if we grant the theistic worldview as the best case for a moral order of the universe, we still have to establish that life without such a worldview is demoralizing. That is, is it empirically true that the moral life without God cannot get going or leads to despair? Adams argues that this empirical question does not admit of a conclusive answer. Many people do find that belief in God sustains moral life, that it helps them to face obstacles and avoid temptations. As Adams's writes: "Seeing our lives as contributing to a valued larger whole is one of the things that gives them a point in our own eyes. . . . Having to regard it as very likely that the history of the universe will not be good on the whole, no matter what we do, seems to induce a cynical sense of futility about the moral life, undermining one's moral resolve and one's interest in moral considerations" (1987, 152).

Still, given that not all people find belief in theism necessary for an engaged moral life, we can only say that the moral life without God *can* be demoralizing, but not that it will inevitable be so. Here, of course, is where I part company with Kierkegaard, for Kierkegaard's claim is stronger: he would say that it is humanly impossible to escape the power that constituted us with a *telos* toward unity, with a task toward interpenetrating the finite with the infinite, and hence to bypass our need for God. The cost of escape is spiritual death. Adams's conclusion is that this is a practical argument that provides emotional and motivational support for belief in God, but not theoretical support; theoretical support cannot be gained from pragmatic arguments. Indeed he seems to go so far as to claim that even our justification for morality cannot be purely pragmatic; we must have grounds for moral convictions independent of moral helpfulness, else we are in a vicious circle. But I would argue that when it comes to moral and spiritual matters this may concede too much to a more positivistic conception of the scope of reason; surely a pragmatist like James would argue that the divide between the cognitive and the noncognitive is not always so sharp.

I propose that Anti-Climacus's existential argument for God, an argument we found in Climacus too, can get us only so far. Given that we are committed to morality and have grounds in human experience and reason for our commitment, then it is not irrational to be swayed by the moral helpfulness of theism. Anti-Climacus's relational achievement theory of the self provides a rationale for the moral life; the moral life satisfies our deep interest in bringing our cognitive and volitional capacities to bear on our finite life, on the social and biological exigencies of the human condition. The ideal of objective reengagement is one that is attractive to creatures such as us. The alternative, demoralization and despair, is not attractive. So there is a pragmatic point to Anti-Climacus's claim that I need to relate myself to God: belief in God can be morally helpful, can help us stay the moral course against the slings and arrows of outrageous fortune. To bring William James back in again: "In a merely human world without a God, the appeal to our moral energy falls short of its maximal stimulating power" (1897, 212). Kierkegaard would, I think, make a stronger claim, but maybe this is strong enough. Kierkegaard thinks he is in even more certain territory with the "subjective" than with the "objective," and so he reasserts a strong traditional moral realism; the demands of morality are sovereign, and then God (the source of the moral demands, the ground of the traditional conscience) is not an optional relation for the individuals but is humanly necessary.

Christian Existential Identity

There is one other matter that I have not yet explored, and that is the question of the content for the self when it is explicitly committed to God: what content is discerned when the self relates to the power that established the entire relation? I am to will as God would have it, and not as I would have it. But as we asked earlier, how would God have it? What does the notion of "resting in God" come to in practice? And then how does the revelation of Christ, or the self's relation to Christ, impact on this theological self before God? As I have indicated already, I do not intend to examine Kierkegaard's christological reflections, for it is my conviction that Kierkegaard's "argument" for Christian existence rests on his vision of the normatively human, and the epistemic supports for this vision are more fragile than Kierkegaard thought. If the move to theism is in question, or not as compelling as Kierkegaard would have, the next move to Christianity is even more questionable. Put another way, the final affirmation of traditional Christianity, like the theism that preceded it, is not humanly or existentially necessary. The end result is a more pluralistic vision of human existential identity.

Initially it seemed like the self had to actualize itself, to maintain the strenuous task of relating itself to itself and willing to be itself, and it would thereby stand in relation to God. This seemed to be Climacus's view, and it was essentially reaffirmed by Anti-Climacus in part 1. But in part 2 of *The Sickness unto Death* the formula becomes even more relational: to be before God and to will to be one's self. Even if we grant that there must be a divine ground for our self-transcending self to rest in, we need to remember that this power for Anti-Climacus serves as a measure for the self, thus establishing the self as a theological self. The only way I can become the self I am essentially intended to become is to stand in a conscious and free relationship to my creator, to God. But what exactly does God require of me? That is, what am I to will if I am to will to be my true self and realize theological selfhood?

In part 2 of *The Sickness unto Death,* entitled "Despair Is Sin," Anti-Climacus begins to fill in a more substantive vision of the self in its relation to God. He says that now "the self has a conception of God and yet does not will as He wills, and thus is disobedient" (SUD 80). Or slightly further on: sin is now the state of the spirit, and this signifies a "self-willfulness against God, a disobedience that defies his commandments" (81). When the self is before God it looks like this: the human self has a deep "obligation in obedience to God with regard to its every clandestine desire and thought, with regard to its readiness to hear and understand and its willingness to follow every hint from God as to his will for this self" (82). This does not tell us much yet, but it suggests that we need to "listen to God," that we need to be obedient to God and his commandments. It becomes clear, however, in part 2, that the substance of "before God," the source of spiritual rest, will be filled in by the Western Jewish and Christian vision of God and by the revelatory clarity afforded therein: despair is sin and "sin is—after being taught by a revelation from God what sin is—before God in despair to will to be oneself or in despair to will to be oneself" (96). There must, says Anti-Climacus, as "orthodoxy emphasizes," be a "revelation from God to teach fallen man what sin is, a communication that, quite consistently, must be believed, because it is a dogma" (96). In the final analysis, a human being, says Anti-Climacus, "has to learn what sin is by a revelation from God" (95). According to Climacus, we knew what despair was by honest self-examination, and we even knew (as Climacus put it) a "tranquility and restfulness in all this strenuousness, because it is not contradiction to relate oneself absolutely to the absolute *telos,* that is, with all one's might and in renunciation of everything else, but it is the absolute reciprocity in like for like" (CUP 422). But now sin (the intensification of despair when the self is directly before God) we know only by divine initiative. We are no longer talking about a general religious faith; we are talking about a specific Christian faith. We are, I would submit, now operating from within a specific restoration of a tradition-constituted *telos*—the Jewish/Christian tradition as creatively retrieved and reconstructed by Kierkegaard. As MacIntyre puts in his early *A Short History of Ethics:* "It is only when writing from *within* a Christian position that Kierkegaard can find any reasons for answering the question, How shall I live? in one way rather than another" (1966, 218). The only way Anti-Climacus can regain any substantive content is to return to the Western theistic presuppositions that orient his whole effort.

But these considerations do not yet lead us to what is distinctly Christian. So far we have really simply stepped into Judaism, or the theistic religious view, and into the demand of righteousness, the call to perfect moral conscience, of the high God Yahweh. To get to Christian existence we need the further step of the revelatory act of God becoming a human being, of the transcendence of existence within existence. Climacus has already set the stage: "Christianity has declared itself to be the eternal, essential truth that has come into existence in time; it has proclaimed itself as the paradox, and has required the inwardness of faith with regard to what is an offense to the Jews, foolishness to the Greeks—and an absurdity to the understanding" (CUP 213). Even Anti-Climacus takes a considerable number of pages to get to what is distinctively Christian; indeed I think that a good deal of the time when he refers to Christianity he really means to speak more broadly of the theistic revelation. For example, when he says "sin is not to be found at all in paganism, but only in Judaism and Christendom, and there again very seldom" (SUD 101), this means that sin is a unique qualification of the individual consciousness afforded by the Jewish and Christian revelation and cannot be expected of those poor souls outside this circle of faith. There seems to be something of a transitional form of religious consciousness: no longer immanent religiousness, Religiousness A, which has only human nature as its presupposition, and not yet Christian existence proper, Judaism (and perhaps Islam) is in between. There also seems to be some tension here, for is it the theistic religious revelation that is an offense to the understanding, or is it the specific Christian claim that God has become human?

Maybe there are increasing degrees of offense. In any event, it is clear that the very high standard of "before God" no longer has to pass muster before human reason and experience, because we have taken the final step outside of even *finite* human reason and experience and are before the infinite. And so it is that "men are offended by Christianity because it is too high, because its goal is not man's goal, because it wants to make man into something so extraordinary that he cannot grasp the thought" (SUD 83). But as we noted above, if Anti-Climacus is right, as well as Climacus, this theological self is the self he or she really wants to be; he or she has just not realized it yet. Slightly further on Anti-Climacus begins to accuse those who would hesitate of a lack of courage and comprehension: "Everyone lacking the humble courage to dare to believe [Christianity] is offended. But why is he offended? Because it is too high for him, because his mind cannot grasp it, because he cannot attain the bold confidence in the face of it, and therefore must get rid of it, pass it off as . . . nonsense and folly" (85–86). Can his mind really be expected to grasp it? Yes and no. That the overwhelming demand for moral transcendence, for the impossible demand to bring together the infinite and finite, might be substantively known (revealed to us) or, better, achieved, or even has been achieved with Christ, is beyond human comprehension, but it is something that we (or so Kierkegaard argues) desperately desire. It is then existentially reasonable to believe what is intellectually or, more narrowly, "objectively" nonsense.

But what is it that the Christian believes; what then is distinctively Christian for Anti-Climacus? Almost predictably, he announces that there is "a further intensification of the consciousness of the self" with "the knowledge of Christ" (SUD 113). This intensification is a result, of course, of being before the highest criterion: Christ. After the self that has a human criterion, Anti-Climacus reminds his reader, comes the self directly before God, the theological criterion, and then, not surprisingly, and finally, a self comes "directly before Christ": "That Christ is the criterion is the expression, attested by God, for the staggering reality that a self has, for only in Christ is it true that God is man's goal and criterion" (114). There is a tension here between whether this is finally our goal or God's goal for us, and then is it this only after a normative revelation from God? It seems that in Anti-Climacus's Christian hands our goal can be reached only within God's revelatory goal for us.

The position of the self that leads to this final stage is that the self knows itself as a sinner; it is in sin before the revelation of God, but despite the fact that it yearns now for forgiveness of its sins, it tends toward defiance. In the rejection of the Christian revelation, or proclamation of Christ, the self is once again, and finally, not willing to be itself. At this point what the self is is a sinner in need of forgiveness. Those not *willing* to go forward in Christian faith are failing to be selves. They are in the deepest state of despair, they are defiantly living in sin. Their release is in willing to believe, in willing to believe one very traditional image of the message and meaning of Jesus. That Anti-Climacus is a defender of a traditional orthodox understanding of Christ is evident in this ultimate declaration: "A self directly before Christ is a self intensified by the inordinate concession from God, intensified by the inordinate accent that falls upon it because God allows himself to be born, become man, suffer, and die also for the sake of this self" (SUD 113).

So where does this leave us? Human reason, as Kierkegaard portrays it, sees that it has reached its limit with the content of the Christian claim; it cannot comprehend this event, that within the historical the infinite appears. But, on the other hand, the theological self is in such desperate straits that this appearance, this impossible content, is eminently rational for the self, the self in the throes of existential despair. Indeed, the Christian gift is the Kierkegaardian wish realized; it is, as Kierkegaard says in his journal, really *immediacy attained:* "From a Christian point of view, immediacy is lost and it ought not be yearned for again but should be attained again" (SKJP 2.377). Or somewhat latter (1849) this journal entry: "Immediacy is attained again only ethically; immediacy itself becomes the task—you shall attain it" (1.424). With Christ the self is immediately with God and so is directly satisfied and positively refreshed, but this is only after the ethical, or holding fast to the ethical. This, it is proclaimed, is not another delusion of the positive thinker. Of course, one difficulty is that this content must be accepted on faith, must just be believed: "All Christianity turns on this, that it must be believed and not comprehended, that *either* it must be believed, *or* one must be scandalized and offended by it" (SUD 98). We have reached a final either/or. We have existential *reason* to adopt what is nonsense, but why *this* nonsense? Admittedly this "Christian nonsense" is answering what the theistic revelation proclaimed was required, high righteousness and moral perfection; it is accommodating that demand, but why this theistic revelation or, better, why the first move to God? The existential argument for God we reviewed above, and again we are driven back to the vision of the normatively human; only when this vision is in place does the "Christian nonsense" become existentially compelling. But then so might other "nonsense" that proclaims itself "immediacy attained" or the final revelation.[3]

Climacus repeatedly told us that our task was exceedingly strenuous; indeed at many points he seemed to say it was really impossible. I concluded in reviewing Climacus that the strenuous requirement issues from a conviction that nothing less than a standpoint outside of existence will do, but this cannot be had while still within existence. Despite the fact that this high ideal is seen as a contradiction, even an impossibility, nonsense really, it is held out as the ideal. As Anti-Climacus says, "Truly if there is anything to lose one's mind over, this [Christianity] is it!" (SUD 85). Why do I want to lose my mind at all? Not for no reason, but for existential reasons: for spiritual grounding, for secure purposes, to live from the ultimate goal; in short, I yearn to realize the Kierkegaardian ideal. The whole Kierkegaardian project is designed to provide an existential motivation, a spiritual rationale, for Christianity, for what is finally said to be intellectual nonsense. Such a project is built on an ideal for humans that, I am convinced, lives from a specific faith that the ideal is required by sources beyond the conditions of existence.

This conclusion is supported by Kierkegaard's clear and strong commitment to a sharp and deep divide between what "the ethical" demands, what the Kierkegaardian ideal requires, and what humans beings can, on their own resources, achieve. Owen Flanagan refers to this exaggerated position as "the autonomy" thesis. We will explore this sharp divide and its implications in the next chapter. At this point I want to conclude with a brief suggestion. The idea that Christianity (and for that matter, numerous other moral and spiritual views) is substantive nonsense follows if one begins with foundationalist presuppositions. In many respects Kierkegaard himself was still under the sway of the strong objectivist aspiration. He inherited Cartesian foundationalism. Kierkegaard is compelled to view Christianity as nonsense, and an offense to the understanding, because he thinks that objective inquiry measures religious matters only in terms of a rationalistic metaphysics or the traditional arguments for God's existence. Kierkegaard sees no way to provide a justification for moral and spiritual matters given the modernist terms within which he assumes justification must take place—strong objectivist foundationalist terms. Moreover, the Christianity he inherited was the Christianity of strong rationalism or metaphysics and not of moral and spiritual existence. This Christianity had lost touch with the individual and his or her existential questions. So Kierkegaard himself provides a subjective or existential rationale for Christianity, reconnecting religion to the vitality of lived experience. But this route then opens up to wider spiritual horizons for us, wider than Kierkegaard imagined, because other deep construals of life's meaning cannot be ruled out if they prove to be pragmatically helpful or existentially edifying. Kierkegaard opens the door to a plurality of existential identities; other forms of spiritual wisdom can speak to us. The crucial step then, or so I conclude, is to find a moral and spiritual path through which you can self-consciously engage your history (the social and cultural resources at your disposal) in such a way that you extend that history so it becomes your own as you move effectively and fruitfully into the future. You must find, as Kierkegaard says, truth for you.

Notes

1. As Hannay argues, the two primary resources for understanding Kierkegaard's analysis of despair are *Either/Or* and *The Sickness unto Death* (1998, 330).

2. MacIntyre's more recent *Dependent Rational Animals* (1999) provides, however, a new more naturalistic dimension to his thought and actually leads in some of the directions I will propose.

3. Besides other religious traditions, I am reminded of humanistic psychotherapy and its claims about living from one's "inner vision," which seems like a sort of immediacy attained. Bugental sees the ideal of therapy this way: "*When I am preoccupied with* how to *get myself to do or not do something, then I am surely out of my own center. . . . When I am in my own being, there is no meaning to the question of* how to—*of how to discover what I feel, understand why I am reacting as I do, and so on. I am the feeling, the acting, the intending.* To the extent that I truly have my inner vision, my intention is my process; *in other words, what I want is apparent and I don't need some 'procedure' to discover it*" (1976, 235).

4 *In the Twilight of Modernity: Kierkegaard and Contemporary Reflections on Existential Identity*

> All philosophers share this common error: they proceed from contemporary man and think they can reach their goal through an analysis of this man. Automatically they think of "man" as an eternal verity, as something abiding in the whirlpool, as a sure measure of things. Everything that the philosopher says about man, however, is at bottom no more than a testimony about the man of a very limited period. Lack of historical sense is the original error of all philosophers.
>
> —Nietzsche, *Human, All-Too-Human*

So where does this analysis of Kierkegaard leave us, those of us who are searching for existential identity by way of Kierkegaard? Thinking after Nietzsche means understanding our situation as one of multiple perspectives with no clearly noncontroversial uncontested framework, a pluralistic context. Perhaps it is this confidence in sociohistorical consciousness over against a confidence in common human experience and reason that signifies that postmodernity has overtaken Enlightenment modernity, that the twilight of modernity has arrived. Although Kierkegaard writes after Hegel, this strong sense of historical consciousness does not yet have the upper hand for him. He is still confident that historical consciousness poses a challenge that must and can be met. Nietzsche is the turning point.

Although Nietzsche's position cited in the epigraph is an overstatement, for it is implausible to think that none of our claims about humans can be said to transcend our period, it does capture a good deal of the problem I have been developing for Kierkegaard. Kierkegaard does not exactly develop his analysis from contemporary humans, but he does proceed from an analysis of culturally embedded consciousness (especially his own consciousness), and he does seem to think of "subjectivity" as having an epistemologically privileged status, as a sure point of departure. I have argued, however, that Kierkegaard was practicing a pragmatic retrieval and reconfiguration of certain traditional concepts and arguments. A careful analysis of his thought reveals just which concepts and arguments he finds attractive. Why he finds these attractive has as much to do with their measuring up to the bar of human experience and reason (a slippery bar at best) as with the fact that they are just the concepts and arguments that resonate with his own sensibilities as an individual who has drunk deeply from the Western Christian intellectual tradition. It was these cultural resources that helped him through the crisis of traditional conscience and existential affirmation firmly in place for him as a nineteenth-century intellectual.

As many authors have documented, in the early nineteenth century the West was increasingly experiencing a breakdown of the Enlightenment confidence in a common human nature and reason, a breakdown that lead to a crisis of, in Basil Mitchell's phrase, "the traditional conscience." Many people during the nineteenth century followed the Victorian emphasis on conscience and character, but the rationale for such an allegiance was increasingly strained. The general problem of the time, in Mitchell's words, "was to find a satisfactory rationale for [moral] convictions and a framework that could give meaning and purpose to life" (1980, 87). This is the very predicament within which Kierkegaard comes of age. The romantic reaction in the early nineteenth century to this perceived collapse of moral authority is to put the responsibility for charting a moral and spiritual course on the shoulders of each individual. Iris Murdoch sums up the predicament the romantic faced, perhaps more honestly than the more conservative Victorian: "Human life has no external point or *telos*. . . . There are properly many patterns or purposes within life, but there is no general and as it were generally guaranteed pattern or purpose of the kind for which philosophers and theologians used to search. We are what we seem to be, transient, mortal creatures subject to necessity and chance" (Mitchell 1980, 86). The question then becomes one of making a new case for the moral and religious life as traditionally conceived, for a notion of *the* human *telos,* or finding one's own path forward through the thicket of existential options. Ultimately Kierkegaard ends by making an innovative case for an orthodox Christian conscience, but in the beginning he is clearly more of a romantic. In an early letter written from Gilleleie in 1835 we see a brilliant young Kierkegaard, age 22, struggling with just these questions of existential identity: "What I really need is to get clear about *what I am to do,* not what I must know, except insofar as knowledge must precede every act. What matters is to find my purpose, to see what it is that God wills that I shall do; the crucial thing is to find a truth that is truth *for me,* to find *the idea for which I am willing to live and die. . . .* Of what use would it be for me to be able to formulate the meaning of Christianity, to be able to explain many specific points—if it had no deeper meaning *for me, and for my life?*" (E/O 361–62).

The young Kierkegaard relates how he searched for an existentially secure point of departure, how he "sought an anchor in the boundless sea of pleasure as well as in the depths of knowledge" (E/O 363). He even took up the path of "resignation," but all these avenues were blind alleys. The key was an inward journey toward the self, his own self: "One must first learn to know oneself before knowing anything else. Not until a man has inwardly understood *himself* and then sees the course he is to take does his life gain peace and meaning; only then is he free of that irksome, sinister traveling companion—that irony of life. . . . Only when a man has understood himself in this way is he able to maintain an independent existence and avoid surrendering his own *I*" (E/O 364–65).

I dwell on Kierkegaard's early personal existential voice not because I think it reveals the direction of his mature vision of the normatively human, but because I think that it reveals a truth that the mature Kierkegaard neglects as he engages in his unique defense of orthodox Christianity and of the more conservative stance of the strong moral conscience. The search began in a search for a meaning for his life, but it increasingly becomes (and maybe this is a deep human tendency) a defense of what he takes to be *the* meaning of human life. As Charles Taylor says: "The really difficult thing is distinguishing the human universals from the historical constellations and not eliding the second into the first so that our particular way seems somehow inescapable for humans as such, as we are always tempted to do" (1989, 122). Kierkegaard begins by searching for a path forward that grips him, that he finds engaging, but as his confidence grows he thinks that it is just in taking the inward path forward that all will discover just what he has discovered—if only they will have the courage to take that path—namely, that a sincerely earnest search for existential identity can find its rest only in an orthodox and paradoxical Christianity. In the end, he mistakenly takes too much of what is *his* way to be *the* way.

The central point that has been pervasive in my analysis is that Kierkegaard overstates his case for the normatively human; he draws excessively strong conclusions about the essence of the human condition as one where human beings as human beings are compelled toward a specific sort of ethical, religious, and finally Christian existence. His confidences run too high. I base this claim largely on a second main claim: that while Kierkegaard's epistemological reflections on the conditions necessary for human knowledge suggest a very high standard, when it comes to his own efforts to develop his vision of the normatively human, his "method" is a radically empirical and pragmatic examination of the conditions of human existence. He is in fact moving away from the "presuppositions of epistemologically centered philosophy" and toward a radically empirical and edifying or pragmatic hermeneutical posture, a stance where practical rationality and judgments about reasonableness take center stage. The irony (as I see it) is that an equally strong epistemic framework does not support Kierkegaard's high confidence in the substantive vision; Kierkegaard's epistemic approach leads us to a more modest conclusion. When the strong substantive vision is subject to a careful analysis, the result is more pluralism when it comes to existential stances. What then supports Kierkegaard's strong confidences? The early social relations and practices that constituted Kierkegaard's life-contexts have created deep structures, enduring intuitions, which are the inescapable results of his more introspective analysis and search for satisfactory spiritual identity. In the end, while we cannot endorse his strong conclusions, properly reconstructed, Kierkegaard's thought on existential identity has much to commend it.

My final task is to explicitly state where I think Kierkegaard goes too far (and is better understood through explanations that deconstruct) and where he gets it right (and gets it nearly enough right that we can reconstruct his views). Following Hilary Putnam's point that "deconstruction without reconstruction is irresponsibility" (1992, 133), I will state my reconstructed Kierkegaard. I have already argued for my criticisms of the normative vision and the epistemic tactics that Kierkegaard's pseudonymous voices use. This chapter will involve an excursion into several contemporary discussions, in particular Owen Flanagan's critique of selected portions of Charles Taylor's thought, Alasdair MacIntyre's analysis in *After Virtue* of contemporary social and moral identity after the failed Enlightenment project, and Jeffrey Stout's critique of MacIntyre's efforts in *After*

Virtue. As I mentioned in the opening chapter, both Taylor and MacIntyre lean toward restoration of the traditional conscience with a more theistic backing for this conscience. At the risk of simplicity, they both are convinced that traditional Christian positions can be restated in ways, as MacIntyre says, that "restore intelligibility and rationality to our moral and social attitudes and commitments" (1984, 259). My critique of Kierkegaard's thought is similar to Flanagan's critique of Taylor and Stout's critique of MacIntyre's communitarian efforts. I do not think we need to restore traditional Christian convictions to have an engaging and meaningful and even morally informed life; this tradition might be one way forward, an attractive way if one is committed to maintaining strong and overriding moral realism, but there are other important aspirations and multiple ways of realizing these in a life. There are even other more contemporary construals of the meaning of Christian faith. So in the final analysis I present a more pragmatic, more pluralistic Kierkegaardian vision of the normatively human.

Ethics, Psychology, and the Kierkegaardian Vision

In *The Sickness unto Death* Anti-Climacus begins part 1 section B, entitled "The Universality of This Sickness [Despair]," with the comment that the claim that despair is universal "will strike many people as a paradox, an overstatement, and also a somber and depressing point of view" (SUD 22). I have argued that Kierkegaard's position is an overstatement. Kierkegaard himself seemed to admit that he had not realized his high spiritual ideal, so that he remains in despair, but that only raises the question whether it is in fact possible for anyone to achieve that state in which despair is rooted out. Indeed, Kierkegaard seems to suggest that the higher forms of spiritual despair are really rare, and so, presumably the successful cure, radical faith, is rarer still. In the second part of *The Sickness unto Death,* Anti-Climacus refers back the first part of his analysis and notes that "it was pointed out that the more intensive despair becomes, the rarer it is in the world. But if sin is now despair qualitatively intensified once again, presumably this despair must be extremely rare" (SUD 100–101). Even within the circle of theistic faith, Anti-Climacus concludes, "seldom is there a person who is so [spiritually] mature, so transparent to himself, that this can apply to him" (101). And before Anti-Climacus, Climacus noted that the "task is ideal and perhaps is never accomplished by anyone" (CUP 431).

The upshot is that in the final analysis Kierkegaard's ideal is so high that it is impossible. Does it matter? Stephen Crites frames the issue well:

"If only the hyper-Christian can avow the faith that in our text [*The Sickness unto Death*] is the sole antidote to despair, the question arises as to whether there are any nonfictive examples of such a faith" (1992, 146). One quick response to this is to say that despair can be eradicated only with divine assistance from outside the human condition, with grace.[1] But I do not want to too quickly simply say that humans find themselves in (or have been placed in) a no-win position, that despair can be eradicated only from the outside, if only because it seems odd that God creates us in such a condition. Before we move to more religious and theological considerations, I want to consider a related issue: whether it makes any difference if a proposed normative perspective is even possible for beings like us. This issue is crucial, for the despair that we hope to eradicate is itself a consequence of the impossibly high ideal of Kierkegaardian personhood. What is the relationship between our ethical ideals and our understandings of what human beings are like and what is possible for them? Should we reject a moral and spiritual stance if it sets the bar so high that it is on reflection clearly impossible for us? What possibly could be the rationale for such an ideal?

This is an issue that Owen Flanagan examines extensively. He notes: "There are definite strands of thinking in ethics which seem to imply that psychology is irrelevant to its aims and thus that psychology—and the human sciences generally—simply do not matter to moral philosophy" (1991, 24). The position that psychology does not matter to moral philosophy Flanagan calls the "autonomy of ethics thesis," and I think such a view is deeply embedded in Kierkegaard's whole discussion.[2] Of course there are a wide variety of ways that one might see ethics and psychological considerations as distinct or maybe distantly related. One way that Flanagan mentions, a way that seems closest to Kierkegaard, is found in forms of religious nonnaturalism, which "deny that ethical properties are in the world or that ethical requirements have their (complete) source in human needs and desires, in human understanding, in social life" (1991, 25). But, asks Flanagan, do these views really cut ethics off from psychology and from our natural world? I think it is clear that, while Kierkegaard wants a degree of distance, there are also important relations between the human constitution as he understands it and his high ideal of human selfhood. Do we contain within our human constitution a demand, or the ability to perceive a demand, that we cannot even hope to fully realize?

Kierkegaard has his pseudonym Vigilius Haufniensis in *The Concept of Anxiety* state that "the more ideal ethics is the better. It must not permit itself to be distracted by the babble that it is useless to require the impossible" (CA 17). We have already seen that the core of Judge William's view is that personality is the absolute which has its *telos* in itself. And I argued that there was clearly a natural-law view of spiritual development there, but we saw early on that the Judge really has a bar so high that even his heroic efforts to reengage on spiritual terms seem somewhat truncated. Humans are subject to conditions not of their choosing, conditions which constitute standards for their existential identity, but standards that are finally from a source beyond finite existence, transcendent standards.

In *Concluding Unscientific Postscript* Climacus makes the intriguing, if contradictory, claim that "ethics focuses upon the individual, and ethically understood it is every individual's task to become a whole human being, just as *it is the presupposition of ethics that everyone is born in the state of being able to become that.* Whether no one achieves it is irrelevant; the main thing is that the requirement is there" (CUP 346, emphasis added). From an ethical view ought implies can, human beings *are able* to become whole human beings, to pull off the synthesis of infinite and finite, but then Climacus says it is irrelevant whether anyone really achieves it and that there is a contradiction in human life. Overall Kierkegaard affirms something of the "autonomy thesis," but he also thinks that there is an important relationship between human beings, their psychological make-up, and the normative dimensions of humans, their ethical and spiritual concerns. He claims that we can advance closer to the ideal; some of us are closer than others. Kierkegaard paints a portrait of human existence that has a natural-law dimension; I judge that he is a committed moral realist: there is a pattern of moral and spiritual development set for all individuals by the basic structural dynamics of the human condition. But while these dynamics are not totally daunting, they seem to be such that their ultimate outcome is despair; moral failure and spiritual despair are the final result of a tension, a contradiction even, within the heart of the human condition. The ethical ideal implanted in our breast is first discovered (or better, revealed to us) and earnestly approached, but then difficulties emerge as we push the horizon of our consciousness out, striving to situate ourselves in wider and wider horizons, until finally we see that our task is beyond us, it is impossible for us, and we despair. But if we can put on the reflective and evaluative brakes earlier, then we might not be in such dire straits. Kierkegaard thinks we cannot legitimately and authentically stop; I think that we can. What is the difference between us?

Kierkegaard is a strong moral realist; I am more of a modest realist, a pragmatic realist. Kierkegaard thinks that the demands of ethics are demands set in anthropological, metaphysical, even theological stone, and then the realization of the demands, high demands, are nonnegotiable. But can this strong moral realism stand? This question is still with us today. I have already agreed with Flanagan that Kierkegaard's vision of personhood goes far beyond what can be empirically supported; human beings do not need to become strong spiritual evaluators, do not need to become individuals with ethical and spiritual self-realization defining their identity, to avoid a mental breakdown, an identity crisis. Charles Taylor seems to argue, however, for a moral realism.[3] In a fashion similar to Kierkegaard, he claims that persons must make strong qualitative distinctions, they must be strong evaluators, they must have an articulated metaphysical and moral framework for their lives, else they fall victim to an identity crisis and they fail as persons. This is, says Taylor, not just "a contingently true psychological fact about human beings." It is, he continues, "constitutive of human agency" and what counts as "undamaged personhood" (1989, 27). Overall, he claims: *"I want to defend the strong thesis that doing without [spiritual/ethical] frameworks is utterly impossible for us"* (1989, 27, emphasis added). I think that Taylor's thesis, like Kierkegaard's, cannot be carried through. To defend the strong thesis, Taylor leans toward a moral realism that begins in considerations of human selfhood. How does this go according to Taylor?

"My identity is defined by the commitments and identifications which provide the frame or horizon within which I can try to determine from case to case what is good, or valuable, or what ought to be done, or what I endorse or oppose" (Taylor 1989, 27). And, Taylor continues, if I lose these commitments or identifications, I "wouldn't know any more, *for an important range of questions,* what the significance of things was for [me]" (1989, 27, emphasis added). But what is this important range of questions? It involves, Taylor argues, "discriminations of right or wrong, better or worse, higher or lower, which are not rendered valid by our own desires, inclinations or choices, but rather stand independent of them and offer standards by which they can be judged" (1989, 4). Clearly Taylor is talking about normative matters and what we have called our existential identity, our life-purposes and basic values and attitudes, and this is not optional for us; we must have some deep commitments and identifications. But when he says that we must have an identity or else we suffer an identity crisis because we cannot (or can no longer) orient ourselves with regard to existential matters, does he mean that we have not *found* a framework for ourselves, or that we cannot *articulate* the terms of our framework, or that we do not have a satisfactory *defense or justification* of our framework, or (finally) that there simply are *no ultimately satisfactory* frameworks? These are distinct questions, and I am inclined to think that some are more plausible than others. Taylor leans toward the latter strong questions, questions that demand strong evaluative identity for an answer. It is one thing to lack a settled set of commitments and identifications, quite another to be unable to adequately articulate or ultimately defend a set you affirm.

Taylor intends to develop a "moral ontology" of our distinctly modern moral identity, an identity he says that affirms the objective value of human life, dignity, and the flourishing of the human community. He wants to provide a strong backing for our moral conscience in traditional realist terms; if not a metaphysics for our deep sense of moral matters and spiritual concerns, then at least something as strong—an "ontology of the human." But, and this is where the real difficulties emerge: he also cannot deny that our modern sensibility accommodates (even affirms) a deep sense of individual variation as regards existential identities. This issues from his deep sense of legitimate social and cultural pluralism. Taylor is deeply affected by historical consciousness. He admits that ontological "frameworks today are problematic. . . . No framework is shared by everyone, can be taken as *the* framework tout court, can sink to the phenomenological status of unquestioned fact" (1989, 17). In this situation, many intelligent people identify with a framework or frameworks in a tentative, provisional way, and "they may see themselves, as, in a sense, seeking. They are on a 'quest,' in Alasdair MacIntyre's apt phrase" (1989, 17). But then Taylor concedes that we must acknowledge that this quest might fail: "Failure might come from there being *no ultimately believable framework*" (1989, 17, emphasis added). This will be a spiritual crisis for us, because, he continues, such a "framework is that in virtue of which we make sense of our lives spiritually. Not to have a[n ultimately believable] framework is to fall into a life which is spiritually senseless" (1989, 18).

The odd situation on this analysis is that while we live in a world where individuals with multifaceted, complex identities are flourishing and living meaningful lives, where a variety of existential postures are not easily ruled out as irrational and unacceptable, Taylor says that not only are individuals without a well-defined and well-justified moral and spiritual orientation already disintegrating as persons, even individuals who have taken on the quest, who are seeking moral and spiritual grounding, are treading on perilous ground—especially those people in fact! As Flanagan points out, on Taylor's view, we seekers after existential identity, are in the grip of a deep spiritual identity crisis—at least if we are honest with ourselves. What we cannot do without, namely an ultimately believable normative framework, we cannot in fact discover; we are all on the edge of an existential crisis. And Taylor fully admits that "this articulation of moral ontology will be very difficult" (1989, 10). But this means, to follow Flanagan again, that Taylor's requirement of strong personhood has "a particularly disturbing downside—it makes identity and agency prone to coming undone by demanding that our frameworks pass tests they cannot pass" (1996, 159).

So what Taylor is claiming is not so different from Kierkegaard. The striving for existential identity, for a framework for our lives, is a necessary project and one that the individual increasingly discovers as more and more difficult to pull off: finding firm foundation or making our lives ultimately secure becomes impossible. But if we do not secure it outside of the finite conditions that confront us, if we do not find a transcendent ground for our projects, commitments, and identifications, we will suffer a spiritual crisis that resonates within us, undermining our identity-constituting relations; the meaningful life is in question and spiritual despair is the result. There is a need for something more than naturalistic or communitarian rationales for our lives if they are going to be lives that affirm objective value and the ultimate worth of life. Moderns, Taylor says, want to draw a clear distinction between "the higher, the admirable life, and the lower life of sloth, irrationality, slavery or alienation" (1989, 23). Although Taylor finally opts for a theistic response, he admits that our choice is not just God or arbitrariness. Modern moral culture, Taylor tells us, "is one of multiple sources; it can be schematized as a space in which one can move in three directions. There are the two independent frontiers [expressive individualism and deep naturalistic humanism] and the original theistic foundation. The fact that the directions are multiple contributes to our sense of uncertainty. This is part of the reason why almost everyone is tentative today" (1989, 317).[4] He continually shows much more sensitivity to the final existential alternatives for individuals than Kierkegaard; Kierkegaard is convinced that there is finally one existential trajectory for all: the ideal of strong personhood that ends in Christian existence. But how then does Taylor finally defend his moral realism? This will provide a contemporary point of comparison to Kierkegaard's efforts.

Taylor says that we cannot live without a normative identity that is objective, that incorporates high standards, strongly valued goods, for judging our desires and choices, for having an identity that is securely defined and justified. It is part of being a moral agent and having identity that we can ask such questions and demand answers: we need to know who we are in moral and spiritual space. If we do not have this we are no longer a person, or at least an "undamaged person," and we are in crisis. But I think that Taylor (like Kierkegaard) is referring to a specific sort of normative identity crisis, a spiritual identity crisis, not a crisis in ego or personal identity. The crisis they refer to is a crisis in strong evaluative identity. Flanagan puts the attitude of the strong evaluator this way: "A person who is a strong evaluator understands that desires can be evaluated in terms of their value, their worth. She does so with the aim of creating a character that is not merely self-governing but that governs with the highest standards. The strong evaluator is concerned that her desires, commitments, plans and character satisfy high ethical or spiritual standards. The strong evaluator is morally serious" (1996, 205). But do we need to be a strong evaluator to avoid a disintegration of our ego identity? I think not. Having a well-functioning identity and not engaging in strong evaluation are perfectly compatible. The person who rarely considers his or her ethical commitments and has never deeply reflected on his or her life-purposes, what Flanagan calls a weak evaluator, but has a settled set of moral values and attitudes, attitudes that are decent and not seriously out of kilter with his or her wider community, is not disintegrating as a person; he or she still has a firm and motivating identity.[5]

So what is the problem for individuals who are in an identity crisis? If we follow Erik Erikson, people who have identity crises have no sense of what defines them because they have no "significant identifications," and as a result they may suffer from a motivational paralysis. Most fundamentally, says Erikson, they lack "the sense of inner continuity and sameness" (1980, 135). This is usually the result of some traumatic external social conditions in childhood, or in later life, that brought about the undoing of a basic set of identifications or forestalled their initial development. The classic adolescent identity crisis is a matter of having more than the normal difficulties in settling on self-conscious aims and interests, usually as a result of absent or overbearing social models for role identifications. Getting on through this psychosocial crisis is not always easy; many an individual has a hard time getting the inner strength to, as Erikson says, "accept the historical necessity which made him what he is" (1980, 50). Judge William has made just that step, but his young friend A is still floundering in a sea of possibilities, unable to self-consciously integrate and settle on his necessity, on his actual identity.

The successful negotiation of identity issues and the resolution of an identity crisis leads to self-represented autonomy; the individual now has a self (those actual preconscious identifications he has accepted and reaffirms) to be conscious of, to comprehend, to control, to move forward with. Erikson writes: "The individual feels free when he can choose to identify with his own ego identity and when he learns to apply that which is given to that which must be done" (1980, 50). Finding this liberation, this freedom, is, however, not yet Kierkegaard's ideal. It is a truth that Judge William at least knew, and it is one that Kierkegaard affirms, but the more spiritual aspirations for transcendence overshadow it.

The problem for the strong evaluator, by contrast, is a different one; it is a more intellectual and philosophical one. The crisis for strong evaluative identity comes from an intellectual grasp of the historical contingency, the empirical arbitrariness of the content of our actual identity, the identifications and commitments that make us who we are. While this might lead, as Flanagan admits, to a "complete surrender of moral seriousness in the face of the ridiculous arbitrariness of human life and living," this is not necessary (1996, 211); it is a specific problem for a specific late-modern reading of human life and not a deep truth of human psychology. It is, however, a problem that we see Climacus wrestling with and one that comes to increasingly occupy Kierkegaard. My argument is that it might be a problem for those influenced by Kierkegaardian sorts of existential analyses, but its solution does not have to lie in the position that Kierkegaard seemed to settle on.

Furthermore, and this may be the really important point, even a person who has reflected deeply on moral and spiritual matters, who has pursued strong evaluative seriousness, need not end in a crisis of existential identity with the discovery of historical, social, and personal contingency. A person may self-consciously adopt a framework, an orientation to life, and still not have the aspirations of a strong evaluator. A person can, as Flanagan points out, "identify fully with one's framework while at the same time seeing it as imperfect, subject to revision, and as hardly the only or best framework" (1996, 170). I call such a stance the modest evaluator. What the modest evaluator lacks (as well as the weak evaluator, a person who does not really reflect serious at all on existential matters, but who has an identity) is the spiritual agony of the strong evaluator. While the moral and spiritual seriousness of the strong evaluative attitude are goods, they can, Flanagan rightly claims, "be too demanding. [The strong evaluative attitude] engenders moral self-indulgence and has no hope in ending one up in a state of reflective security, despite a pretense to do so" (1996, 206). Like Kierkegaard's radically self-transcending self, the strong evaluator begins with hopes for reflective security, but inevitably ends with despair; reflection can find no stopping point that will satisfy the demands of radical transcendental reengagement.

So Taylor's effort to defend a moral realism is tied to his ideal of the strong evaluator; the high ideal, the moral seriousness, needs a strong source, needs firm foundations. But he admits to having a great difficulty with making the case, to finding sources strong enough to provide a foundation for the spiritual transcendence of the strong evaluator. He hopes that Christian theism might again serve as that source. But it is clear that he has yet to make good on this aspiration, and the fact is that his position (at least in *Sources of the Self*) is finally so historically nuanced and so generous that his "realism" accommodates a wide variety of normative positions. His rich historical consciousness allows him only a very modest claim, and the effort to say that we must be strong evaluators and so must have a strong source for our identity fails to convince. If this is realism, it seems that we live in a pluralistic universe.

As I suggested when we started, all this runs parallel to Kierkegaard. While I am clearly critical of the Kierkegaardian ideal at its extreme, Kierkegaard's (and Taylor's) reflections leave us with a heightened sense of the importance of moral and spiritual identity, but also with a sense that this spiritual journey has no single source or destination. Journeying is important, but the outcome is not decided. This points to a core psychological truth in Kierkegaard's analysis: a person is well advised to make a serious effort to find his or her own way of self-expression and existential orientation and not simply accept the de facto preferences and orientations given him or her by society. That is, a person will discover that the exercise of their abilities to evaluate, to choose, and to act, in short, to engage their practical reason, leads to a more meaningful and fulfilling life. Not to do this is to lack an essential ingredient of human well-being; the activity of reflective self-development is critical to human flourishing. This is more than simply achieving an ego identity, a significantly important step crucial for psychic health and well-being.[6] But then more than this is needed for a full affirmation of the Kierkegaardian ideal of personhood. In fact, to even engage existential matters, one must already have an ego identity. As Erikson says, to be an existential rebel who is spiritually restless and on the journey "is one of the choices of mature man; to have that choice the immature person must, with our help, first find a home in the actuality of work and love" (1964, 99).

So why continue to make strong demands for firm moral and spiritual orientation? Much has slipped in the whirlpool of history. Why not the yearning for firm and secure grounding too? My suggestion is that this yearning is part of what it means to be a human with self-reflective and imaginative capacities, but it can take various forms and receive multiple plausible articulations. Some fundamental orientation to life is necessary, but as Taylor himself notes: "Our identities, as defined by whatever gives us our fundamental orientation, are in fact complex and many-tiered" (1989, 28–29). This fundamental orientation need not be taken as securely grounded and finally founded; it can be self-consciously seen as open to revision and further articulation. This is not to say that it is not plausible and worth defending; it is not simply thought of as a "useful fiction." We have to learn to limit the yearning to what works for us, we informed twenty-first-century thinkers. Still it seems that the human spirit does seek fundamental orientation, but that orientation can, if we have confidence and courage, be acknowledged as tentative and provisional, as the best results to date of our efforts as culturally connected critics. Taylor ends by affirming an intuition: that "we tend in our culture to stifle the spirit," and he intends only to "bring the air back into the half collapsed lungs of the spirit" (1989, 520). That intuition seems right but more careful consideration is needed of spirit, especially of Kierkegaardian claims about its status.

Behind these psychological considerations lies a claim about human identity formation: there is a basic difference between simply having a personality in the sense of a settled set of dispositions, beliefs, and values and achieving a personality or becoming a self. The difference is the role of rational and responsible agency in the constitution of the individual. All individuals have some degree of rationality and self-consciousness, but in many cases the individual himself or herself is not the predominant force in selecting and ordering what makes up the content of his or her consciousness. Rather, the unity that is their conscious experience is largely a result of whatever biological, social, and cultural context they live in. So, for example, such individuals will understand themselves and make choices that further structure their lives, on the basis of what is given to them. This does not mean that they cannot be held accountable for their actions, but it does mean that it is often a struggle for them to give an account of themselves, to articulate their beliefs and values, to even minimally justify their thought and behavior. The passion of reflective engagement is weak, and their lives are mediated to them largely through the beliefs and values of their society; who they are is largely a reflection of these contexts. This is not to say that they are morally bad; they may be living morally decent lives, but something is lacking. It is the good of freedom or autonomy—not simply freedom of the will, but freedom in the sense of shaping the course of one's life according to self-chosen principles and standards and thereby having one's self in one's own hands. The interest in spirit as spirit is missing, and so a crucial element of human well-being is missing.

In the end I see four distinctions, distinctions not so different from those seen by Kierkegaard: (1) just having a personality, a given identity; (2) achieving a personality, self-consciously adopting and maintaining a self-represented identity; (3) achieving an existential identity, a morally and spiritually informed self-represented identity (modest evaluative identity); and (4) despairing of an ultimately secure existential identity, the Kierkegaardian ideal of transcendental personhood (strong evaluative identity). In the first case one measures one's self more or less directly from the social and historical circumstances in which one finds one's self. In the second case, an individual gains some distance from the conventional wisdom, but does little to step (as we say today) "outside the box" of the mainstream options available; she measures her life but decides not to push things too far. In the third case the individual forgoes ready-made identities and searches for some existential orientation (with ethical and spiritual dimensions) and some medium for self-expression that she can rationally and responsibly affirm. The measure is not ready-made; the moral *biocoleur* or culturally connected critic is the best characterization of the activity of the search. Her final position (if there ever really is one) is not easily located on any social spectrum of existential postures. This is the stance of existential identity. And here is where the really interesting questions emerge. Does the content, the measure, of this self-expression need to be just my own, or can it be my self-conscious participation in social practices and living traditions?

Sometimes the idea of autonomy and personality feeds a romantic ideal that I must find an orientation all my own, a unique identity, and that I can find an inner sense, a subjective experiencing that can adequately orient my life. This is popular today. MacIntyre argues that two character types dominate our times: the manager and the therapist. The therapist represents the social instantiation of this romantic ideal for personal life. The therapist frees individuals, frees them from their past, their social identity, but where is one to land, where to go? Mitchell (1980) also analyzes this ideal, referring to romantic humanism, and identifies the fatal weakness as a radical subjectivism that leaves the individual without resources to rationally adjudicate between various options. Certainly there are times when an individual's identity is so enmeshed in the identifications simply given to her that she must make a radical shift to discover that she can renounce such identifications and reclaim her life. She must discover her capacity for imaginative transcendence of the given, the given rules and roles that have structured her life in ways that have taken her life from her. This is not an easy step, and much psychotherapy is occupied with such matters. But finally this is a transitional ethic; it will not sustain a perdurable existential identity. For one thing, it lacks a clear moral dimension, and some moral concern for others seems necessary for undamaged personhood. In fact, more than is often acknowledged supports the psyche of the romantic. Speaking of one of his former patients, an existential therapist says: "He never replaced his former identity; he discovered that he could let go of the need for it if he was truly and subjectively alive in the moment" (Bugental 1976, 52). The existential therapist knows the transcendence of the self, but what he offers to fill up consciousness, the listening to one's inner sense, is really the listening to the message of a community of likeminded therapists, who draw on a socially available assemblage of maxims and roles to fashion freer, more flexible identities. In any case, what is missing is an explicit understanding of the role of social and cultural context in the finding and fashioning of an existential identity.

Moral Identity and Socially Situated Selfhood

Climacus (if not Kierkegaard) thinks that the ethical deliverances of conscience escape sociohistorical contingencies; his criticism of objective philosophical efforts is that ethics "has indeed been shoved out of the system and at most has been replaced with a surrogate that confuses . . . the bellowing demands of the times with the eternal demands of conscience upon the individual" (CUP 346). But does conscience ever really escape the times? While I certainly do not want to insist that the current conditions dictate what our norms should always look like, for such a view lacks resources for criticism of our times, I am even less confident that individuals have on tap a faculty, a sense, that will provide normative guidance free of social and historical conditions. There is elbow room for normative criticism, but no one escapes the times completely and starts from nowhere. Now freed from dependence on his or her past, on what basis does our existential seeker proceed? How to think about what sort of person to become?

More than almost any other philosopher writing today, Alasdair MacIntyre has examined the implications for ethics and for our moral lives, given the deep ways that we are socially and historically constituted. In his provocative and widely read *After Virtue,* he argues that we live in the ruins of various moral traditions, and as a result our lives are fragmented and lacking coherence. The only way for us to restore intelligibility and wholeness is, he argues, to restore a final goal, an overarching objective *telos* for human life. This is what made the classic moral traditions intelligible to their participants. But this *telos* is ultimately (unknown to its classical advocates) a tradition-constituted *telos,* a *telos* rooted in a social context of established and shared practices. Any effort to provide a foundation for normative discourse outside of all social contexts, a universal goal for all times and everybody, such as the Enlightenment attempts, is bound to fail. MacIntyre rightly sees Kierkegaard as inheriting this Enlightenment project and working from within some of its terms, but he misunderstands his full response to it. As we have seen, Kierkegaard does not simply announce an irrational subjective choice for the ethical over the merely esthetic as MacIntyre reads him; his response moves to restore more traditional Christian claims about moral existence. Does he then commit the same mistake that MacIntyre identifies in classical thought; does he take his vision of the human *telos* as an anthropological, even theological, truth when it also relies on the heritage of a particular tradition-constituted truth?

MacIntyre argues that classical moral thought, premodern thought, adheres to a scheme where there is "a fundamental contrast between man-as-he-happens-to-be and man-as-he-could-be-if-he-realized-his-essential-nature" (1984, 52). The precepts of ethics are designed to enable humans to make the transition from the former to the latter state. In short, the premodern ethical scheme is "a three-fold scheme in which human-nature-as-it-happens-to-be (human nature in its untutored state) is initially discrepant and discordant with the precepts of ethics and needs to be transformed by the instruction of practical reason and experience into human-nature-as-it-could-be-if-it-realized-its-*telos*" (1984, 53). This is the basic ethical equation; without it one cannot think ethically. Modernity cannot think ethically because it has lost the notion of an essential human *telos.* MacIntyre again: "The joint effect of the secular rejection of both Protestant and Catholic theology and the scientific rejection of Aristotelianism was to eliminate any notion of man-as-he-could-be-if-he-realized-his-*telos*" (1984, 54). Although MacIntyre accuses modern thinkers of this rejection, it is not completely accurate in Kierkegaard's case. As I have shown, Kierkegaard attempts a restoration of a theistically grounded essential human *telos.* But what I want to note now is that MacIntyre does not argue for a direct return to Aristotle or Aquinas, rather he says that the notion of an essential human function, a *telos* for humans, is really derived from "the forms of social life to which the theorists of the classical tradition gave expression. For according to that tradition to be a man is to fill a set of roles each of which has its own point and purpose: member of a family, citizen, soldier, philosopher, servant of God. It was only when a man is thought of as an individual prior and apart from all roles that 'man' ceases to be a functional concept" (1984, 58–59). (He seems to agree with Taylor on one point: it is next to impossible to get past the historical construction of society and selves. But unlike Taylor he is much less sanguine about the state of modern moral identity.) The upshot is that we must see all theological, metaphysical, and even naturalistic purposes as really sociocultural purposes in disguise. If I know who I am in the social ordering of my world, then I know what I am to do, and the virtues and rules of ethics become intelligible to me as the means to realize myself. MacIntyre's point is well taken. And in certain respects, Kierkegaard's ideal of personhood will seem intelligible only to those who are embedded in the community of faith to which he subscribes.

But how then, for MacIntyre, do we proceed? Given our postmodern condition, that we live in a time when many see themselves as radically free individuals, where are we to find our *telos?* Like Kierkegaard, MacIntyre does not think we can turn directly to our given nature, our facticity, to find a secure point of existential departure. But his reasons for turning away from our nature are more sociohistoricist than Kierkegaard's. Why can we not look to human nature or to conceptions of human flourishing for guidance? In his earlier *A Short History of Ethics* he puts it this way: we cannot "look to human nature as a neutral standard, asking which form of social and moral life will give it the most adequate expression. For each form of life carries with it its own picture of human nature. The choice of a form of life and the choice of a view of human nature go together" (1966, 268). In *After Virtue* MacIntyre says much the same thing: "In our cultural history [there are] deep conflicts over what human flourishing and well-being do consist in" (1984, 52). But as MacIntyre begins to unfold his vision, several key claims strongly suggest that he does have a conception of human nature which constrains and structures our conceptions of social and moral life, which does some normative work. Conceptions of human nature are not simply or completely reflections of social forms of life. Some of these notions will bring us back to the truth of Kierkegaard's reflections, reflections linked to human nature, but some will act as counterweights, correcting Kierkegaard.

The first point I want to pursue is MacIntyre's notion of a practice, a notion that is central to his effort to defend moral virtues and attitudes in our contemporary context of crumbling traditions that once provided a rationale. A practice, MacIntyre tells us, is "any coherent and complex form of socially established cooperative human activity through which goods internal to that form of activity are realized in the course of trying to achieve those standards of excellence which are appropriate to, and partially definitive of, that form of activity, with the result that human powers to achieve excellence, and human conceptions of the ends and goods involved are systematically extended" (1984, 187). Core to this definition is the idea of "goods internal to practices." Such goods are distinguished from goods merely external to a practice. For example, the practice of teaching has external goods, such as social respect and (some) money. These goods are not internal to the practice, for these can be gotten in other pursuits, but certain goods can be had only by actually engaging in teaching, goods such as wider understanding, capacity for intellectual exchange, ability to think on one's feet, and so on. It is not that these are unique to teaching, but that only in teaching (or some similar social practice) can these goods be acquired and extended. One cannot achieve these good by just pretending to be a teacher or repeating what was once teaching but is no longer, but only by seriously and continually striving to achieve those standards that are constitutive of what we (teachers) understand as the excellences of teaching. Furthermore, such reasons for engaging can "only be identified and recognized by the experience of participating in the practice in question. Those who lack the relevant experience are incompetent thereby as judges of internal goods" (1984, 188–89). These goods provide *reasons* for engaging in the practice, but more specifically, reasons for taking up the virtues that are necessary for participating. For a virtue, MacIntyre tells us, is an "acquired human quality the possession and exercise of which tends to enable us to achieve those goods which are internal to practices and the lack of which effectively prevents us from achieving any such goods" (1984, 191). So there is a link between an experienced good and moral virtue; it is only through *virtuously* engaging in social practices according to standards and rules that I can experience the goods. By not participating, or participating in a way that sidesteps virtues—virtues such as wisdom, justice, courage, and temperance—I will miss out on vital human goods.

There is, here, an important experiential, if not naturalistic, dimension in MacIntyre's thought. It is only with my lived experience in an activity, an activity that is socially structured, that I can recognize how a certain activity promotes my flourishing. Indeed, MacIntyre himself goes so far as to suggest that his notion of goods internal to practices has certain parallels to John Stuart Mill's thought, where Mill "distinguished between 'higher' and 'lower' pleasures" (1984, 199). Such a view would seem to have some connection to human needs and interests. I take it that any human being, if he or she internalizes the standards and rules of a social practice, can come to realize the internal goods of participating in that social practice in a morally appropriate manner. The goods provide a strong rationale for participating, and it is not just a rationale I happen to prefer: "In the realm of practices the authority of both goods and standards operates in such a way as to rule out subjectivist and emotivist analyses of judgment" (1984, 190). The authority of moral virtues comes from the authority of social practices and their standards, but also the goods internal to these practices. MacIntyre's *telos* might better be thought of as a *psychosociological* *telos,* for it is not only grounded in socially established forms of human activity, but in the feedback of human experience; we are creatures who can flourish better in some activities than in others, especially in activities that develop our capacity to evaluate, to choose, and to act as rational creatures. This is truth that Kierkegaard knew better than MacIntyre.

MacIntyre goes on to argue that we need to remember how deeply human selves are social selves. This is another claim about human nature that seems critical to his overall case. MacIntyre begins by proposing "a concept of self whose unity lies in the unity of a narrative" (1984, 205). By this he means to argue that a person's identity is always related to a narrative, and he or she has a unity of self only to the degree that he or she participates in narratives with unity. It is "natural," MacIntyre claims, "to think of the self in a narrative mode" (1984, 206). Narratives, however, are always embedded in socially constituted forms of life. Only with narratives do we know who we are and what we should be doing. Narratives are critical to our flourishing as selves; the self is essentially a narrated entity. Although human agents can be held accountable for their lives, "what the agent is able to do and say intelligibly as an actor is deeply affected by the fact that we are never more (and sometimes less) than the co-authors of our own narratives" (1984, 213). In fact, on MacIntyre's view, individuals can know what to do and what to become only if they have the resources of narratives: "I can only answer the question 'What am I to do?' if I can answer the prior question, 'Of what story or stories do I find myself a part?'" (1984, 216).

So the first step is to locate the moral particularities of my life; only with these resources can I begin to narrate myself, to have some overarching story that identifies my life. But if this is not to be exceedingly narrow, disparate, and conflict ridden; if it is to provide a unity of self, we must enter into a narrative quest. The question that drives the quest is: "What is the good for me?" I begin with this question but as I pursue this quest in word and deed I am compelled to ask: But what is the good of a human life? So this quest for unity of self will have at least a "partly determinative conception of the final *telos,* [or else] there could not be any beginning to a quest. Some conception of the good for man is required" (MacIntyre 1984, 219). But how does my moral understanding develop, how does a self move forward? "A quest is always an education both as to the character of that which is sought and in self knowledge" (1984, 219). As I answer the question of the quest, I learn more and more about who I am and what I am to do. MacIntyre believes then that whatever differences images of the good human life may have it seems that there is one essential element: "The good life for man is the life spent in seeking the good life for man, and the virtues necessary for the seeking are those which will enable us to understand more and what else the good life for man is" (1984, 219). This more ambiguous and process approach, a "how" rather than a "what" model, to discerning who I should become, parallels Kierkegaard.

But another crucial element plays into MacIntyre's image of the moral life. This element speaks to his seemingly paradoxical claim about the good life as the life spent seeking the good life. The story or stories that make up any person's self are always embedded in larger meaning structures; traditions are crucial to the quest for moral identity. When we see our lives in terms of a tradition, the moral virtues make sense as the means to realizing the *telos,* the goal, that the tradition holds out for us as the good for humans as such. The terms provided by tradition-generated resources provide an answer to the question of the moral quest on a more universal level. As Gary Gutting puts it in his careful study of MacIntyre: "Tradition is the communal counterpart of the narrative of an individual life" (1999, 96). Stepping outside of tradition is stepping into incoherence and disunity, into aimlessness and anomie; not only do I lose the moral life, but also I lose myself. Traditions are necessary for thought and action, necessary for the exercise of practical reason and for intelligible and meaningful action: together this adds up to a moral identity, a unified and motivating self. Traditions speak to the larger question of the good for humans. Fortunately, as a matter of fact, all of us, MacIntyre concludes, operate from with certain traditions: "The individual's search for his or her good is generally and characteristically conducted within a context defined by those traditions of which the individual's life is a part" (1984, 222). Only with the help of tradition-embedded resources can the good of rational deliberation be had; only within the parameters and resources of a tradition can one exercise rational evaluation and rational choice and become autonomous. Nor can the good of a relatively unified and motivating self be realized outside of tradition. From the social facts about human life, MacIntyre connects certain normative truths about the good life for us. But notice that MacIntyre refers here to "traditions" in the plural. This raises a crucial issue about pluralism. Before we look more carefully at the issue of a plurality of traditions, I want to return to Kierkegaard.

As should be clear from my analysis of Kierkegaard, this is a strikingly Kierkegaardian image of moral self-development and self-understanding.

As others have pointed out, MacIntyre's position has a good deal in common with Kierkegaard.[7] In the first place, I have brought MacIntyre into my conclusion because he is, like Kierkegaard, concerned primarily about existential identity in a pluralistic world. MacIntyre asks "what sort of person should I become?" (1984, 118). And he is passionately concerned because he knows that the question is inescapable: "An answer to it is given *in practice* in each human life" (1984, 118). His answer is only partly Kierkegaardian. One way it is Kierkegaardian is that like Kierkegaard he believes that the only intelligible approach to ethics is teleological. And the way a *telos* gets a grip on someone is that it is seen (at first dimly) as essential to who they are becoming, to their self-conscious identity. This occurs only if an individual actually begins an ethical quest. So I *need* to become a person that pursues a goal in thought and action; the posture of the intellectual esthete is a failed posture, the engaged ethicist is more successful when it comes to individual flourishing. That MacIntyre cannot completely escape some naturalistic claims, some ties between what humans are and how they should be living, as he develops his case for tradition embedded virtue ethics, ties him even closer to Kierkegaard.

Macintyre claims that in the course of my ethical quest I will expand my ethical self-understanding, which will then further modify the shape of my quest: beginning with only a dim awareness and little self and advancing to richer vision and fuller self-consciousness. Gutting captures this point in MacIntyre: "The quest-narrative that is my life must be guided throughout by a normative conception of the human good. Initially this will be a quite thin conception, perhaps amounting to little more than the need to search for a fuller, more adequate conception of the human good. But, to the extent that my quest is successful, I will arrive at ever 'thicker' conceptions of the human good" (1999, 96). Journeying is important, but the outcome is not decided. And another Kierkegaardian-related theme in MacIntyre: The way we advance is to rely on feedback from experience and our practical intelligence in discerning what edifies and builds up and what tears down and disintegrates our life-praxis. As I argued when reviewing Climacus's thought, practical wisdom (*phronesis*) is at the core of the Kierkegaardian approach to envisioning selfhood.

But where the way swings off from Kierkegaard is when MacIntyre claims that I cannot carry out this quest as an individual independent of social context and cultural traditions. Traditions are the necessary soil of human life and thought; they provide the content base for intelligent praxis. In *Whose Justice? Which Rationality?* MacIntyre writes: "The person outside all traditions lacks sufficient rational resources for enquiry and *a fortiori* for enquiry into what tradition is to be rationally preferred. He or she has no adequate relevant means of rational evaluation and hence can come to no well-grounded conclusions, including the conclusion that no tradition can vindicate itself against any other. To be outside of all traditions is to be a stranger to enquiry; it is to be in a state of intellectual and moral destitution" (1987, 367). So although I might be carrying out my quest in heroic isolation from the masses, from popular opinion, I am not carrying it out in complete and total isolation; and although I might think I am, I am not. Our initial question was about conscience; our answer is that the content of conscience is social practices and specific traditions. A content-less conscience is nonfunctional. In the Judge's letter Kierkegaard affirms the crucial connection to social life for realizing ethical selfhood. Only by reengaging my full concretion do I have any content to synthesize and to begin to realize myself as a strong moral evaluator. Kierkegaard's moral psychology clarifies how the relational self expands its ties to the social world of practices, roles, and commitments and in so doing becomes more unified and stable self. And such social practices are often given as well as chosen. My social roles already provide some initial structure to my life, some normative particularity: for example, I am a daughter in this family, in this time and place.

Up to a point, Kierkegaard can affirm some of MacIntyre's socially situated and morally engaged self. As we have seen, however, both Climacus and Anti-Climacus seem to be less inclined to think that this reengagement with life can be pulled off; either the finite or the infinite, more than likely the infinite, will be truncated in the process. But they do not grasp how deep social and cultural influence goes. As Rudd puts it, the "simple fact that I grow up speaking one particular language initiates me into a certain tradition, a way of seeing and evaluating the world. [I am] an inheritor of a certain culture: these things are part of my identity—I cannot just shrug them off as if they were alien to me" (1993, 95–96). Anthropologist Victor Turner refers to "root cultural paradigms," instead of traditions, but the point is the same: "A [cultural root] paradigm goes beyond the cognitive and even the moral to the existential domain. . . . Cultural root paradigms reach down to irreducible life stances of individuals, passing beneath conscious prehension to a fiduciary hold on what they sense to be axiomatic values, matters literally of life and death" (1981, 149–50). But if Rudd and Turner are right (and I think they are) that even my language, my vehicle of thought, binds me to a certain root cultural paradigms, to ways of seeing and evaluating the world, it seems more plausible to see Kierkegaard's teleological natural-law ethic as MacIntyre proposes to see it, as providing a tradition-constituted *telos.* At least Kierkegaard's vision should find some connection to a specific tradition or assemblage of traditions.

These points are deeply unsettling for Kierkegaard's project. Kierkegaard did not fully comprehend how deep our subjective experience is shaped by social and cultural context. His claims about human beings, and the ideal vision of a human nature driven with a deep *telos* toward ethical then religious and finally Christian existence, reflects as much some truth about us as some truth about Kierkegaard's own social and cultural context. As Macintyre puts it: "The content of Kant's morality was conservative in just the way that the content of Kierkegaard's was, and this is scarcely surprising. Although Kant's Lutheran childhood in Königsberg was a hundred years before Kierkegaard's Lutheran childhood in Copenhagen the same inherited morality marked both men" (1984, 44).[8] And in Kierkegaard's case the Christian religion had an even deeper hold. Let us explore the evidence for this contextualist point a bit further.

In her essay "Judge William—A Christian?" Julia Watkin argues that one crucial issue in analyzing Judge William's views is "what 'ethical' is to mean" (1995, 113). I have argued that its meaning is intimately intertwined with the Protestant Christian tradition within which Kierkegaard was nurtured. There is no question that Kierkegaard was so nurtured; as he says in his *Journals:* "Humanly speaking, I was given a strict Christian upbringing" (JSK #892). Watkin sharpens this point and makes a persuasive case that Kierkegaard's ethical and religious reflections are deeply constituted by his instruction in Christian texts as a child, especially Nikolai Edinger Balle's (1744–1816) then widely used catechism. Watkin details the striking parallels between Kierkegaard's portrayal of the ethical and religious and what one can find in Balle's writings. As Watkin puts it, quoting Climacus's commentary on *Either/Or,* while it is "true that the Judge is 'an ethical individuality existing on the basis of the ethical' (CUP 1.253), his ethics are based on Christianity, and in his two letters to the young aesthete, he makes both a direct and an indirect connection to Balle's catechism" (1995, 120). In Watkin's words, Balle's catechism "inevitably forms part of the spiritual tradition directly influencing Kierkegaard" (1995, 115). Although Watkin believes that Kierkegaard's final Christian religiousness cannot be *fully* traced to this influence, it is clear that he was deeply constituted by his instruction in this strand of Protestant Christianity.

My claim is that Kierkegaard sticks to the highest righteousness, maintains an ideal aspiration which he knows is not possible for existing temporal creatures such as ourselves, because his past influences his perceptions and interpretations. How does our past influence us? Perhaps the most critical element in our past is the sense of trust derived from early caregivers, a basic trust that the world, especially others, can be relied upon. Following Erikson, Anthony Giddens (1991) argues that the psychological ground of an "ontological security," and then an adult hope and courage, is this basic trust. Without it individuals are crippled in their development toward identity and then toward mature existential stances. But perhaps most telling is Giddens's claim that "basic trust links self-identity in a fateful way to the appraisals of others" (1991, 38). Who I am at a deep level is related to how those early others receive me; what they commend and recognize, and what they denounce and ignore, forms me. Built on this basic trust and these early signals are our adult confidences and concerns. Kierkegaard's deep confidence is that our lives are primarily and finally about religious concerns, concerns of ultimate meaning, and his equally deep faith is that the terms for answering the existential question of ultimate meaningfulness have been revealed. Both deep trusts are intertwined with his effective history, with certain social and cultural resources on which he drew. *Early social relations and practices cultivate our enduring intuitions, our ways of being in the world; they constitute our effective history from which we can never fully escape.*

I think a strong argument can be made that Kierkegaard was restoring an inherited vision of human life that he found compelling because he read the terms of this vision out of the effective history of his own immersion in just those strands of moral and Christian culture. MacIntyre is right that the substance of Kierkegaard's ethical and religious vision is "an older and inherited way of life"; but his genius is in his providing a "new practical and philosophical underpinning for this tradition" (1984, 43).[9] Karen Carr supports this claim, arguing that "while much of the vocabulary he [Kierkegaard] introduced (and to some extent the approach he employs) is new and innovative, the underlying view of the human self and its relationship to its surroundings is not and has in fact a long history within the Christian tradition" (2001, 174). Norman Lillegard also suggests this point in his analysis of Judge William's thought on the self and its virtues. The Judge, Lillegard claims, defends the ethical life over against the esthetic, but the "picture of selfhood" therein is "rooted at least partially in a particular tradition or set of related traditions—theistic, biblical, even Lutheran" (2001, 225). Further, says Lillegard, following MacIntyre's line, any effort to defend a view of the self and a set of virtues requires, "for the full specification of the nature of such virtues," reference to a "specific tradition" (2001, 225). He later notes that despite the fact that Kierkegaard is aware that different ages have different customs, standards, views of life that shape an individual's existential identity: "Nonetheless Kierkegaard assumes that some structural dynamics within persons are more or less invariant from age to age. Behind every 'morality' or ethics, behind the *Sittlichkeit* of different ages, there seem to be on Kierkegaard's view a limited number of psychological/spiritual conditions" (2001, 228). This is correct, but Lillegard does not take on the difficult question of just how much we can confidently assert about invariant structures of human existence and how much we should admit is contributed from "a particular tradition or set of related traditions." In my judgment, more is contributed from cultural traditions than Kierkegaard would have us believe.

Some interpreters of Kierkegaard[10] argue that Judge William's ethical position shipwrecks on the cultural contextualist problem, but not Kierkegaard's final view. The self-transcending individual cannot rest in the relativities of social and cultural context. What projects, what practices, do I engage in? Or what stories, what traditions, should I affirm? How, in other words, do I move forward as a rational and responsible agent. I have my moral starting point, but that does not define my moral trajectory in an unambiguous fashion. Kierkegaard's final position, it is argued, is not Judge William's Hegelianism; Kierkegaard transcends the contextualist dilemma that shipwrecks Judge William; Kierkegaard finally goes religious, which means that he is oriented to a transcendent source of value.

I am not so sure about this reading. First of all, it is interesting to note that Climacus denies that the Judge is opting for a Hegelian solution altogether. Clearly Climacus is critical of Hegelian ethics: "The desperate attempt of the miscarried Hegelian ethics to make the state into the court of last resort in ethics is a highly unethical attempt to finitize individuals, an unethical flight from the category of individuality to the category of the race." The ethicist in *Either/Or,* says Climacus, "makes a concession to the religious," but *"the ethics he champions, . . . is diametrically opposed to Hegelian ethics"* (CUP 503n, emphasis added). Admittedly, Climacus is saying the Judge's ethic opens up to the religious, to the infinite, but as I emphasize in italic type, his ethic was never simply Hegelian. What was it? It was more of a natural-law ethic, almost Kant naturalized, where that natural urge toward personhood is first anthropologically, but finally theologically, rooted. I have argued that this is one of Kierkegaard's core convictions, and it indicates that his thought lives from a cultural paradigm that affirms rational and responsible personhood.

My overall point, however, is that much is right in MacIntyre: there is no way to completely escape traditions; Kierkegaard's vision never really escapes social practices and cultural traditions. Where Kierkegaard identifies a theological anthropology that contains an ultimate human *telos,* I see certain needs and interests getting cultural elaboration and emphasis and then informed and reformed by other elements active in Kierkegaard's own effective social history. While certainly not the first richly pluralistic society, we twenty-first-century Westerners live in one of the most richly pluralistic. And pluralism is a concern for late-modern individuals. As Jeffrey Stout begins his *Ethics after Babel:* "Disagreement and diversity in ethics beget worries" (1988, 13). While MacIntyre begins by announcing our contemporary existential disarray, he provides mixed messages about our final ability to surmount it. MacIntyre begins by claiming that the traditional moral equation included a *telos* for humans as such. He sees our ethical quest as a quest for "the good for man." Yet when he talks about the quest he admits that it is a quest that begins with a "partly determinate conception of the final *telos,*" the "good for man." He identifies his own indefinite process conclusion about the "good for man" as "provisional." And perhaps most striking, when MacIntyre speaks about our quest he makes the empirical claim that our conception of the good is "defined by those *traditions*" of which our life is a part. Much in MacIntyre's thought suggests that while the classical thinkers aimed for one overall *telos* or good for humans as such, we today cannot realistically achieve such a conviction. I think that we might not even want to.[11]

Jeffrey Stout is one of the most perceptive and careful philosophers writing today, and he has followed MacIntyre's thought closely over the years as he developed his own unique brand of liberal pragmatism. He points out that MacIntyre himself seemed to realize this pluralistic dilemma in his earlier historicist conclusions. At the end of his *Short History of Ethics,* MacIntyre says that "we are liable to find two kinds of people in our society: those who speak from within one of the surviving moralities, and those who stand outside of all of them. Between the adherents of rival moralities and between the adherents of one morality and the adherents of none there exists no court of appeal, no impersonal neutral standard" (1966, 266). Stout then points out that MacIntyre later announces that all we can do is "choose both with whom we wish to be morally bound and by what ends, rules, and virtues we wish to be guided" (1988, 205). Here is a disengaged postmodern thinker, telling us as a Sartre might, that we are radically free and must simply choose when it comes to normative matters. In *After Virtue* this position is wrongly identified with Kierkegaard. But *After Virtue* (and subsequent works) is also MacIntyre's effort to come to terms with this situation.

We have already examined that standpoint, and we found that in fact it did contain some limited claims about human nature, and these do some normative work for MacIntyre in making his case for a return to the Aristotelian tradition of the virtues (although more recently it is the Thomistic synthesis of Augustinian Christianity with Aristotle.)[12] Our main use of MacIntyre was to affirm his conclusions about social and cultural context, to concur that the Enlightenment project to find an ahistorical nonsocially relative foundation for ethics fails. What is our alternative? His conclusion in *After Virtue* is that our contemporary world is so morally impoverished that all we can do is construct "local forms of community within which civility and the intellectual and moral life can be sustained through the new dark ages which are already upon us" (1984, 263). Stout argues, however, that our situation is not so dire and provides a more pragmatic answer to the problem of pluralism.

In his later *Whose Justice? Which Rationality?* MacIntyre admits that few contemporary individuals are completely estranged from traditions; most accept "usually unquestioningly the assumptions of the dominant liberal individualist forms of public life, . . . [but draw] in different areas of their lives upon a variety of tradition-generated resources of thought and action, transmitted from a variety of familial, religious, education and other social and cultural sources" (1987, 397). And what contemporary individuals must do, he says, is to "learn to test dialectically the theses proposed to him or her by each competing tradition" (1987, 398). This is precisely what Stout thinks we can and should do.[13] Stout begins by noting that MacIntyre downplays the limited agreement we do have in our wider society about human nature and the human *telos:* "We are not united in consensus around a particular theory of human nature or man's ultimate *telos,* . . . but our disagreement about what human beings are like and what is good for us does not go all the way down" (1988, 212). And most of us, he argues, do agree on what might be called a "provisional *telos* of our society" (1988, 212). In short, liberal society is built around an overlapping consensus that has advantages, possibly advantages over anything yet realized to date. Stout reminds us (repeatedly) of a point that MacIntyre forgets: "What I find lacking in *After Virtue* is a sufficient recognition of what our [liberal] society has going for it as a form of life" (1988, 224).

Stout, however, is not a straightforward liberal; he advocates what he calls a "nonstandard" form of liberalism. When he says that it "would indeed be fortunate for all of us, even atheistic fellow travelers, if people like Robert Bellah got their wish and a form of Biblical tradition essentially continuous with republican virtues began to flourish and enrich public life,"[14] he suggests that what makes his liberalism nonstandard is that it is more aware of the role of cultural traditions in our social life and in our philosophical arguments (1988, 223). Stout modifies MacIntyre's views, pushing them closer to his own pragmatic liberalism. He claims that MacIntyre's own "metaphysically austere and historically informed teleological framework" can be used to defend versions of liberalism, versions that do not deny the need for a provisional definition of the good, but include in that definition of the good "a healthy degree of individual freedom." Indeed, MacIntyre does not, claims Stout (1988, 237), intend to advocate a "fixed conception of the good, derived once and for all from a philosophical view of the human essence." MacIntyre is not following the *universalism* of the Aristotelian tradition, at least not in any strong sense. As Stout (1988, 238) notes MacIntyre has, since *After Virtue,* claimed that "there is not one kind of life the living out of which is the *telos* for all human beings in all times and places." Kierkegaard's preferences run closer to Aristotle than MacIntyre here.

Still there is, argues Stout (1988, 238), "a truth of the matter about what constitutes our *telos,* given our time and place. And the good life for us is one in which the necessity of a self-consciously provisional, contextually sensitive, conception of the good life is recognized." This point takes us to questions about philosophical tactics and epistemic strategies in thinking about the good human life *for us* and about *our* existential identity. These matters take us to questions about practical and theoretical reason and return us to the edifying hermeneutics that I earlier identified in Kierkegaard.

Practical Rationality, Self-Understanding, and Understanding Selves

One of my main claims is that despite the fact that Kierkegaard moves away from the "presuppositions of epistemologically centered philosophy" and toward a radically empirical and edifying or pragmatic interpretive stance, he still tends to think that if we do not have knowledge in a strong objective sense, we simply have groundless decisions to believe, arbitrary subjective convictions. But when we ask about the epistemic status of the whole existential framework, the grounds for his vision of the normatively human, his "method" is a radically empirical and pragmatic examination of the conditions of human existence. These conditions, this vision of selfhood, is not simply what he happened to prefer or what his tastes enjoyed, but it is what his practical experience and wisdom led him to believe was the case. Because this is the most innovative and radical side of Kierkegaard's project, it was not completely clear to him just how the existential or radically empirical and pragmatic analysis was carried out. Kierkegaard never dwells on the conditions of relative knowing. But we uncovered clear signals in Climacus's reflections; the direction was toward *phronesis.* He was engaged in immanent thinking, in the more or less of practical reason. Was he making decisions, willing to believe? Sure, but it is one thing to just decide on whatever strikes one's fancy and a different thing altogether to carefully weigh the available evidence, consult those knowledgeable in the field, and come to a considered opinion after much experience.

In most contexts individuals accept a belief when they think the preponderance of the evidence weighs in its favor. Think of a jury deliberating the evidence in a case. Is the final outcome knowledge? Not in a strong sense, not in a sense that it might not be revised by further evidence, by more time, by smarter jurors. But does this make it groundless and mere personal preference? Does this make it just a passionate subjective stance? No, it makes it a relatively well-founded conviction. If we consider the conclusions of a community of scientific inquirers on a topic, are their conclusions knowledge? They are our best-justified beliefs, and this is knowledge the only way it can be had for limited human cognition. So there is a big difference between the person who accepts whatever he or she likes and one who accepts a belief (although it might undermine some of his or her current beliefs) just because it is rationally warranted to do so, that is, because he or she has good reasons to accept the belief. Then it is not the efforts of faith or the willed belief that makes possible approximate knowledge, it is the evidence and rational warrants that support the belief that is decisive, and this is the element that Kierkegaard misses or rather ignores since it is not the ultimately secure and total vision that the objectivist desires. Is this cause for despair?

Kierkegaard claimed that unless I can achieve wholeness, unless I can put myself together as a synthesis of finite and infinite, of eternity and temporality, I am in despair. It is clear that Kierkegaard knows that the aspiration is impossible to achieve: we are finite existing creatures engaged in approximations. As Rudd notes: "Kierkegaard will not permit any attempt to think of reality as a *whole,* as though we could stand outside of it" (1993, 32, emphasis added). But to achieve coherence and wholeness is his most fervent yearning, and hence the craving for the absolute standpoint. As Rudd later says: "For Kierkegaard the factor that drives us from one stage of life to the next is an—at first unconscious and inchoate—desire for *wholeness,* for an *ultimate* integration and coherence in our lives. This is what brings us to make ethical commitments, but, if it is strong enough, it may drive us out of the ethical altogether in the search for an *absolute telos*" (1993, 134, emphasis added). We cannot think reality as a whole, but we are constantly trying to approach it: this is nothing other than the interests of reason at work. But Kierkegaard's desire for epistemic and moral transcendence is impossible to fulfill. What sort of response should we take to this contradictory situation?

One thing that seems clear is that on this analysis Kierkegaard's own substantive vision of human existence is itself an objective uncertainty held fast in Kierkegaard's passionate inwardness. If so, then his conviction that humans are in deep spiritual despair must be seen as linked to the vision of humans aspiring for totality but failing, a vision that is itself another limited human effort. The aspiration is impossible, and we return to our relatively well-founded opinions on existential matters, we continue to make the moves of life with our best lights. So when it comes to such transcendental aspirations, perhaps the best posture is Stout's pragmatist one: "Adopt a Buddhist-like attitude toward incoherent desires that add nothing but disappointment to life. That is, . . . try to extinguish such attitudes" (1988, 255). It makes sense to reject the aspiration, for what does it add to the content of our understanding? If it is like all other human knowledge, it is an objective uncertainty, a judgment more or less well founded. Kierkegaard, however, thinks it is secure knowledge because it is an inwardly apprehended knowledge, and apprehended by that which never changes, my eternal infinite self-spirit. This is where he begins to go wrong.

We have glanced already at the question of the status of introspection. Climacus seemed to follow the Cartesian legacy of introspective infallibility. On this view our knowledge of our own current mental states is both certain and infallible; in short, our mind is "transparent" to itself. But does this Cartesian image hold? While we do have access to our own mental states that others do not, it does not seem to follow that what we perceive about ourselves is infallible. Whenever we grasp ourselves, we are doing so in some description or another. Just as the pragmatist says that it makes no sense to talk about correspondence to reality where reality is undescribed, or not symbolically construed at all, so it makes no sense to think that I have grasped myself apart from some description of who I am. The self as-it-is-in-itself does no epistemological work in the formative processes of self-represented identity or even existential identity. While we have an access to our own mental states and activities that others do not, our construals of these states are really no more certain than anything else, than any other construals of our world.

William James, in his classic *Principles of Psychology,* begins the scientific investigation of the mind, and his writings are still one of the best places to begin to address this issue. James considers both the question of psychological method and the notion of a soul, or transcendental I, lying behind the empirical construals we make of ourselves. James gets close to the right view in his claim that while we need to rely heavily on introspective observation in psychology, "*introspection is difficult and fallible; and . . . the difficulty is simply that of all observation of whatever kind*" (1890, 191). He notes that some authors claim for introspection "a sort of infallibility," but others go to the opposite extreme and say that we have "no introspective cognition of our own minds at all" (1890, 187–88). James opts for an empirical approach, where even introspection is corrected by the experimental and the comparative approaches. Flanagan points out that while James's psychology is the beginning of a naturalistic and empirical psychology, his heavy reliance on introspection limits his psychology to a "theory of conscious mental life" and not to the full range of our mental life (1984, 27). Increasing evidence indicates that much is taking place "behind the scenes" of conscious awareness.

James is most persuasive when he sticks to a phenomenology of consciousness. He argues that we can understand consciousness without insisting on a spiritual some "thing," a pure ego, or without going to the other extreme and denying that consciousness plays an active role in life. Personality identity, James notes first, is simply a matter of judging sameness in a class of phenomena, in this case my apprehensions of my psychic life, my emotions, perceptions, and so on. But who is doing the apprehending? Common sense, says James, is sure that behind the unity of self-consciousness that I call me there is "a real belonging to a real Owner, to a pure spiritual entity of some kind" (1890, 337). What we call the "I," James suggests, is a functional capacity of human creatures; it is active as it is efficacious in navigating the environment. Thinking and judging, like walking and breathing, name functions, not entities. Introspection, on a radically empirical method, can only conclude that this "owning" capacity is inherent in thought itself, as it is continually repossessing itself. In James's words: "Each thought is thus born an owner and dies owned, transmitting whatever it realized as its Self to its own later proprietor. . . . It is this trick which the nascent thought has of immediately taking up the expiring thought and 'adopting' it, which is the foundation of the appropriation of most of the remoter constituents of the self. Who owns the last self owns the self before the last, for what possess the possessor, possesses the possessed" (1890, 339). It is hard even today to put it better. The striking thing is that while this analysis denies that there lies at the depth of every self a spiritual "reality," an eternity in Kierkegaard's sense, it affirms the sort of identity construction, or active relational achievement theory of self-formation, that Kierkegaard affirms: "The identity found by the I in its *me* is only a loosely constructed thing, an identity 'on the whole,' just like that which any outside observer might find in the same assemblage of facts" (James 1890, 372). The way we look at ourselves is not a difference in kind, just a difference in degree and scope. And how we understand who we are is roughly similar to how we understand others, by their showings and tellings.

Kierkegaard's inward grasping is not an infallible apprehension, nor is it (if we stick to the evidence) an apprehension of eternity, not a transcendence of temporal conditions, but the subject's effort to represent itself to itself, and this too is subject to the dialectic of doubt and belief. Admittedly, James is influenced by evolutionary biology, but it is his strict adherence to an empirical experiential psychology that is compelling. But what of spirit on this functional reading, what of the aspirations for wholeness and coherence, for ultimate perspectives and transcendence? As James says in his later *Pragmatism* (1907, 125): "For pluralistic pragmatism truth grows up inside all the finite experiences. They lean on each other, but the whole of them, if such a whole there be, leans on nothing. All 'homes' are in finite experience; finite experience as such is homeless. Nothing outside the flux secures the issue of it. It can hope for salvation only from its own intrinsic promises and potencies." This suggests a spirituality within the finite, a spirituality that remains within nature, and perhaps the way forward lies here. But at this point I want to consider the dialectic between experience and interpretation in pluralistic pragmatism.

Hilary Putnam puts the pragmatist perspective best. Putnam draws by now a widespread distinction between what he first called external realism and internal or pragmatic realism (see Flanagan 1996, 195). The external realist is the classic metaphysical realist who claims that truth "involves some sort of correspondence relation between words or thought-signs and external things or sets of things." The internalist perspective holds "that *what objects does the world consist of?* is a question that it only makes sense to ask *within* a theory or description" (Putnam 1981, 49). And then truth on this view is a "sort of (idealized) rational acceptability—some sort of ideal coherence of our beliefs with each other and with our experience as those experiences are themselves represented in our belief system—and not correspondence with mind-independent or discourse-independent 'states of affairs'" (1981, 49–50). The crucial point, a point I made in discussing Piety's reading of Kierkegaard's epistemology, is that experience never comes without interpretative coloring. This does not mean that experience is not important; just that it is not without the influence of the conceptual resources we have on hand. Putnam puts the interface between experience and conceptualization right: "Internalism does not deny that there are experiential inputs to knowledge; knowledge is not a story with no constraints except internal coherence; but it does deny that there are any inputs which are not themselves to some extent shaped by our concepts, by the vocabulary we use to report and describe them, or any inputs which admit of only one description, independent of all conceptual choices" (1981, 54).

The upshot is that not only does metaphysical realism disappear, but also theological perspectives that think we have some sort of access to God or God's views shorn of our interpretative contribution. The pragmatic point about knowledge of the world and ourselves holds true for religious knowledge as well: "There is no God's eye point of view that we can know or usefully imagine, there are only the various points of view of actual persons reflecting various interest and purposes that their descriptions and theories subserve" (Putnam 1981, 50). Furthermore, individual interests and purposes are bound up with the wider social practical and cultural traditions. As Stout writes: "You can't somehow leap out of culture and history altogether and gaze directly into the Moral Law, using it as a standard for judging the justification or truth of moral propositions, any more than you can gaze directly into the mind of God. You can, if you possess the requisite virtues, search your available resources for all relevant considerations and deliberate wisely" (1988, 23). Kierkegaard yearned to gaze into the mind of God, and his final faith was that we did have an avenue for discerning God's will. But what he in fact did was take up the journey for existential orientation, and, as Stout says, he did what really only the more courageous and clever can do: "You can even expand your own culture's horizons in a way that brings new or long-neglected considerations into view" (1988, 23).

In the final analysis, our epistemic situation is one where there are still parameters within which well-founded beliefs fall, and since these do not stand separate of our biology, our psychology, and our culture, they define "objectivity for us." As Putnam says, speaking of our criteria for rationality: "They define a kind of objectivity, *objectivity for us,* even if it is not the metaphysical objectivity of the God's eye view. Objectivity and rationality humanly speaking are what we have; they are better than nothing at all" (1981, 55). Stout puts it this way, stressing the limits that constrain intelligence: "What you can't do, if you are human, is have your judgment determined solely by the matter under consideration without relying on beliefs, habits of description, and patterns of reasoning that belong to a cultural inheritance" (1988, 23). So while the metaphysical realism of the strong objectivist is gone, the result is not nihilism and despair. This is only the result when one still hankers after the classic metaphysical image of a God's-eye view. In Putnam's words: "Pragmatists hold that there are no metaphysical guarantees to be had that even our most firmly held beliefs will never need revision" (1995, 21). But, he continues, this is not cause for radical skepticism, for on pragmatist terms one "can be both fallibilistic *and* antiskeptical" (1995, 21). Perhaps Albert Camus put it best some time ago: "Our appetite for understanding, our nostalgia for the absolute, are explicable only in so far, precisely, as we can understand and explain many things. It is useless to negate the reason absolutely. It has its order in which it is efficacious. It is properly that of human experience" (1942, 27). This is an important point: if intelligence did not have some capacity to penetrate experience, the appetite for the infinite perspective would never arise. If this yearning is given up, deconstructed, then the result is not a loss of intelligibility but simply a locating of intelligence in its proper domain, limited interpreted human experience.

So Kierkegaard's positive proposals emerge from his practical reasoning, from *phronesis,* and thereby prudential considerations (broadly taken) figure in his analysis. This is hard to see because he often criticizes prudence as an escape, but prudence can be narrow or generous. A narrow prudence is tied to the store of current common sense, to the majority views and conventional wisdom of a culture. In philosophical matters this tends nowadays toward a scientistic view, a view that wraps itself in the esteem of the positivist view of science; in Kierkegaard's day it was a rationalistic metaphysics with universal aspirations. But a more generous prudence is nothing other than practical reason operating out of a broader scope for reason than do forms of strong objectivism. Generous prudence in existential matters can even be involved in traditions of alternative and subversive *wisdom.* There are, as Marcus Borg (1994) points out, the resources of more subversive and alternative wisdom traditions. But, of course, these alternative and subversive wisdoms are not created anew by the individual himself or herself; it is in deconstructing, reconfiguring, and extending the resources supplied by the living cultural traditions to the exigencies of the times that they are reconstructed. Consider Jesus's message in relation to the Pharisees or Buddha's in relation to the Hindu Brahmins; they both are radical reformers, not creators of wisdom from nothing. But most important here, and perhaps more critical of Kierkegaard, *this alternative wisdom is not nonsense or an absurdity to the understanding*—unless that understanding is completely bound up with conventional wisdom and especially with more objectivistic scientistic attitudes. Kierkegaard brings us to a place where what we have is the dialectic of doubt and belief; a place where, as Stout says, we have "only practical wisdom and our own justified beliefs" to go on (1988, 260).

Finally, then, we do best to read Kierkegaard as an edifying hermeneutical philosopher. Kierkegaard was concerned with awakening and upbuilding, a pragmatic project that lives from our existential need to advance our spiritual interests in living purposeful and worthy lives. But edifying discourse does not escape its times. As James says: "We plunge forward into the field of fresh experience with the beliefs our ancestors and we have made already; these determine what we notice; what we notice determines what we do; what we do again determines what we experience" (1907, 122). And this pragmatist point explains why many of us (students of existential matters through Western Christian culture) find, not surprisingly, as Evans says, that Kierkegaard's construal of our life provides us with "interpretive power" and can "illuminate our situation" (1995, 94).

Religious Aspirations and Human Flourishing

Kierkegaard presents an analysis of sickness and health. He diagnoses sickness and prescribes measures to restore health. He promises to root out despair and provide peace. In my view his promise is overstated and the peril of the project is not fully realized. We have already seen that on Kierkegaard's analysis of existential development human beings need to become strong spiritual evaluators, need to become individuals with ethical and spiritual concerns defining their identity; in this is their hope of unity and wholeness and the avoidance of losing themselves as rational and responsible agents, a situation that results in despair. But it seems clear that this claim is overstated if it is meant to be a straightforward empirical claim. Individuals do not need to maintain the stance of the strong evaluator to avoid an identity crisis. Furthermore, Kierkegaard's own analysis of human selfhood, and the dynamics of identity formation, strongly suggests that individuals become selves to greater or lesser degrees. The more they can achieve personhood, can take their lives into their own hands and move forward toward greater horizons of understanding and self-conscious action, the more they surmount despair. The individual without any or without sustained self-conscious relations to "the world" is the person in despair. But Kierkegaard tells us that our striving for existential identity really only accentuates our dire predicament; we discover a "higher" despair, a despair over our inability to ever pull off the demands with success.

Here is another of Kierkegaard's missteps. First, as I have already suggested, trying to be a strong evaluator seems to be identity undermining and may itself be the cause of a spiritual identity crisis. Why should I want to pursue that path? Perhaps because I think that only if I have absolute and firm foundations will I have real security, will I have exorcized the relativist's anxiety. In the final analysis, it is the relativism issue that propels Kierkegaard toward the religious stage; it is an issue that is still with us, but our worries are overstated. Anthony Rudd's reading of our options in this situation is worth noting in full:

> Within the contemporary disintegration of *Sittlichkeit*, the individual is, to some extent anyway, forced into disengagement. He may react to that by immersing himself in the crowd—that is, by adopting whatever values and norms the majority of people accept, following them as they change. This is different than the attitude of the ethicist, in that he [the ethicist] adheres to a stable set of values defined by institutional roles. Or he may retain his individuality in personal commitments to freely chosen ground projects, which are without much institutional definition, and which must therefore generate their own norms and standards. It is accordingly difficult for this to avoid collapsing back into aestheticism. There remains Kierkegaard's preferred option: the leap of faith to the religious level, where each individual is related, as an individual, to a transcendent source of value. (1993, 131)

I think this captures our options pretty accurately but not altogether fairly, and insofar as these are Kierkegaard's options, Kierkegaard is right, up to a point. In the first place, the effort to avoid the objectifying abilities that indicate my lack of a naturally unifying standpoint, a secure moral and spiritual home, is virtually impossible for intelligent twenty-first-century individuals. The subsequent effort to return to conventional wisdom, at least without some degree of conscious clarity that this is one's choice, is intellectually dishonest. Although I have doubts about the degree to which this means a person's identity will disintegrate, it does seem clear that their existential identity (as an identity that they autonomously fashion as they engage in social practices and cultural traditions) is denied. To some degree they are missing out on a significant human good.

Second, perhaps the slippage back into estheticism, and the acknowledgement that I cannot transcend my time completely, cannot locate the uncontested framework, is a healthy realism. Flanagan mentions the attitude of the ironist, an attitude that Kierkegaard thought was finally despair, but what does it look like within pragmatism? Flanagan writes: "The ironist relishes and is amused by contingency, including the contingency of her character, aspirations, projects and so on. She is not confident that her final vocabulary has things right. Indeed she is confident that it doesn't" (1996, 207). But taking up an strong ironist attitude (just like the strong evaluator) cannot sustain a person, and I am inclined to think that some things are more contingent than other things; if we look from far enough out everything looks contingent, but if we come closer it does not look that way. On the other hand, I am inclined to agree with Flanagan that sometimes adherence to a transcendent source of value makes for a pompous attitude. It creates intolerance and moral self-righteousness; it does not have to, but it has that tendency. (We do not want to be the person who, as Mark Twain reportedly said, "is so full of what's right that he can't see what's good.") So this seems, on the whole, something to avoid, at least if the ironist has some of the truth.

Third, as I have argued, and Rudd admits, the Judge is not simply following the crowd, he has only so much institutional definition when it comes to norms and standards. So, does the Judge's position need to be overcome with an individualistic leap of faith to a transcendental source? His view is Hegelian enough that Rudd seems to think it will flounder in a social and cultural relativism. Rudd spends considerable time arguing that Kierkegaard is on to something when he rejects the relativism of a Hegelian social morality. I have spent considerable time arguing that a modified Hegelian view, a pragmatic realism, is good enough. The worry of relativism is overblown. If we have a society with social practices and cultural customs that value and provide both support and elbow room for *modest* moral and spiritual evaluators, we are headed in the right direction.

But the religious aspiration remains: how best to accommodate it? As I mentioned in the last chapter, William James's pragmatic argument for theistic convictions is about as good as it gets for Kierkegaard's approach to God. James argues that we lack an absolutely public or universal normative perspective but that we nevertheless strive to expand our consciousness and act from such a view. The "strenuous liver" (as James calls her) is the individual who affirms her intuition that there is an ideal reality, a higher demand, whose terms we yearn to approach. But what are the terms of this higher demand, what is (if we use theistic language) the will of God? James answers: "Exactly what the thought of the infinite thinker may be is hidden from us even were we sure of his existence; so that our postulation of him after all only serves to let loose in us the strenuous mood" (1897, 214). Judge William affirmed such an open-ended religious ethic, and up to a point Kierkegaard does as well—if Climacus's Religiousness A captures Kierkegaard's view. But if Anti-Climacus tells us where Kierkegaard ended, then we have a faith that the thought of the infinite thinker has been revealed to us in Christ. Even on this faith, *what* has been revealed is still vague; clarity of content emerges as we engage

Christian cultural traditions, embodying frames of ultimate significance. Living cultural traditions can function as an ideal *Socius,* as a power not ourselves, within which we can have some reflective peace, some spiritual roots. Spiritual despair, life's despair, is supplanted as much as can be reasonably expected when we are actively engaged in living traditions.

So finally, I want to suggest that the advantage of Kierkegaard's vision revised is better seen as a pragmatic advantage, a matter of moral and spiritual helpfulness. It is better seen as making the case for the plausibility of a normative ideal where the radically self-transcending self is always kept in view and where reengagement is always seen as slightly suspect, and so never taken too seriously. I want to explore this posture by contrasting it with C. Stephen Evans's argument that the stance of transcendent theism is secure against the temptations of idolatry and so superior to other life-stances.

Evans argues that there is a certain advantage to aligning ourselves with the transcendent God: we can inoculate ourselves against false "religious" pretensions if we hold firmly to the true transcendent measure (1997, 12). And given that religious needs cannot be denied, this is the best way to hold "idolatry" at bay. If we do not have this ultimate security, the anxiety of self-consciousness and existential homelessness, our lack of a naturally unified standpoint, drives us to elevate the merely finite to the status of the infinite, to commit the sin of idolatry. The assumption is that we cannot live without God or a God-substitute; we inevitably invest something with ultimate authority. Evans, in defending Kierkegaard's moves, puts the danger this way: "When the 'criterion' of the self is derived *solely* from relations to other humans, then that *finite human identity becomes invested with ultimate authority.* God in the sense of what is of ultimate worth is completely immanent; there is no place left for transcendence" (1997, 13, emphasis added). But why do we need to invest the finite with ultimate authority? And what is the content of this transcendence? Rudd suggests that our practical moral life will be less than adequate without strong backing: "Can I commit myself with passion to a way of life without believing it to be defensible in universal terms? Does not this sense that absolute foundations are missing for our social morality actually have the effect of undermining our commitment to it" (1993, 133)?

This is similar to Adams's argument that we reviewed in the last chapter. The lack of a strong backing is demoralizing. I do not see why this should necessarily be the case. It is, as Evans said, the anxiety of self-consciousness in the face of our existential homelessness that drives us to elevate the merely finite to the status of the infinite. But I am not so sure that it necessarily does. This formulation of the dilemma poses a set of false alternatives. Must we either have a God's-eye view or be totally lost? Perhaps "the relatively more adequate rather than less adequate" will do, where "adequate" is defined in whatever terms we can best discern as conducive to our flourishing. While humans do have a tendency to fasten onto an ethical perspective and an existential orientation and not let go, to take one identity posture as ultimate and exclusive, this tendency of humans does not seem necessary. We do not have to invest our ideals of human selfhood with ultimate authority to consider them worthy of pursuing. One could argue that this tendency is (like some other human tendencies) best acknowledged and deconstructed. If it was not possible to live without appeal to transcendence no one could live without binding themselves to a substantive orientation that they take as ultimate. But this seems clearly not the case; people do live, as we say, secular lives, and they are lives that have existential significance and are motivationally compelling. And while it is true that sometimes a so-called secular orientation takes on "religious" ultimacy for a person, there is no necessity in this occurring. But perhaps more important, many people bind themselves to explicit religious perspectives and traditions but do not understand them to have absolute authority, for as humans they are cognizant of the limitations of these humanly refracted moral and religious worldviews. Like their secular counterparts, they too live lives of meaning and worth, *despite the fact that they cannot affirm* (what a strong realist like Kierkegaard affirms) *that these convictions are universal eternal truths.*

In addition, it would seem that if this was not possible, religious tolerance and respect for others might be in very short supply. There is a moral point here as well. Now tolerance and respect clearly are in short supply in some locations today, but ironically those seem to be where a religious perspective is most deeply ingrained and widespread in an uncritical social consciousness. As Evans himself notes: "We live in a world in which the identity of human selves is fundamentally shaped by relations such as those of family, clan, nation-state, religion, class, race and gender. Such relations are a necessary part of our finite human selves; we exist as concrete selves—as men and women, North Americans and Europeans and Africans, Christians and Muslims, Catholics and Protestants, rich and poor. It seems perilously easy for us humans to move from an affirmation of our identity based on those relations that define us to a negation of all those who do not share that identity" (1997, 12–13).

But although it may be "perilously easy," it is not necessary, and is not the solution to this tendency to back off the strong affirmation of this specific identity as the truth for all and practice a more modest critical angle? Unless it is clear that there is in fact a secure spiritual perspective, an identity resource that is not infected with the social and cultural, then all selves are relatively spiritually insecure. Moreover, the hankering after a secure stance might be an equally potent recipe for idolatry; if Anti-Climacus is right, that we are in despair because our identity lacks "infinite interest and significance" or is not "eternally steadfast," we might well fasten onto a perspective that claims ultimacy and refuse to give it up. We are, of course, back to questions about the stance of the strong spiritual evaluator, about drawbacks and benefits, and about plausible alternatives.

In the end, the ideal of the strong evaluator is one of several possible and plausible life-postures linked to worldviews. There are other well thought-out and fulfilling life-postures than that of the strong moral and spiritual evaluator. Taylor mentioned two other contemporary fronts for existential identity: expressive individualism and deep naturalistic humanism. The scientific empiricist, the Asian contemplative, the Native American spiritualist, the liberal social activist, the political libertarian, and even the postmodern ironist are some expressions of a more modest moral and spiritual stance. And of course there are a variety of Christian and theistic postures. All involve resources for existential identity and rational and responsible choice. A strong moral realism that eliminates these other views is overly self-confident. Furthermore, I would argue with Putnam that, unlike Aristotle (or Kierkegaard) "who seemed to think that ideally there was some sort of constitution that everyone ought to have," we should affirm that in "the ideal world there will be different conceptions of human flourishing, that diversity and pluralism is part of the ideal" (1981, 148). There are moral reasons not to affirm the ideal of strong spiritual evaluation as the way.

There is a tendency for the spiritual to supplant the moral, especially when the social dimension of the self is pushed to the background. If a person was to begin their study of Kierkegaard with Anti-Climacus's reflections in *The Sickness unto Death,* what seems not as central is the moral earnestness of the Judge. Anti-Climacus speaks of becoming a self, but this self is not primarily a moral self, although it must be a self that is responsive to the relational web that is its self-identity. One must search *The Sickness unto Death* carefully to find mention of moral concepts such as conscience and duty. In the final analysis it is the self's relation to the Western God of high righteousness that assures that Kierkegaard's vision of existential identity is not simply a eudemonistic ethic of self-actualization in a humanistic vein. But the overall vision is so decisively spiritual that it is not concerned primarily with moral matters, with how I live in relation to others, but more directly with *my* life's ultimate meaning and final purpose, with the state of *my* soul. A single-minded focus on moral matters, on the claims of others on me and my responsibilities to them, will, one is inclined to conclude (from Anti-Climacus's reflections), lead one further away from a secure higher theological selfhood.

There is some evidence that this is not Kierkegaard's final position, but I will not address the argument here. In his nonpseudonymous *Works of Love,* Kierkegaard seems to affirm an ethic of love of neighbor based in human equality, and in *Practice in Christianity,* Anti-Climacus says that Christianity is "the healing of the sin-conscious self and the indicative ethics gratefully expressive of the redemptive gift" (PC xiii). I suspect that this substantive ethical development is again tied more to his social nurturing and cultural connection to Christianity and less to his analysis of human selfhood and its dynamics; it is Kierkegaard unpacking the implications of his Christian measure for selfhood. On the whole Kierkegaard's ideal, I have argued, is finally less a strictly moral ideal (such as a stringent utilitarian who calls for the continual superiority of moral considerations) than a spiritual ideal, although I think that the ideal's connection to the God of the West, a God of justice and righteousness, moderates the distance. A spiritual ideal may very well assert that an individual's meaningful engagement with life, with flourishing as a complete human being, sometimes conflicts with strictly moral considerations, considerations of other's interests, and when it does, the spiritual ideal can trump the moral; the religious call is not equivalent to the call of the moral.[15]

The Kierkegaardian ideal of personhood is not simply focused on moral virtue, but is broader; it is concerned with existential meaningfulness, with flourishing as a self-transcending spiritual self. One reason for saying this comes from Kierkegaard's aversion to social engagements. As we explored in the last chapter, Anti-Climacus makes numerous negative remarks about individuals who are involved in the world to the exclusion of their "self," and not all the remarks can be glossed as remarks critical of only an immediate person encased in the crowd. Some of his remarks seem clearly critical of anyone who does not take the path of becoming a strong spiritual evaluator, does not strive for the higher authentic self. Such individuals, says Anti-Climacus, "waste" their lives, because they never become "conscious as spirit, as self, or, what amounts to the same thing, never become aware . . . that there is a God, and that 'he,' he himself, his self, exists before this God. . . . What wretchedness that they are lumped together and deceived instead of being split apart so that each individual may gain the highest" (SUD 26–27). Distance from the crowd and awareness of one's capacities for self-transcendence, and hence for distance from given social and cultural meanings, is good, but take it too far and others are just in the way; take it to the level of the strong spiritual evaluator, and a degree of spiritual dis-ease can infect all one's finite relations, as even moral concerns slip into the whirlpool of radical spiritual transcendence. The *modest* spiritual evaluator retains moral seriousness, for she retains a deep awareness of the importance of social relations for the flourishing of herself; the more spiritual aspirations can live in relative harmony with the moral life, never overshadowing moral reengagement, but always restraining moral self-righteousness and pomposity.

Notes

1. Kierkegaard may have held such a view. In speaking of the requirement of Christian ideality, he says in some of his latest writing, "you admit that this is the requirement, and then have recourse to grace" (PC xv).

2. Alastair Hannay concurs here and sees the autonomy of ethics as indicating that for Kierkegaard "ethical principles and concepts . . . contain specifications of irreducible, and in that sense ultimate and absolute, *desiderata.* In this sense, to say that ethics is autonomous is to say that one *cannot* go beyond ethics" (1982, 158). Why? Because ethics "lies beyond the self and its world." But then Hannay understands that this must be reconciled with ethics and its clear connection to human nature in Kierkegaard's thought.

3. See Gary Gutting (1999) and Gary Kitchen (1999) for valuable examinations of Taylor's moral realism. As for Taylor's connection to Kierkegaard, John Davenport is the only philosopher who notes an affinity between Taylor's comments about the strong evaluator and Kierkegaard's ethical ideal (2001, 271).

4. Claiming three options for us is strikingly similar to Mitchell's (1980) claim that there is romantic humanism, scientific humanism, and, the position he argues for, Christian theism. Mitchell, however, admits a fourth, liberalism humanism, which tries to get the best of the first two worldviews, but he thinks that it finally fails to provide an adequate rationale for the traditional conscience, a rationale that theism can provide.

5. As Flanagan says: "There is nothing in the canonical descriptions of persons who are suffering identity crises, and who thereby are immobilized and alienated from their own lives, that requires that we think of them as former virtuosos at strong evaluation or alternatively as persons who have never discovered the good of strong evaluation and have thereby come undone" (1996, 152).

6. As Erikson notes, the increasing sense of identity "is experienced preconsciously as a sense of psychosocial well-being. Its most obvious concomitants are a feeling of being at home in one's body, a sense [of] 'knowing where one is going,' and an inner assuredness of anticipated recognition from those who count" (1980, 127–28).

7. See especially Davenport and Rudd (2001).

8. Interesting Rudd points this out in Kant's case, but not in Kierkegaard's. Kant

mistakes his own Christian Lutheran background for a common rational morality (1993, 136).

9. This is true, we might note, of MacIntyre's efforts as well.

10. In particular Rudd (1993), but also Evans (1997) and Westphal (1987).

11. Charles Taylor, in his recent *Varieties of Religion Today: William James Revisited,* makes a similar point. Considering the more conservative call to return to a thicker socially informed spiritual identity, he concludes that we should stick with our individualistic cultural, even with its downsides: "Even if we had a choice, I'm not sure we wouldn't be wiser to stick with the present dispensation" (2002, 114).

12. And as Stout notes this now seems to make MacIntyre's sociocultural *telos* something more of a metaphysical/theological *telos* and raises the difficult question of defending these "thicker" convictions in public life (1989, 224–25).

13. Indeed, Stout makes a persuasive argument that MacIntyre himself has been doing just this throughout his philosophical career, and so one does not (contra MacIntyre) need to be too firmly tied to a tradition to exercise rational thought.

14. Robert Bellah is the lead author of a popular analysis of American life, *Habits of the Heart: Individualism and Commitment in American Life,* which was deeply influenced by MacIntyre's *After Virtue.*

15. Climacus says of Religiousness B, Christianity, that it is "isolating, separating," and that "as I absolutely bind myself to it, I thereby exclude everyone else" (CUP 582).

Conclusion: Reconstructing Kierkegaard

Kierkegaard, I have argued, is compelled to postulate a transcendent standard as the only adequate measure because he thinks that the human desire for existential orientation can mean only *ultimate* security and *final* rest in the flux and contingency of everyday life. But what does the human desire for existential orientation and identity come to? My answer has been that humans need an existential identity because they are radically self-transcending selves and so discover that they have no naturally given standpoint, no unambiguous perspective. Humans find themselves existentially homeless and so seek a home; they seek a life-perspective they can ground themselves in that will orient them morally and spiritually. And by spiritually I mean some meaningful life-purposes, something we can live for that is not simply our given desires or social context, but which we can self-consciously and rationally affirm. *The question has been what counts as an adequate answer to such existential matters.*

It is perhaps necessary, at this point, to mention that although one might think that I am explaining away theism, or Christianity, the thrust of my argument is that Kierkegaard's efforts to provide a "subjective rationale" for theism cannot be decisive; there is no way to approach religious matters that ignores the "objective" side: metaphysical and even historical/empirical questions cannot be bypassed in making the case for a religious worldview. The subjective rationale is too subject to incursions from the social and cultural side to be decisive. I do not claim to have pronounced on the truth of theism or Christianity; I have claimed that the truth of theism or the Christian vision of life cannot be settled once and for all with existentially edifying arguments about what makes for human flourishing. It is not that I think a traditional metaphysics must be attempted and made good, for I think this is forever beyond our reach. Rather, I think that even a cumulative case for a worldview, one that employs both existential practical psychological and theoretical metaphysical arguments, will finally be seen as one rationally permissible view among others for our allegiance. For those of us who live and think after Nietzsche, our answer must deal with historical consciousness and the lack of one secure and noncontroversial normative perspective. Pluralism is the final story or, better, the final stories.

Traditionally, and for the most part (although there have been dissenters), theologians and philosophers have sought to discover an Archimedean point, a firm foundation, a God's-eye perspective. Is there an ultimately secure place for the strong spiritual evaluator to rest? In the strong terms that Kierkegaard lays out, I do not think so. The history of human thought on the matter of the correct ethical and spiritual posture gives us great reason to be skeptical. The current philosophical climate (one of deep and pervasive pluralism) gives even more reason to be cautious in declaring our answer. At least it will lead us to conclude that an attitude that thinks it is philosophically finished is probably only just beginning. Most striking, perhaps, is that Kierkegaard's own terms strongly suggest that the ultimately secure foothold is unintelligible to us; there is no way we can get to it on terms acceptable to the human understanding. Admittedly we have a desire for it, but our intelligence shows that this desire cannot be satisfied—short of giving up on our intelligence. But then anything goes.

We are, Kierkegaard concludes, fallen creatures in need of rescue; the human situation is simply despair. But Kierkegaard did not end up frustrated and in despair, and many others who follow the terms of his Christian existentialism do not. Why not? In the first place I do not think that Kierkegaard or his disciples have followed the terms of his analysis to their radical conclusion; to use Climacus's terms, they have slipped into the delusions of the positive thinkers, or in grander terms, they have taken the leap of faith. But this leap truncates the tension, the contradiction, that comes with being a *synthesis* of the infinite and finite, and the wound of limitless self-transcendence is covered over. But to some degree that is as it should be for earthbound creatures. The pragmatist sees our reengagement as suspect, and so never taken too seriously, but also as always the necessary condition for thinking and acting, and so beyond radical doubt. The pragmatist, again, is both fallibilistic and antiskeptical; the modest evaluator is skeptical of the strong skepticism in the radical Cartesian and Climacian sense.

What is disturbing is when those who leap think that they have really pulled off the synthesis. Or that they know which way to leap, where to stand, in a pluralistic world; and in this sense Kierkegaard's final leap is disturbing, if he did leap. (Indeed, his extended deliberation over whether to claim the writings of Anti-Climacus as his own, whether to announce that he was now speaking to his reader from his own finished and final position, suggests that he realized how complex and even controversial his own existential analysis had become.) My alternative explanation for the sense of well-being discovered by those who would genuinely affirm paradoxical Christian views is this: humans find spiritual satisfaction, resolve despair, in pursuing and developing a self-consciously expressed life-project that draws on social and cultural resources and that they should understand to be limited and finite but which if well informed by an understanding of humans and their world is just good enough. The ideal of the strong spiritual evaluator generates a gap between an infinite possibility and finite conditions that is unbridgeable. The answer is to jettison the strong ideal in favor of a more modest ideal. The advocate for the modest ideal argues that our objectifying reflection shows us that our vision is never fully complete and final, never the whole truth; there is always a limitation in our view, and so the most adequate view, most things considered, is a more modest objectivism. While we may try to follow and realize the terms of Kierkegaard's ideal exactly and carefully, it is neither possible nor advisable for us to do so. A meaningful and satisfying life is found in pursuing a more modest moral and spiritual path. That path will inevitably involve, as Jeffrey Stout puts it, beliefs, habits of description, and patterns of reasoning that belong to a cultural inheritance. The trick is to move critically within these constraints, testing them dialectically against one another for overall coherence and satisfactoriness. The Kierkegaardian ideal threatens to make life thoroughly absurd and frustrating, or alternatively, healing a huge gap would not be salvation but a peace beyond understanding—something no human being should want. It would drain life of its meaningfulness; meaningful life lives in the gap between what is and what ought to be or what might be.

More specifically, I would claim of Kierkegaard that he found fulfilling the affirmation of an existential identity, a spiritual self, informed by a worldview that constituted him even before he could self-consciously realize it. The Protestant Christianity that his father's guiding hand instilled in him as he matured is in essence the very Christianity that he later discovers is his salvation. Our early identifications and social practices can provide the deep structure for adult existential confidence. When Kierkegaard comes to rest transparently in God, he really rests in an enduring and powerful narrative of Western Christendom, a narrative reinforced by familial context and cultural conversation. I think this true for all of us. We find relative reflective peace when we are involved in cultural frameworks that (if we are lucky) early significant others instilled in us and in which we now are self-consciously and actively engaged. The ontological other which the spiritually serious reflective self comes to know is best seen as a culturally constituted frame of significance that, while crucial to our flourishing, is finally metaphysically opaque. This realization does not drain the project of its meaning, although it should make us less confident that we have discovered God's own way. While we will never have complete confidence in our evaluative stance, such confidence is not needed for a life of value and significance. To yearn for complete confidence and the ultimately believable framework is a recipe for despair. To live the life of the culturally connected critic, the modest evaluator, is to learn to live without the ultimate ground, the final vision—and perhaps it is to live a life of faith.

I am then reconstructing Kierkegaard with two positive arguments. One is that the split in our being is not so deep; we can, to various degrees, bridge the distance between finitude and transcendence. While we have no naturally unified standpoint, our biological nature does provide parameters in our construal of the good for creatures such as ourselves; we are to some degree biologically fitted for the world. Obviously my post-Darwinian sensibilities influence me here, but I also think that there is empirical evidence for certain human lives and activities leading to more satisfactoriness overall than others sorts of lives. Kierkegaard's view of the self as a relational reality that is meaningfully constituted to the degree that it establishes relations to its construals of the empirical world is correct. I conclude that the achievement of an invigorating motivating self can be a more-or-less affair. The more we are able to establish successful relations to the world, to engage in tradition embedded practices, the less we are in despair because the less we are without a web of relationships that constitute a meaningful and invigorating self. The self without self-conscious relationships, without social engagement and commitment to institutional and cultural practices, is the self narrowed down and impoverished, the self in despair. In the final analysis, to still despair, even with rich and invigorating self-constituting relations to a world, is to hold to the ideal of the strong evaluator who will never end up in a place of secure existential identity. Only when the terms of the strong evaluator are subtly (and reasonably) settled down can a mature existential identity flourish. Perhaps Kierkegaard himself should be read, in the final analysis, as a more *modest* moral and spiritual evaluator.

My second point is that cultural embeddedness goes deeper than Kierkegaard knows. When Anti-Climacus says that despair is dispelled and faith is victorious when the self rests transparently in the power that constituted it, we can read: "When the self has deeply and self-consciously assimilated the resources of a living tradition, it is psychically sustained and volitionally empowered by these relations." The metaphysical/ontological question concerning the self's ultimate ground is finally either opaque or requires a serious metaphysical effort that Kierkegaard seeks to bypass, an effort that I would argue ends inevitably in pluralism. In any case, the empirical fact is that individuals who are self-consciously and critically engaged in a living tradition or traditions rest in "powers" by which they are spiritually constituted, are existentially rooted and empowered, for they have satisfied a need of the human creature for existential orientation and identity. We might even say that they have a "higher" self than those who merely live from the de facto social rules and roles current in their time.

This more Kierkegaardian normative claim will need to be carefully stated. Many, it seems, do not crave a "higher" self; the social and cultural resources as they happen to have them are sufficient for their existential needs, and the question is what normative advantage does becoming a "higher," more "authentic self" confer. The best way to state the advantage is in terms of a significant human good, the good of autonomous self-expression, and the advance in well-being and confidence that issues from self-conscious reengagement within social and institutional practices, practices related to cultural traditions. When Alasdair MacIntyre talks of goods internal to practices, he is referring to the goods that the modest evaluator pursues, the goods that lend fulfillment and meaning to life, but goods that are always related to specific social and institutional contexts. Owen Flanagan refers to the "ironic strong evaluator," an individual who is confident that she does not have it all right, the "confident unconfident," but who is evaluatively serious just the same and strives to advance the meaning-giving goods of life (1996, 211). Robert C. Solomon, whose recent book *Spirituality for the Skeptic* covers some of the same issues as this work, says, "spirituality is a synthesis of uncertainty and confidence" (2002, 47). He goes on to develop a view that he calls "naturalized spirituality." Drawing heavily on Nietzsche, he argues for spirituality as a thoughtful and passionate process of expanding and transforming the self. Spiritual reflection is uncertain, Solomon argues, because "we always view our world from *somewhere,*" and he notes that there is "no possibility of God-like objectivity, strictly understood. *Nor does this impossible God's-eye perspective make sense even as an aspiration, an ideal*" (2002, 68, emphasis added). These authors affirm the project of self-criticism and moral seriousness, but with the modesty that an awareness of historical contingency brings. These attitudes, so far as I can see, capture the best sense of a "higher" self and what advantages it confers. Here we see all it can mean not to stifle the spirit, but to allow the spirit to breath.

If we say, alternatively, that a self is a "secure" and "higher" self because it justifies its identity-constituting relations against rigorous and high standards, even transcendent standards, standards that are thought higher than our practical wisdom and relatively well-justified beliefs, then we are fooling ourselves. I have already said that this is a temptation and one that has repeatedly proved to go bankrupt. Given the deeply pluralistic lessons we have learned, we should be cautious about strong conclusions. As reflective social animals, all of us do well to find a set of broadly moral convictions, a vision of our world and our place in it, and a way forward for our self-expression, on pain of frustration and unhappiness. But if I am right about the limitations of Kierkegaard's approach, then I must be more generous to my neighbor's views and existential orientations, remembering that they too may be living in equally plausible and satisfying stances. My answer is the modest spiritual evaluator who is a culturally connected critic regarding his or her beliefs and values. The "connected critic" is Michael Walzer's (1987) term, and he uses it to talk about the work of the social critic in a pluralistic world, but since selves are social and culturally embedded, it can be seen as the most plausible position from which to fashion and define ourselves in a pluralistic world. The modest moral and spiritual evaluator is such a connected critic; indeed, Kierkegaard himself was a culturally connected critic.

One rebuttal to this reading of Kierkegaard reflecting his social and cultural context is his rejection of any normative view that reduces the individual to a one-dimensional reflection of his or her society. Was not Kierkegaard's whole authorship calculated to demonstrate that being a "self," and finally a Christian, was not simply a matter of reflecting the social and ethical norms current in one's time, but a matter of self-consciously and freely choosing to become a unique and authentic self before God? To say that Kierkegaard simply reflects his time is surely wrong. And I agree that Kierkegaard certainly does not advocate the self-satisfied bourgeois Christianity widespread in his time and in ours. But my claim is that the individualist who breaks with his time and its assurances does so in the name of yet older assurances. Kierkegaard uses his rhetorical and psychological skills to portray a more traditional Protestant stance that many in his day could intellectually identify but only faintly feel. But Kierkegaard, with his intensely Christian background and deep drinks from the Western tradition, discovered that his lived-experience resonated with a more traditional Christianity. From then on his task was to reinstate the existential power of a cultural perspective that was losing its grip.

Kierkegaard presents us with a powerfully persuasive view of authentic human existence, but he overstates its strength. It, like other normative views, is subject to the dialectic of doubt and belief, to the evolving standards of earthbound socially embedded critical inquirers. The various appeals that Kierkegaard makes for the ideal, the appeal of self-reflexivity, the appeal to inward experience, the appeal of moral and spiritual helpfulness, are not sufficient to close the case. What he also has in fact appealed to, an authority not clear for him, is the effective history of Western Christian culture as it appears in his own person. Introspective reflection gone deep enough reveals effective history. Kierkegaard's unyielding affirmation of the ideal of the morally serious strong spiritual evaluator, an affirmation that generates the rationale for the move to theism and Christianity, rests on the powers that constituted him: his social and cultural context. While Kierkegaard's efforts to ground faith and morals in human subjectivity extend our grasp of humans and their religious life, he overstates his case. His analysis is only one provisional and opened-ended piece of our ongoing effort to conceptualize ourselves and our moral and religious interests and intuitions. In the final analysis we can learn much from Kierkegaard's vision of the normatively human, but we should not think that his trajectory for existential identity is demanded with the urgency that he conveys.

WORKS CITED

Kierkegaard's Works

CA *The Concept of Anxiety.* Edited and translated by Reidar Thomte in collaboration with Albert Anderson. Princeton, N.J.: Princeton University Press, 1980 [1844].

CUP *Concluding Unscientific Postscript to Philosophical Fragments,* 2 vols. Edited and translated by Howard V. Hong and Edna H. Hong. Princeton, N.J.: Princeton University Press, 1992 [1846].

E/O *Either/Or, part II.* Edited and translated by Howard V. Hong and Edna H. Hong. Princeton, N.J.: Princeton University Press, 1987 [1843].

FT *Fear and Trembling.* Edited and translated by Howard V. Hong and Edna H. Hong. Published with *Repetition.* Princeton, N.J.: Princeton University Press, 1983 [1843].

JC *Johannes Climacus or De Omnibus Dubitandum Est* [Everything must be doubted]. Edited and translated by Howard V. Hong and Edna H. Hong. Published with *Philosophical Fragments.* Princeton, N.J.: Princeton University Press, 1985 [1843].

JSK *The Journals of Søren Kierkegaard.* Edited and translated by Alexander Dru. London: Oxford University Press, 1940.

PC *Practice in Christianity.* Edited and translated by Howard V. Hong and Edna H. Hong. Princeton, N.J.: Princeton University Press, 1991 [1850].

SKJP *Søren Kierkegaard's Journals and Papers,* 7 vols. Edited and translated by Howard V. Hong and Edna H. Hong, assisted by Gregor Malantschuk; with index, vol. 7, by Nathaniel Hong and Charles Barker. Bloomington: Indiana University Press, 1967–78.

SUD *The Sickness unto Death.* Edited and translated by Howard V. Hong and Edna H. Hong. Princeton, N.J.: Princeton University Press, 1980 [1849].

WL *Works of Love.* Translated by David Swenson and Lillian Swenson. London: Oxford University Press, 1946 [1847].

Other Works

Adams, Robert M. 1987. *The Virtue of Faith.* New York: Oxford University Press.

Bellah, Robert N., Richard Madsen, William M. Sullivan, Ann Swidler, and Steve Tipton. 1985. *Habits of the Heart: Individualism and Commitment in American Life.* Berkeley: University of California Press.

Bernstein, Richard. 1985. *Beyond Objectivism and Relativism: Science, Hermeneutics, and Praxis.* Philadelphia: University of Pennsylvania Press.

Borg, Marcus J. 1994. *Meeting Jesus Again for the First Time: The Historical Jesus and the Heart of Contemporary Faith.* San Francisco: Harper Collins.

Bugental, James F. T. 1976. *The Search for Existential Identity.* San Francisco: Jossey-Bass.

Butler, Joseph. 1727. *Fifteen Sermons.* In *British Moralists, 1650–1800,* vol. 1. Edited by D. D. Raphael. London: Oxford University Press, 1969.

Camus, Albert. 1942. *The Myth of Sisyphus and Other Essays.* Reprinted New York: Knopf, 1955.

Carr, Karen L. 2001. "After Paganism: Kierkegaard, Socrates, and the Christian Tradition." In Davenport and Rudd 2001.

Connell, George B. 1992. "Judge William's Theonomous Ethics." In *Foundations of Kierkegaard's Vision of Community.* Edited by George B. Connell and C. Stephen Evans. Atlantic Highland, N.J.: Humanities Press.

Crites, Stephen. 1992. "'The Sickness unto Death': A Social Interpretation." In *Foundations of Kierkegaard's Vision of Community.* Edited by George B. Connell and C. Stephen Evans. Atlantic Highland, N.J.: Humanities Press.

Davenport, John J. 2001. "Towards an Existential Virtue Ethics: Kierkegaard and MacIntyre." In Davenport and Rudd 2001.

Davenport, John J., and Anthony Rudd, eds. 2001. *Kierkegaard after MacIntyre: Essays on Freedom, Narrative, and Virtue.* Chicago: Open Court/Carus.

Elrod, John. 1975. *Being and Existence in Kierkegaard's Pseudonymous Works.* Princeton, N.J.: Princeton University Press.

Erikson, Erik H. 1964. *Insight and Responsibility.* New York: Norton.

———. 1980. *Identity and the Life Cycle.* New York: Norton.

Evans, C. Stephen. 1995. "Kierkegaard's View of the Unconscious." In *Kierkegaard in Post/Modernity.* Edited by Martin J. Matastik and Merold Westphal. Bloomington: Indiana University Press.

———. 1997. "Who Is the Other in 'Sickness unto Death'?" In *Kierkegaard Studies.* Edited by Niels Jorgen Cappelorn and Herman Denser. New York/Berlin: de Gruyter.

———. 1998. "Realism and Antirealism in Kierkegaard's *Concluding Unscientific Postscript.*" In Hannay and Marino 1998.

Flanagan, Owen. 1984. *The Science of the Mind.* Cambridge, Mass.: MIT Press.

———. 1991. *Varieties of Moral Personality: Ethics and Psychological Realism.* Cambridge, Mass.: Harvard University Press.

———. 1996. *Self Expressions: Mind, Morals, and the Meaning of Life.* New York: Oxford University Press.

Frankfurt, Harry G. 1988. *The Importance of What We Care About.* Cambridge: Cambridge University Press.

Giddens, Anthony. 1991. *Modernity and Self-Identity: Self and Society in the Late Modern Age.* Stanford, Calif.: Stanford University Press.

Gutting, Gary. 1999. *Pragmatic Liberalism and the Critique of Modernity.* Series in Modern European Philosophy. Cambridge: Cambridge University Press.

Hannay, Alastair. 1982. *Kierkegaard.* London: Routledge & Kegan Paul.

———. 1998. "Kierkegaard and the Variety of Despair." In Hannay and Marino 1998.

Hannay, Alastair, and Gordon D. Marino, eds. 1998. *The Cambridge Companion to Kierkegaard.* Cambridge: Cambridge University Press.

James, William. 1890. *The Principles of Psychology,* vol. 1. Reprinted New York: Dover, 1950.

———. 1897. *The Will to Believe and Other Essays in Popular Philosophy.* Reprinted New York: Dover, 1956.

———. 1902. *The Varieties of Religious Experience.* Reprinted New York: Modern Library, 1936.

———. 1907. *Pragmatism and the Meaning of Truth.* Reprinted Cambridge, Mass.: Harvard University Press, 1975.

Kant, Immanuel. 1793. *Religion within the Limits of Reason Alone.* Translated by Theodore Green and Hoyt Hudson. New York: Harper & Row, 1960.

Kitchen, Gary. 1999. "Charles Taylor: The Malaises of Modernity and the Moral Sources of the Self." *Philosophy and Social Criticism* 25.3:29–55.

Lillegard, Norman. 2001. "Thinking with Kierkegaard and MacIntyre about Virtue." In Davenport and Rudd 2001.

MacIntyre, Alasdair. 1966. *A Short History of Ethics.* New York: Macmillan.

———. 1984. *After Virtue.* 2d edition. Notre Dame, Ind.: Notre Dame University Press.

———. 1987. *Whose Justice? Which Rationality?* Notre Dame, Ind.: Notre Dame University Press.

———. 1999. *Dependent Rational Animals.* Chicago: Open Court/Carus.

Marino, Gordon. 2001. "The Place of Reason in Kierkegaard's Ethics." In Davenport and Rudd 2001. (First published in *Kierkegaardianna* 18 [1996]: 49–64.)

Mill, John Stuart. 1859. *On Liberty.* Edited by Currin V. Shields. Indianapolis: Bobbs-Merrill, 1956.

Miller, Bruce. 1987. "Types of Autonomy and Their Significance." In *Bioethics: Readings and Cases.* Edited by Baruch Brody and Tristram Engelhardt Jr. Englewood Cliffs, N.J.: Prentice-Hall.

Mitchell, Basil. 1980. *Morality: Religious and Secular.* Reprinted Oxford: Clarendon, 1985.

Mooney, Edward. 1996. *Selves in Discord and Resolve: Kierkegaard's Moral-Religious Psychology from "Either/Or" to "Sickness unto Death."* London: Routledge.

Nagel, Thomas. 1986. *The View from Nowhere.* New York: Oxford University Press.

Nietzsche, Friedrich. 1878. *Human, All-Too-Human.* In *The Portable Nietzsche.* Translated by Walter Kaufmann. New York: Viking, 1968.

Piety, Marilyn. 2001. "Kierkegaard on Rationality." In Davenport and Rudd 2001. (First published in *Faith and Philosophy* 10.3 [1993]: 365–79.)

Pojman, Louis P. 1984. *The Logic of Subjectivity.* University: University of Alabama Press.

Putnam, Hilary. 1981. *Reason, Truth, and History.* Cambridge: Cambridge University Press.

———. 1987. *The Many Faces of Realism.* LaSalle, Ill.: Open Court.

———. 1992. *Renewing Philosophy.* Cambridge, Mass.: Harvard University Press.

———. 1995. *Pragmatism.* Cambridge: Blackwell.

Rorty, Richard. 1979. *Philosophy and the Mirror of Nature.* Princeton, N.J.: Princeton University Press.

———. 1982. *The Consequences of Pragmatism.* Minneapolis: University of Minnesota Press.

Rudd, Anthony. 1993. *Kierkegaard and the Limits of the Ethical.* Oxford: Oxford University Press.

Solomon, Robert C. 2002. *Spirituality for the Skeptic: The Thoughtful Love of Life.* Oxford: Oxford University Press.

Stout, Jeffrey. 1988. *Ethics after Babel: The Language of Morals and Their Discontents.* Boston: Beacon.

———. 1989. "Homeward Bound: MacIntyre on Liberal Society and the History of Ethics." *Journal of Religion* 69.2 (April): 220–32.

Taylor, Charles. 1989. *Sources of the Self: The Making of the Modern Identity.* Cambridge, Mass.: Harvard University Press.

———. 1992. *The Ethics of Authenticity.* Cambridge, Mass.: Harvard University Press.

———. 2002. *Varieties of Religion Today: William James Revisited.* Cambridge, Mass.: Harvard University Press.

Turner, Victor. 1981. "Social Dramas and Stories about Them." In *On Narrative.* Edited by W. J. T. Mitchell. Chicago: University of Chicago Press.

Walzer, Michael. 1987. *Interpretation and Social Criticism.* Cambridge, Mass.: Harvard University Press.

Watkin, Julia. 1995. "Judge William—A Christian?" In *International Kierkegaard Commentary: "Either/Or, part II."* Edited by Robert L. Perkins. Macon, Ga.: Mercer University Press.

Westphal, Merold. 1987. "Kierkegaard's Psychology and Unconscious Despair." In *International Kierkegaard Commentary: "The Sickness unto Death."* Edited by Robert L. Perkins. Macon, Ga.: Mercer University Press.

INDEX

PETER J. MEHL is a professor of philosophy and religion and an associate dean in the College of Liberal Arts at the University of Central Arkansas. His recent publications include "Edifying Hermeneutics: Kierkegaard's Existential 'Method' and Its Limits," in *Kierkegaard and the Word(s): Essays on Hermeneutics and Communication,* edited by Gordon D. Marino and Poul Houe; "Kierkegaard and the Relativist Challenge to Practical Philosophy, with a New Postscript," in *Kierkegaard after MacIntyre,* edited by John J. Davenport and Anthony Rudd; and "Moral Virtue, Mental Health, and Happiness: The Moral Psychology of Kierkegaard's Judge William," in *International Kierkegaard Commentary: Either/Or, vol. 2,* edited by Robert L. Perkins.

The University of Illinois Press
is a founding member of the
Association of American University Presses.

Composed in 9.5/12.5 Trump Medieval
by Type One, LLC
for the University of Illinois Press
Manufactured by Maple-Vail
Manufacturing Group

University of Illinois Press
1325 South Oak Street
Champaign, IL 61820-6903
www.press.uillinois.edu